Forever Blue!

By Debbie Fletcher

Acknowledgments

Many people have contributed to my adventures and memories in this book and if I miss any of you out I apologise but please be assured that you are in there amongst my memories. All of my family including my mom, sister Annette, brother Neil, nephew etc supported and encouraged me during the writing of this book. I would also like to mention Bluenoses that we lost during this time such as Snowy, Ken and Squid – gone but not forgotten.

I would like to thank my best mate and Blues sidekick June Humphreys for being there every step of the way. I would also like to mention my loyal travelling army of James Humphreys, James Gough, Terry Dolloway, Nigel Williams, Harry Wilson and Charlie Turner – we have had some brilliant and very funny adventures together following Blues. Also my Bluenose nephew Stephen who I meet up with for our London adventures amongst other trips. Thanks also go to other Blues mates such as Steve Woolley, Brendan and family, Paul Fidler, Dawn and her sister (my St. Andrews neighbour – seat next to me) Pete and family (also sit by me – Forza Blues) Baz, Linda, Redditch Pete and Lynda, Liam and Stuart and many more of you. To Ballie (Julie Borland) my best mate from my time playing for Blues Ladies who I don't see enough of these days as she lives in Liverpool now but it is great when we see each other at Blues games.

And of course for Birmingham City FC who have given me so many joys and sorrows over the years. What a team, what a club, what a City! Never boring and always an adventure to be had. Thank you all and Keep Right On!

Chapters

Chapter One – Highest Top Flight Finish In 51 Years

It was brilliant being back in the Premier League and I was really looking forward to our first season back after only one season in the Championship. Not much had changed during the summer break, I was still working as a charge midwife at the Corniche Hospital in Abu Dhabi and as usual the summer months had been long and hot. I must admit that I dread the summers in Abu Dhabi as it's way too hot and humid to go out and there isn't that much to do really, that I haven't already done over the last 12 years that I have been here. I am starting to miss the normality of life in England and the friendliness of the English people, as well as my family and my beloved Birmingham City of course!

As I had missed my moms birthday for many years due to my living abroad, I decided to travel home to spend the special day with her this year. It meant I would miss the start of the season though, as her birthday is on the 3rd of August, but I really wanted to spend it with her, which I did. However, I was still determined to get to as many pre season friendly's as possible.

Mom was having a family get together at her house to celebrate her big day, which was also the day that Blues were playing away at Nottingham Forest in a friendly. I did the only thing possible and missed the game to spend it with my family. We all had a lovely day which was spent mostly in the conservatory drinking, dancing and celebrating moms birthday.

A few days later, after texting Brendan to see if he was going to Crewe (which he was) I was preparing to see my first pre season friendly of the 2009 to 2010 season. Brendan had kindly offered to take me along with him and his son, and he arrived to collect me in Marie's lovely yellow beetle.

The trip didn't take too long and we were soon pulling into a car park not far from the ground in Crewe. We headed for the pub closest to the ground where we found other Bluenoses enjoying a pre match pint or two. It was good to see other bluenoses that I knew or recognised from following Blues. After catching up with a couple of them and chatting to Brendan, his son and Ron, we headed off to the ground just before kick off time.

It was a night game and the Blues fans were situated in the stand along one side of the ground where a few hundred hardy souls were already knocking out a few songs. The game itself left a lot to be desired and ended in a crap

4-1 defeat. Blues fans sang 'I wanna go home, This is the worse trip I've ever been on!'.

Not all doom and gloom though, as us Bluenoses are pretty optimistic and I got to meet even more people that I hadn't seen for a while. The Crewe fans celebrated like they had won promotion but they were still pretty much out sang by the entertaining Blues following who never lost faith. I must admit to being a bit worried about the coming season after this showing though. Perhaps we tried to play too much football against lower level opposition? Who knows eh? I met Alan again and we chatted and reminisced about bygone times. He remembers going to Crewe many years ago – I think he said 50 years. I really admire Alan, he is always at every Blues away game that I get to.

A couple of days later I went on a trip to London with mom, Annette and Nicola on the coach from Weoley Castle Square. It was like being a tourist and I got to visit the Tower of London for the first time, which was really cool as I am quite interested in history and the royal family over the years. It is only when you live abroad that you realise just how much history we have in Britain and we don't seem to visit half of the historic sites that we have on our doorstep.

Knowing how much I love doing things like this, Steve (my sisters boyfriend), Annette (my sister) and mom took me on the old steam railway that runs to Bridgenorth on a real old steam train for a day out. That was pretty great too and the weather was lovely all the time I was home this trip.

My last game was to be the friendly against the Spanish team Sporting Gijon at St. Andrews and I was really looking forward to this especially as it was a beautiful sunny day. Annette, Nicola and I had tickets for this game and we set off early as I had decided to travel back in time and get the bus to town then walk to St. Andrews like I used to do in the 70's and 80's. It was brilliant, just like I used to love so much as I walked to the ground on match days in bygone days. It had been so long since I had done this and it was lovely and sunny.

We decided to do a bit of a pub crawl and we started at The Old Crown, which is the oldest pub in Birmingham. It's really cool, with the outside being of Tudor style with the old black and white front. Inside was 'Olde world' and I have heard that the ladies toilets are haunted. With this in mind I decided that I needed to use the toilet whilst Annette got the drinks in. Somewhat out of curiosity Nicola decided to join me and off we headed. Whilst in the cubicle I heard a noise and I called to Nic 'which toilet are you in Nic?', 'left one' she replied. 'Thank god for that' I said 'I thought it was the ghost for a minute!', 'did I say left?' She replied. I think she has the Fletcher sense of humour!

We decided to have our beers outside (Nic was on coke) as it was so hot. Therefore we headed for the beer garden to enjoy our pints along with the Cornish pasties that mom has packed for us. Wonderful! Then we headed up the road and cut up the back way to the Wagon & Horses for our next stop. We took our drinks outside to enjoy in the sunshine with the other Bluenoses that were enjoying their pre match pints.

It was also the anniversary of our dear friend Dave Brueton's tragic death and we decided to head to the pub where he always enjoyed his pre match drinks in – 'The Cricketers' to raise a glass to him, so off we set. When we arrived at The Cricketers, Brendan and his wife Marie and their sons Sam and Liam, and Ron were all already there so we obtained our drinks and joined them outside in the sunshine. We quietly raised a glass to Dave and chatted and enjoyed the sunshine that was blazing down on us. Then we all headed off to the ground where we enjoyed a good game of football which ended 0-0 and was much better than the Crewe showing! We also got free programmes, which was a treat.

After the game we headed to the club shop which was full of Spanish fans who were all happily buying Blues souvenirs. I thought this was really cute, especially as one guy was buying a bib which stated '50% dad 50% mum 100% Bluenose!' One woman came in and took off her Blues shirt and swapped it with a Spanish fan. Priceless! He looked really pleased with the deal. I obtained the new Blues shirt for the coming season which I then changed into in the toilets down the road in McDonalds before jumping the bus back to town.

As we passed the 'Burberry Arms', sorry, 'The Clement', I desperately wanted to get off the bus as I noticed all the Spanish fans in their red and white shirts happily drinking outside. I would have loved to have joined them for a chat. Annette insisted that I couldn't get off as we were heading to meet Steve at the 'Green Man'!

When we arrived at the Green man, Graham was amused to see that I already had the new shirt on, especially as when he had seen me earlier at the game I had been wearing last season's shirt! So, after giving Steve lots of stick about missing the game, we enjoyed a meal and headed back to moms.

Because of the way our holiday is done at work, I had to head back to Abu Dhabi the day before the first game of the season away at Manchester United – which had already been changed to accommodate Sky TV. I couldn't believe that I would have to miss such a big game but at least I would be off work and would be able to watch it live on my satellite Chanel.

So, back in Abu Dhabi the next day, my suitcase remained unpacked, and I sat down with my pint of cider (in my Birmingham City pint glass) with my flag and scarves draped around the room, to watch the first game of the season away to Old Trafford. What a start to the season, I thought, Manchester United away, at least it gets it out of the way early on. I thought Blues played really well and we were only narrowly beaten 1-0, which is no shame really. I had still hoped in my heart that we might have pulled off a shock win but, alas, it wasn't to be. Next season maybe? And then it was back to work!

On the Wednesday night Blues played our first home game and I stayed up to watch it, even though it was really late here. I was rewarded with our first win as Blues beat Portsmouth 1-0 with James McFadden scoring in the last minute. Fantastic!

The next few games seemed to pass quickly and I was busy at work and planning my next trip home. Blues drew the next match at St. Andrews 0-0 against Stoke City and then played away at Southampton in the second round of the Carling Cup and won 2-1 with goals from Bowyer and Carsley. I really like Bowyer. He has loads of passion and will run his heart out for the Blue cause.

Next up was an away game at Tottenham which we lost really unluckily 2-1. At 1-1 we were cruising and I thought there was only one team that would win it but then Stephen Carr fell over the ball in the last minute and a Spurs player was on it in a flash and the next minute it was in the net and we were robbed again.

Lady Luck has definitely deserted us and we lost the big one against our neighbours 1-0, again against the run of play. Blues did everything but score in a passionate display. Our time will come though if we continue to play so well. Personally I think we lack a decent striker.

I was rewarded for my faith in the next game with Blues first away win of the season at Hull City as I watched live as Blues won 1-0 with a goal from Garry O'Conner. Then the Blue roller coaster crashed downwards again as we were knocked out of the Carling Cup at Sunderland 2-0. I would love to win a major cup but we still had the FA Cup to look forward to so I will be hoping for a good draw in that competition.

Then followed three defeats on the trot – against Bolton at home 2-1, which I watched with Trish, Tracey and Pam (who happens to be from Bolton and although not a football fan, enjoyed giving me some stick), than away at Burnley 2-1 (in which Blues were abysmal) and away at Arsenal 3-1.

I was beginning to get despondent but then I was cheered somewhat as Blues beat Sunderland at St.Andrews 2-1 and followed that up with a 0-0 home draw against Manchester City. Blues were now 14th in the league table and I was looking forward to the next match against Liverpool at Anfield. It turned out to be a great game for us Bluenoses as Blues came from 1-0 down to equalise and then Cameron Jerome scored a spectacular goal to put us 2-1 ahead. That goal should have won us the game but we were cruelly robbed when a Liverpool player dived in the box (and it was clearly shown to be a dive on the replay) and up stepped Stephen Gerrard to equalise form the spot and the game ended 2-2.

Next up was a 1-0 win over Fulham followed by a great win at Molyneux over Wolves 1-0 and Blues were up to 11th in the table. Then followed another great win away at Wigan 3-2 and then against West Ham 1-0 at St. Andrews as Bowyer scored the only goal of the game against his old club and Blues were 8th in the league and had won four on the trot. This was brilliant and Blues continued our winning streak against Blackburn Rovers at St. Andrews, winning 2-1. Blues were now unbeaten for 8 games and I was on my way home for Christmas for the first time in ten years! I was so excited.

It was great to see my mom and family again and be back on English soil. My first match would be away at Everton and Steve (Stegga) my sisters boyfriend, had kindly arranged tickets and travel with Brendan for all the games whilst I would be home. I was looking forward to seeing all the lads again at the matches and seeing the Blues play live. You can't beat it.

I was travelling with Stephen (my nephew) as always, and also with Brendan, Marie, Sam and Liam and we were heading to Liverpool by train. I love going to away games by train and this day was no different as we set off from New Street Station bound for Liverpool Lime Street. It always seems funny arriving at Lime Street due to the fact that I lived in Liverpool for nine years and did my midwifery training there. I also made a lot of friends in Liverpool and enjoyed my time in the city.

On arrival in Liverpool we set off for Wetherspoons to get pre-match drinks and something to eat. However, despite the fact that the pub was half empty, the jobsworth behind the bar refused us service because we had children with us (Brendan's children are not especially young though and would not be drinking alcohol). So we went into the pub next door which was much nicer and friendlier and had drinks and meals all round. It was Wetherspoons loss though, as we spent a lot of money on food and drink and we had a nice time before we left to head to a pub closer to the ground to meet up with the others.

We got a taxi to take us to the Taxi Club not far from Goodison Park where we met up with Ron, Graham and Craig and enjoyed drinks and some good pre match banter before heading off in the pouring rain for the short walk to the ground.

The atmosphere amongst the travelling Bluenoses was great inside the ground and we were all enjoying the fantastic run that Blues are on at the moment and we were all feeling pretty positive. The game got underway but it wasn't long before Everton scored, not that it stopped our singing which went on in abundance. I really loved the Scott Dann song which was sang to the tune of 'Gold' by Spandau Ballet, and went 'always believe in Scott Dann, he's got the power to know, he's indestructible, always believe in – Scott Dann, DANN! Always believe in Scott Dann…' Etc. brilliant.

Then Blues won a free kick on the edge of the box and up stepped Seb Larsson to score the equaliser and send the Bluenoses into mass celebration. It was brilliant! The away section made so much noise and I loved it when we sang 'we are invincible, we are invincible, we are invincible ..' Etc. 1-1.

Some of the songs were so funny and even the players seemed to be enjoying them.   Blues sang 'channel five on a Thursday night!' – this being a reference to the Europa League being shown on a Thursday night and Blues aiming for a European place. We sang to the Everton fans 'we're going to Italy - you're going to Coventry, we're going to Italy - you're going to Coventry!'. This was sang several times, again with reference to our chance of Europe and their chance of relegation (Everton were in the bottom half of the table).

The Blues contingent were absolutely buzzing! It was one of the best atmospheres away from home that I could remember for a long time. We also sang 'we're drawing away, how shit must you be, we're drawing away'. Great sense of humour the travelling Blues fans have and I was so proud to be back amongst them again. It was also quite cool when we sang 'we're gonna win the league!'. And of course we also sang 'stand up if you robbed your car' and 'sign on' (to the tune of you'll never walk alone) to the scouters as usual.

As I headed back to my seat at half time I bumped into my mate 'Ballie' who I used to play football with at Birmingham City Ladies and whom I hadn't seen for over twenty years! We were both delighted to see each other and Ballie informed me she is now living and working in Liverpool, although she still has a flat in Birmingham. She commutes at weekends whenever she can make it to see the Blues. I was over the moon to see her and after exchanging hugs we said we would try to meet up at the Taxi Club after the game as that was where I was going with the others for a drink before we headed back to Brum.

It was raining on the way back to the club but once inside it was warm and we met up with Graham, Craig and Ron again and celebrated our away draw. We had a few laughs as always and then we headed back to the station and had a quick drink in the station bar before boarding our train back to Birmingham. It had been a fantastic day out and I was already looking forward to the next away game as I do love travelling with the Blues.

The run up to Christmas was great, especially as I was home in England. I really hate Christmas out in Abu Dhabi these days as it's just not the same as in England even though the malls are decorated with Santa's grotto's and the hotels have Christmas tree lighting ceremonies etc, I miss home. On Christmas Eve my mom did a really nice buffet and we enjoyed that as well as a few drinks and a very Christmassy atmosphere. On Christmas morning I got up and enjoyed the pleasure of opening my presents with my mom and sister Annette for the first time in ten years and it was great! Then Steve came round and Steve, Annette and I headed to Harborne to the 'Green-man' for a lunch time Christmas drink.

It was really Christmassy in the pub with a free glass of sparkling wine or whiskey and a mince pie on the way in. We missed this as we came in the wrong door but we soon obtained one from the bar. Steve – or Woolley as I call him, was wearing his Al Wadha football shirt that I had bought him for Christmas and was having the piss taken out of him by Graham who insisted it was a villa shirt! I had to laugh, it is a sort of browny red colour so I joined in the piss taking too and agreed it looked like a villa shirt! Steve was having none of it though as it's his favourite local team in Abu Dhabi when he visits with Annette, in fact they had just won the league in the United Arab Emirates. Both Graham and Craig were in the pub, so we caught up with them and a couple of others and had a good afternoon before heading back to moms for Christmas dinner.

Christmas dinner was really lovely and we dined in the conservatory and my cousin Bernadette came too and we had a fabulous time with crackers, champagne and Christmas music – it was great! I rang my mate Roxy, who was enjoying Christmas with Rob's family in Glasgow and I said hello to his dad too before ringing my mates Trish and Trace back in Abu Dhabi. All in all it was one of the best Christmases I have had in years. It was great to see all the houses around Birmingham proudly showing off their Christmas lights! It was a fantastic sight – after all – this is our country!

Then it was Boxing Day and our home game against Chelsea. I was really looking forward to going to St. Andrews again, especially to see a game against Chelsea. I was behind the goal in the Tilton for this game and I would be going with Stephen and Annette.

It was a nice day really and the atmosphere inside St. Andrews was buzzing. The game got underway and Birmingham played really well despite the fact that Drogba was diving all over the place as usual. The Blues fans sang 'same old Drogba – always cheating!', very loudly and he smiled in surprise when he realised it was him we were singing at. Then we sang 'Bowyer, knock him out, Bowyer, Bowyer knock him out!' Which I thought was quite funny.

It was a really good game for Blues and we had the ball in the back of the net when Chucko scored in front of the Tilton, only for the linesman (wrongly as it was clearly shown on TV afterwards) to disallow. Stephen and I jumped on each other in celebration and jumped on Annette before we realised that the linesman had his flag up. I should have guessed though as Chelsea always get the decisions in their favour.

The match finished 0-0 and a draw against the champions elect was a good result for us even though we had been robbed of a win. It was great when the Blues fans sang 'we're gonna win the league!'. This meant that we were now unbeaten for 9 games and we are 7th in the Premier League. It was the first time in many games (I think it was 36) that Chelsea had failed to score a goal, so it was a really good point. St. Andrews was fast becoming known as fortress St. Andrews! So it was back to moms and in two days time I had a trip to Stoke to look forward to.

Stephen and I were going by train to Stoke along with Brendan and we were meeting up early in a pub in the City centre due to it being a early kick off to avoid trouble. Neil (my brother & Stephens dad) gave us a lift into town and we arrived at the pub about 1030am and Brendan and Ron were already inside enjoying a pint. Stephen and I ordered bacon and sausage baps and a couple of pints and settled down to breakfast and a chat with the lads. Graham and Craig arrived not long after as we were all planning on getting the same train to Stoke. Brendan had already obtained our train tickets but the others would buy them at the station.

Soon it was time to go and we headed off to New Street Station and onto the platform for the Stoke train. It was really cold and everyone looked frozen on the platform, including the many police officers that were also on the platform waiting to join us on our journey to Stoke. A police escort from Birmingham all the way to the match eh!

The train was packed but Stephen and I managed to get seats next to each other whilst the others were scattered about the same carriage. The train was full of Bluenoses on the way to the game.

I decided to head to the buffet car for drinks, which turned out to be at the far end of the train. There wasn't much left, only bitter or wine. I tried calling Stephen to ask what he wanted but his phone must have been on silent so I called Brendan and asked him to ask Stephen. I heard him shout down the carriage 'hey Stephen, what do you want to drink? Bitter or wine?' Then he spoke to me 'he said he's a student and will drink anything but he prefers bitter', 'okay' I said 'what flavour crisps does he want?'. I heard Brendan relay the message down the carriage and I could hear loads of voices shouting 'I'll have salt and vinegar' or 'I'll have cheese and onion' etc. I had to laugh.

So I made my way back to our carriage and we tucked into our drinks and crisps and chatted about the season so far and the forthcoming match. Stephen was laughing about my phone call and Brendan shouting down the train to him.

When the train arrived at Stoke we were greeted by several double decker buses to take us the the ground which had been laid on by the police in order to escort us. The Bluenoses were already in good voice and boarded the buses singing loudly, followed by the police.

We boarded the loudest bus and joined in the singing. The Blues were singing 'we all hate Stoke, Stoke, we all hate Stoke, Stoke,...' And the bus was literally rocking. The policeman downstairs looked a bit green and said to the driver 'I could do without this' but he was also laughing as he said it.

All the way to the ground the bus was rocking and the Blues fans were singing loudly and I could see people looking up at the commotion as we passed them. As we approached the ground the ground the Stoke fans heard our arrival and looked on as we taunted them with our singing. It was brilliant. The atmosphere amongst the travelling Blues was really fantastic and I was already having a brilliant day.

Once off the bus we all headed into the ground and met up with other Bluenoses that we knew in the bar under the stands in the away end. Then it was up to the seats for the game. Everyone in the Blues end stood for the whole of the match. I was singing my heart out but was situated away from the main singers. I vowed to join them for the second half.

The first half ended 0-0 and Stephen and I headed back down to the bar for refreshments and a catch up with the others. We were chatting to Brendan and were amongst the last to leave the bar when the second half got underway. As we headed up the stairs to our seats we heard an almighty roar and the Blues fans were celebrating wildly. Blues had scored and were 1-0 ahead! Stephen and I had missed the goal by seconds but we soon caught on and joined the celebrations.

This time we stood amongst the singers and I proceeded to sing for the entire second half as Blues secured a great 1-0 away win. My favourite song became 'we are unbeatable!'. What a fabulous run we are on and what a great time to be a Bluenose! We headed back to the buses and were escorted back towards the train station with the Bluenoses in full voice and in celebration mode.

Once back at the station Brendan, Stephen and myself managed to escape the police escort and headed into the hotel across the road from the station entrance. We headed into the bar, which was a nice quiet little bar, and ordered drinks. I had a lovely scrumpy cider and Stephen tried it and also had one. By the time we had enjoyed our drinking session and headed back to the station the train had arrived and, after obtaining more beers from the station shop, we boarded for our journey back to Birmingham New Street Station.

The train was packed with Bluenoses but also had a heavy police presence who were not at all impressed with our singing. Every time someone tried to start a song a miserable copper would appear and nip it in the bud. I received the same treatment myself when I tried to join in the singing. Stephen later told his dad that I gave the copper the fork as he walked away (as if!). We were still happy though and managed to celebrate a little.

Once back in Birmingham we headed to Harborne for a last drink. The next day my brother asked me what I had done to Stephen yesterday! I had to laugh. Apparently he was quite funny when he got home though.

Blues had been drawn away at Nottingham Forest in the FA Cup and I was really looking forward to this trip, Stephen had returned to Leicester where he was at University and he was planning to get the train to Nottingham to meet me there. I had arranged to travel to Nottingham by car with Brendan and some of the lads and we set out early in order to get pre match refreshments.

We arrived in Nottingham with plenty of time to spare and I texted Stephen to tell him which pub we were in. We met up with Graham and Craig in the pub and soon after were joined by other Bluenoses. It was predominantly a home pub and before long it was full of red shirted Forest fans. I was in my usual Blues colours and had to make my way through a sea of red to get to the toilets. No problems though, I made it there and back in one piece! Mind you, I did have Graham as a bodyguard!

During the time we were in the pub I could see the snow coming down outside in large flakes and it was sticking! By the time we left the pub everywhere was white and I was worried that the game would be called off. It was getting really cold too. The walk to the ground warmed me up somewhat, although the snow was still falling and I was glad I had a hat and scarf on. Once inside the ground it was buzzing. There were more that 4,500 Bluenoses in the away end and the atmosphere was brilliant. It was a real old fashioned cup atmosphere and despite the cold the Blues fans were singing their hearts out.

The match got underway and Blues had quite a few chances, even hitting the bar, but we just couldn't score. Then Forest were awarded a penalty and their fans celebrated loudly. Up stepped the Forest player to a crescendo of whistles and boo's from the Blues end and he dispatched it high into the stands to wild celebrations from the Bluenoses – myself included. That certainly warmed me up! The game finished 0-0 and now meant a replay at St. Andrews in two weeks time and I was due to head back to Abu Dhabi once again.

We managed to squeeze Stephen into the car and we dropped him back at Nottingham station for him to catch his train back to Leicester. I gave him the rest of the sandwiches and packed lunch that mom had made me for his train journey back. He had enjoyed his trip to watch the Blues as had I and I wasn't at all ready to be going back. I was enjoying life back in the Premier League and being back in my home country. It was with some reluctance and a heavy heart that I returned to Abu Dhabi. I was beginning to long for my family and home city more and more as time goes on.

Blues followed on from the Forest game with an excellent draw at St. Andrews against Manchester United. A very exciting game ended 1-1 with Alex Ferguson admitting that they were relieved to go in at half time all square and that we were one of the best teams they had played this season. Then it was back to the magic of the FA Cup as Nottingham Forest came to St. Andrews for the third round replay. Blues turned on the style and won 1-0 and progress to a fourth round tie away at Everton in just over a weeks time.

Because of the weather conditions there was no more football played by Blues until theFA Cup game against Everton, which was a bit of a shame as I felt it might have slowed our momentum a bit. I was really looking forward to the cup match as I love the cup and although I thought it was a tough draw I was hopeful that we could bring them back to St. Andrews for a replay and hopefully beat them there. Therefore I was over the moon when Blues beat Everton 2-1 Goodison Park on the day before my birthday. What a birthday present – brilliant! Blues were now unbeaten in 15 league and cup games.

Next up were champions elect Chelsea who were flying and it was perhaps inevitable that our unbeaten run would come to an end at Stamford Bridge. Although we live in hope when we follow Blues we were still a little disappointed to lose 3-0 against the Chelsea. This just shows how times have changed and what a good season we are having at Blues this season. Despite the result we still sit in eighth position in the Premier League and one of our best seasons for many years.

A few days later and St. Andrews witnessed another good result as Blues held Tottenham to a 1-1 draw before hosting our neighbours from Wolverhampton and producing an excellent 2-1 win in front of a very partisan crowd. Still eighth in the league and very happy with life at the moment.

Then followed a small setback with a defeat away at West Ham United 2-0, which came a few days before our FA Cup 5th round tie away at Derby County. Blues are doing really well in the cup this year which I find really exciting. Are we about to realise our dream of winning major silverware this year?

I watched the Derby game live on TV in Abu Dhabi and was impressed by the away support that we took to Pride Park and they were in fantastic voice as usual, I couldn't help but wish I was there. More and more these days I am wishing I was living back in the UK and getting to all the games. I really enjoyed the game, even though it was nerve wracking at times but Blues played well and progressed to the quarter finals with a 2-1 win to send the travelling support into raptures. We're on our way!

We were brought down to earth a little in the next game away at Fulham as Blues lost 2-1 to drop down to 10th place, the lowest since way back in November. However, Blues were soon back up to 8th place with another good victory at St. Andrews, this time against Wigan as Blues won the game 1-0. Then it was off to Portsmouth in the FA Cup quarter final. I was so excited about this game but felt a little let down as I thought we didn't really turn up and didn't play well enough even though Blues were hard done by at times in a really disappointing 2-0 defeat. I had really thought that this was our year. It was probably made worse in the next game, away at Portsmouth again, in which Blues played much better and gained revenge with a 2-1 win in the Premier League. For me, I would have preferred the victory to have been in the FACup rather than the league so there was not a lot of consolation in it for me. I do so love the cup competitions.

Blues were still 8th in the Premier League and remained there after a 2-2 draw against Everton at St. Andrews in the next game but then dropped to 9th after an away defeat at Sunderland 3-1. This was followed a few days later by another defeat this time in Blackburn as Blues went down 2-1 this time. The slide was halted in the next match though, with a great point in a hard fought draw against Arsenal 1-1 at St. Andrews and then another really good draw against Liverpool, again 1-1 at St. Andrews.

Blues then travelled to the a City of Manchester Stadium where high flying Manchester City inflicted our heaviest defeat of the season as we conceded five goals to lose 5-1. Blues remained in 9th place though. We then drew 0-0 with Hull City at St. Andrews before being robbed by our neighbours from Aston with a narrow 1-0 defeat. It hurts just as much though. We did managed to beat the claret and blue of Burnley a week later though, 2-1 at St. Andrews and we remained in our best position for years before ending the season at Bolton with a 2-1 loss, somewhat disappointingly.

The season had been a great success back in the Premier League as Blues achieved a 9th place finish, our best in the top flight for 51 years! We had also reached the quarter finals of the FA Cup. I was really happy with the season and had enjoyed it on the whole.

The Premier League Champions were Chelsea with Manchester United finishing runners up. Portsmouth finished bottom and were relegated along with Hull City and Burnley. Chelsea won the FA Cup, beating Portsmouth (it could have been us!) 1-0 at Wembley and Manchester United won the League Cup beating our neighbours Villa 2-1 at Wembley. Newcastle

United were promoted as champions along with West Bromwich Albion and Blackpool.

So, a great season over and another season in the Premier League to look forward to next season. Life is good!

In April I had been delighted to finally get my book 'Truly Blue' published and I was so excited. I had worked hard on this book since the World Cup in 2006 and I was really looking forward to sharing my many, many memories of following Birmingham City and England over the years. My reasons for writing my memories into a book in this way was to bring back the passion of football as it was in the 70's and 80's which seems to be sadly lacking in the commercialised game we have nowadays. Luckily we still have a lot of that passion at Birmingham City, but for those who have forgotten how good it can be, I wanted to remind them by bringing those distant memories back and igniting their passions once again. By the end of April 2010 'Truly Blue' was on all the major websites such as amazon, WHSmiths, Waterstones etc. I was so excited and really looking forward to coming back to the UK soon to promote the book.

For those of you who have not had a chance to read the book yet, it was inspired whilst I was writing a diary of my adventures following England in Germany in the 2006 World Cup Finals. A fellow football fan suggested that it would be fabulous to share all my football related memories by devoting a book to them and including the Germany experience as a chapter in the book.

Chapter Two   - Blues Sold To Hong Kong!

The summer of 2010 was another hot one in the humid heat of Abu Dhabi and I was beginning to tire of being stuck indoors so often on my days off. It really is too hot to go out during this time, even the shopping malls are beginning to lose their appeal. I was looking forward to the World Cup Finals is South Africa though and once more I thought that England were in with a good chance.

I watched the England games in a pub called Coopers along with my mates. Trish and Tracey were just like me and would get kitted up in England gear which included face paint in the case of me and Trace. We had rattles, big hands, flags and loads of England stuff. It was great. The England v USA game was an entertaining night out as there was a lot of rivalry between us and the Americans! The new management at our hospital were American so you can imagine the mood. It was quite funny really, and the Americans thought they had won the competition by holding us to a draw if their reaction was anything to go by! We were not at all impressed though. A fight broke out at the end of the game between the England and USA fans started by the girls – not me I hasten to add!

The England v Germany game was extremely painful to take! Especially as one of our mates Jessie is German. She goes the whole hog too and had face paint and a large German flag to rival ours. Jessie can be quite fun really as we are always taking the micky and doing the dam busters etc to her on nights out. She takes it all in good faith. I remember us all going out for her birthday on one occasion and the whole table (about 20 of us) did a rendition of the dam busters complete with outstretched arms and pretend goggles, to which she responded somewhat sardonically "I just love my English friends!" to laughs around the table.

On this occasion though England were well and truly robbed by the short sighted referee who failed to see that a Frank Lampard shot that hit the crossbar had crossed the goal line by a good two feet! With the score at 2-1 to Germany this would have put England right back in the game. Instead Germany went on the win 4-1 and our World Cup was over. The pubs in Abu Dhabi emptied and remained that way for the rest of the World Cup without England. Spain won a very dirty final with the Dutch where the only person to come out of it with any credit was the English referee Howard Webb for his excellent handling of such a shockingly dirty Final.

Before I knew it the start of the 2010-11 season was about to begin and I was full of optimism. Following Carson Yeung's takeover of the club in 2009 Blues pre season was to begin with a trip to China for the 2010-11 pre season tour. It began when Blues took on a Hong Kong XI which ended in a 3-2 win for Blues which meant that Blues won the Xtep Cup. Blues then played Beijing Guoan in the Birds Nest Stadium on a dreadful pitch in which Garry O'Conner scored the only goal in a 1-0 win with over 70,000 in attendance. Blues finished their tour of China with a win over Liaoning Whowin by 2-0 with goals by O'Connor and Larsson in front of 20,000.

It was then back to England and a friendly at Derby which Blues won 2-1 with goals from Murphy and Larsson. This was followed by a trip to Northampton by a Birmingham XI and was mostly players who missed out on the Derby game and ended in a 2-2 draw. MK Dons was the next outing and Blues came from 2-0 down to win 3-2 after missing a first half penalty. Garry O'Conner got the winner in the 88th minute. The last pre season friendly was Blues only home friendly and saw Mallorca visit St. Andrews. The Spanish side inflicted Blues only defeat as Emilio Nsue scored the only goal of the game.

The season began on the 14th of August with a very good away draw at Sunderland 2-2. At least while Birmingham are in the Premier League the games are all shown live out here so I can watch them as long as I can arrange my days off around them. Goalkeeper Ben Foster and new signing Nikola Zigic made their debuts at Sunderland and Blues were unlucky on several occasions. Sunderland took the lead when a Stephen Carr foul just outside the area was deemed a penalty! Carr was then unfortunate to score an own goal to double Sunderland's lead. Sunderland then had a player sent off and Blues Scott Dann reduced the arrears before Liam Ridgewell scored a late equaliser to give Blues a deserved share of the points.

Things looked even better a week later as Blues beat Blackburn at St. Andrews 2-1 to go to an amazing 4th place in the Premier – yes I know it won't last! Ben Foster had saved a penalty in this game before Blackburn took the lead which lasted 3 minutes when Craig Gardener equalised. Gardener scored the winner from a cracking 25 yard shot which flew into the net.

Next up was the League Cup and I absolutely love the Cup competitions no matter what stage they are at because I always dream of a trip to Wembley for a major cup final. In round two Birmingham were drawn at home to Rochdale of League One and Alex McLeish played somewhat of a reserve side – which I will never agree with – hence Rochdale gave us a scare before we overcame them winning 3-2 to progress to the next stage of the competition. Nathan Redmond made his debut and at 16 years and 173 days he became Blues second youngest debutant since Trevor Francis.

A trip to Bolton was next on the agenda and a good 2-2 away draw was gained in an eventful game in which the Bolton keeper was sent off for slapping Roger Johnson across the face. This was followed by another draw, this time 0-0 at home against the mighty reds of Liverpool in front of 27,333 who saw Blues home unbeaten run stretch to 17 games. This left Birmingham at the giddying height of 5th in the Premier.

However, a week later Blues were brought down to earth again with a 3-1 defeat at neighbours West Bromwich Albion after taking the lead through Jerome. Prior to the game James McFadden had suffered an injury that would see him out for the rest of the season, Alex McLeish signed a new 3 year contract and football consultant Sammy Yu left the club.

Then it was back to the excitement of the League Cup as Birmingham were again drawn against a League One outfit at St. Andrews. This time it was Milton Keynes Dons who were the visitors and once again our reserves took to the field to despatch the Dons 3-1 to the delight of the 9,450 St. Andrews faithful and saw Blues through to the fourth round and hopefully a journey to the final.

A few days later St. Andrews hosted a League game against Wigan and a hard fought 0-0 draw saw Blues drop to 11th place in the league standings. Craig Gardener received his marching orders in this game and saw Blues one day short of being unbeaten for 12 months and had equalled our 18 game unbeaten record.

It was now September and I was again heading back to Birmingham for my holidays and I was really looking forward to seeing my family, heading to St. Andrews and promoting my book Truly Blue whilst I was home. Unfortunately, much to my disappointment, there was only one game during my time home which was Everton at St. Andrews.

Mike, my cousins husband, had managed to get tickets for the Trevor Francis Suite for me and my sister Annette, so we headed to St. Andrews together and into the TF Suite for a pre match drink. It was the first time we had been in the Trevor Francis Suite and it was really nice inside. We got our match programmes and had a chat and a joke with a few people before going up into the Main Stand to watch the game. I was proudly wearing my new pink Birmingham City scarf only to find that Everton were playing in pink! I had no choice other than to take if off! Luckily I had my Blues shirt on though. It was not a good day though as Blues lost the game 2-0 and I left the stand somewhat dissapointed, to have a drink in the TF Suite. Mike joined us then we all went to a local pub for a couple of drinks while the crowd dispersed.

A few days later I had a visit from the Birmingham Mail photographer for a article they were doing about my book 'Truly Blue', which went very well. While they were taking photos outside my moms a car stopped in the street and the driver asked if I was famous! Very funny. A Bromsgrove newspaper also took some photos and ran a story about my book. I was really pleased. The icing on the cake was a live radio interview with Carl Chin – which I was extremely nervous about. Most of Carl Chin's interviews are done over the phone (live) and last about five minutes but this time Carl had invited me into the studio and the interview went on for about fifteen minutes or more!

On the day of the interview I injured my back in the shower and really struggled to get to the studios, but once there Carl Chin really put me at ease. He was lovely. My mom had come with me and Carl allowed her into the studio whilst we did the interview. Despite being nervous I found the interview flowed very well as Carl asked some great questions and really praised the book. He said it was unique and so far nothing had been written like it before. He said there are plenty of football facts and figures books and plenty of hooligan based booked but nothing written about the passion of football such as I had written in my book. I enjoyed the interview because Carl encouraged me to talk about a topic that I love dearly and it went really well. I still had to be helped out of the studio by my mom though because of my bad back.

The following week I had been invited down to watch the players train and meet up with the Blues programme editor Peter Lewis to do a piece in the programme about my book. I bumped into manager Alex McLeish on my arrival as he came over to see what was happening while club photographer Roy Similaj was taking the photos of me with my book. McLeish was really interested and I got of photo of me, Alex McLeish and my mom who had driven me to the training ground.

It was great watching the players train and they all looked really happy together. The ball went out of play near me and Lee Bowyer came over to collect it and said hello and asked how I was. He seemed really nice. Afterwards I went to their canteen and did my interview as several players came in and said hello. It was fabulous. The article would be in a forthcoming programme which Peter would send to me as I would be back in Abu Dhabi by then. I had a fantastic day though.

I was back home in Abu Dhabi when Blues traveled to the Emirates to take on Arsenal. Nikola Zigic gave Blues the lead but Arsenal equalised from the penalty spot and then grabbed a second to beat us 2-1. Arsenal manager Arsene Wenger had highlighted the problem of reckless tackling which was pretty ironic as Arsenal's Jack Wiltshire was sent off for a two footed tackle on Zigic and Emmanuel Eboue was lucky to escape a red card with his scissor kick on Blues Liam Ridgewell. Blues were down to 16th.

The fourth round of the league cup saw Blues at home to a league one team again as Brentford was the visitors. Brentford had knocked out Premier League Everton on penalties in the last round and 15,166 were in attendance at St. Andrews as we dreamed of a place in the quarterfinals. Brentford took the lead in the 68th minute against a weakened Blues side and when Zigic headed over with only 4 minutes remaining it looked like we could be heading out of the competition. Then in the 92nd minute up popped Kevin Phillips to score and send the game into extra time. No further goals were scored and the game ended 1-1 and went to penalties. It came to Brentford's last penalty before sudden death and Blues keeper Maik Taylor deflected his shot onto the crossbar and Blues were in the quarterfinals. Imagine the excitement a few days later when the draw paired Blues with Villa who would have to travel to St. Andrews for a place in the semifinals of the Cup. Bring it on!

My interview about my new book was in the programme for the Blackpool match as Blues took on the newly promoted team with the best away record in the Premier League. It was a good result too as Liam Ridgewell and Nikola Zigic scored in a 2-0 win that took Blues up to 12th in the table.

Blues had the better of the 0-0 draw away at Villa especially as the referee missed a clear hand ball as well as the same player escaping a red card when he stuck his knee in the back of Craig Gardener.

Against West Ham at St. Andrews the highlight of the first half was when the sprinklers suddenly came on. In the second half West Ham went 2-0 up before Jerome pulled a goal back for Blues before Liam Ridgewell scored to rescue a point in a 2-2 draw.

Away at Stoke, Blues again went 2-0 down before goals from Fahey and Jerome made in 2-2 and Gardener had two great efforts saved by the Stoke keeper. As the Blues players were claiming a hand ball which the referee didn't notice, Stoke went on to score and Blues lost the game 3-2. Next up was a really good away draw at Manchester City came next as Carr cleared off the line and the game ended 0-0.

This was followed by and even better result as Lee Bowyer scored the winner against champions Chelsea in the 17th minute. Ben Foster had been in outstanding form after being criticised for his performance for England against France and Chelsea failed to score from their 32 chances on goal. What a scalp for Blues and we were up to 13th.

Blues took the lead away at Fulham when Larsson got his first goal of the season but Fulham grabbed and equaliser despite the Fulham player climbing all over Fahey to score. Scott Dann hit the crossbar for Blues but the game ended in a 1-1 draw. Not a bad result really.

On the day of the quarterfinal against Villa I had my mom, sister and her boyfriend Steve staying with me in Abu Dhabi so we all sat down to watch it together in my apartment. Apparently West Midlands police were so worried about possible trouble and the effect that might have on England's World Cup bid that they tried, to no avail, to get the game moved to another date. Having failed to move the date the police had four times the usual amount on duty for the game. I was really excited at the prospect of knocking the Vile out of the Cup although a little nervous too.

What a great game it was and I could hear the atmosphere from the Bluenoses and wished I could have been there. On 12 minutes Blues were awarded a penalty when Bowyer was fouled and up stepped Sebastian Larsson to fire home and I ran around the room in celebration. Blues had another perfectly good goal by Zigic disallowed before Villa grabbed an undeserved equalised on the break and I sat down deflated. It looked to be heading for a very late night for me as Abu Dhabi is 4 hours ahead and the match looked to be heading for extra time but with 86 minutes on the clock Zigic scored and I went as bonkers as the Bluenoses inside St. Andrews!

Blues won 2-1 and we were in the Semifinals of the League Cup! I was so happy. I watched as large numbers of Blues fans invaded the pitch at the end of the game and were separated from the Vile fans by the riot police. Missiles, including seats and flares were thrown back and forth which the police believe originated in the away section and the trouble continued outside the stadium. What a fantastic win though! I went to bed delighted and the draw for the Semi Final paired us with West Ham over two legs, the first of which would be played at Upton Park. I would make sure I was home for the return home leg no matter what it took.

Blues fell behind at home to Tottenham in the next game but played much better once Zigic came on and he headed across the penalty area to Gardener to score to give Blues a 1-1 draw.

Blues were poor in the first half of the away trip to Wolves and Alex McLeish said after the game "we didn't turn up at all for the first 60 minutes. We were outfought and then had a go. We need to start games the way we finish them."

In Blues last home game of the season was against Manchester United who took the lead at St. Andrews on 60 minutes in front of 28,242 noisy fans but the ground exploded in celebration when Bowyer scored the equaliser in the 89th minute to make it 1-1.

New Year's Day and Blues were again at home as Arsenal came to town. Disappointingly Blues lost to a good Arsenal team 3-0 in front of another big crowd and after the game Bowyer was banned for 3 matches for violent conduct when television replays seemed to show him stamping on an Arsenal player. Alex McLeish responded by saying that the football authorities are not treating everyone equally when using television evidence. Finally someone has noticed that the football league hate Birmingham City!

Blues traveled to Blackpool with the unwanted record of being the only Premier League side without an away win. After losing to Blues at St. Andrews Blackpool's manager Ian Holloway had said they knew how to deal with us for the return leg. Clearly the didn't as Hleb put Blues ahead before ex-Blues player DJ Campbell got Blackpool's equaliser. Scott Dann scored in the 89th minute to give Blues our first away win this season in the Premier League.

It was the FA Cup next away at Millwall in the 3rd round and it would take place just a few days before our League Cup semi final match with West Ham. Hence McLeish made seven changes to the team, not sure how I felt about this as Millwall were challenging for the play offs in the Championship and I love both Cup competitions. Luckily it didn't make much difference as Blues won 4-1 having taken a 4-0 lead. Goalkeeper Maik Taylor did save a penalty though and Millwall also had a goal disallowed but a great win nevertheless and through to the 4th round. Really exciting times being a Bluenose at the minute.

The away leg of the League Cup Semi Final was soon upon us and I was really excited as I sat down to watch it live in Abu Dhabi in the knowledge that I would be going to the return leg at St. Andrews in a couple of weeks. The first half saw Blues looking nervous and West Ham took the lead through Mark Noble but I was hoping that McLeish would sort them out at half time and we would get back into the game. That is exactly what he did and Liam Ridgewell equalised on 56 minutes as Blues now dominated. West Ham then had a player sent off for kicking Larsson in the Groin and there was now only one team in it and it just looked to be a matter of time before Blues took the lead. Then unbelievably West Ham took the lead when keeper Ben Foster allowed a weak shot to go under him and it was 2-1. I could not believe it as Blues had totally dominated and it was a cruel defeat to take. I could only hope and pray that we could turn in around in the second leg to achieve our dream of a major cup final trip to Wembley.

I was going home again and would manage to get 3 games in and this included the villa game and the League Cup semi final. It was fantastic to be home again and I was seriously thinking of moving back permanently over the next few years and was saving hard for a deposit for a house and would start actively looking around whilst home. I really wanted to come back to my roots in Weoley Castle where all my family, including myself, had been brought up.

My first game back was the lunch time derby game against the Vile at St. Andrews and I headed there with Stephen, my nephew, and we had tickets for the Tilton. The game was an early kick off and me, Stephen and Steve got a taxi to the Cricketers to meet the others and enjoy a pre match drink to calm our nerves!

It was an exciting game which finished all square at 1-1, Roger Johnson scored a great goal but Villa scrambled an equaliser. The highlight of the match was the Blues streaker who invaded the pitch wearing only a gold thong and had 'shit on the villa' written on his back. The stewards made a half hearted attempt to catch him but failed and he eventually jumped into the Tilton and as we were all standing he looked for somewhere to hide. Imagine my amusement when he'd decided to hide behind me and Stephen until his mates arrived with his clothes. Really funny and the footage is still on YouTube where me and Stephen can clearly be seen laughing as he disappeared behind us at the very end of the clip. It's a shame that there were only 22,287 which was the lowest between the teams in the Premier League with both clubs just outside the relegation places. We then made our way to Harborne for a post match drink.

Two days before my birthday and I was off to Manchester for our game against Manchester United and I hadn't been to Old Trafford for many years. We traveled up in plenty of time and we were soon settled in a pub called the Quadrant enjoying a pre match drink. It was funny really as a few different people came over to me to ask about my book. Steve then went about leaving my book 'cards' around the pub. I had a bet at 8 to 1 for Blues to win! We set off to the stadium and it was amazing to see all the changes (I think it had terraces last time I visited) and there was merchandise sellers everywhere.

Once inside the Blues end was packed and in full voice. I was quite shocked as to how quiet the home fans were though. We didn't hear a word from them for the entire time. It was a painful 90 minutes but it was Blues who sang throughout. The usual songs were belted out as well as some amusing ones such as 'your just a ground full of tourists' and 'we support our local team'. Many United fans had green and yellow scarves which is apparently a protest against their American owner (yes I don't get it either) and we sang 'are you Norwich in disguise?' and 'Norwich, Norwich give us a song'. We had loads of fun despite the actual game of football as we lost 5-0. It didn't stop us singing and winding up the silent Manchester United fans. '5-0 and you still don't sing' and 'shall we sing a song for you?' We also sang 'we'll see you on the motorway!' Then it was back to the Quadrant for a post match drink while we waited for the traffic to die down.

It was unbelievable that 3,000 Blues could out sing 72,000 Manchester United fans. I would hate it if Blues ever became a club like that with thousands coming from other parts of the country and being a tourist attraction. Awful thought! It was a bad defeat for Blues but it wasn't helped that we didn't play Gardener, Jerome and Zigic because of the League Cup semi final being only 4 days away. It was a very different team than the one which drew 1-1 with them just 4 weeks ago. Blues are 17th in the table.

I was really excited about the semi final 2nd leg against West Ham as we set off for St. Andrews. Stephen had come down from Leicester where he is at university and my sister Annette was with me today and we headed to Jimmy Spices in town for a meal before jumping a taxi to St. Andrews. It was packed outside the ground and we had to walk up from the traffic island and there was loads of trouble and police everywhere. When we arrived at the stadium it was like a throwback to the 80's as Blues and West Ham fans battled it out as the police ran around with riot shields and were being quite heavy handed in trying to separate them. Some of these clashes were in the car park so we just headed into the ground and took up our places on the KOP/Tilton corner which was already packed.

It was a fantastic atmosphere, the best I have known for many years and everyone was standing! It was absolutely buzzing. As 2 of us were in the back row of the KOP/Tilton corner (one on the KOP) we all squeezed in together. A couple of Bluenoses passed me and said that they had brought my book for their dad. That pleased me as the whole point of my book was to share the memories and help get the passion back into football.

The game got underway and we were stunned and devastated when West Ham scored from a cracking 25 yard shot which beat Foster and put West

Ham 3-1 ahead on aggregate. Blues now had a mountain to climb. We never stopped singing though and Blues were giving their all. Zigic came on for the second half and he seemed to make quite a difference to our performance. Blues should have had a corner when West Ham's Wayne Bridge handled the ball but we were awarded a corner instead. The corner went straight to Lee Bowyer who powered a shot into the net and St. Andrews exploded as we all celebrated and we were filled with renewed hope as it was now 1-1 and 2-3 on aggregate.

Blues were on fire now and with the partisan crowd behind them were throwing everything at West Ham. Then in the 79th minute Roger Johnson powered in a header to make the aggregate score 3-3 and the place went completely bonkers! I was so happy as we jumped around and fell over seats, it was fantastic! In the last minute of the game Gardener hit a cracking long range shot which the West Ham keeper got his fingertips to and diverted onto the post as we came so close to winning it.

So the game went to extra time and with only 4 minutes in, Gardener repeated his shot from the same distance which was hit with so much power that it flew into the net and St. Andrews went crazy! Unbelievable scenes all around the Stadium as we realised what had happened and that this remarkable comeback could mean a trip to Wembley! Blues saw out the remaining minutes and scarves all round the stadium were waved as everyone sang an incredibly loud 'Ka sa ra sa ra whatever will be will be, we're going to Wembley, ka sa ra sa ra'.

When the final whistle sounded it was absolutely amazing - the best night at St. Andrews for many many years and Blues were in our first major Cup Final at Wembley for 50 years. I was so excited and I returned back to Abu Dhabi very happy and looking forward to returning for the trip to Wembley in February. It had been a great trip home and I had viewed a couple of houses while home as well and I was busy trying to arrange an expat mortgage.

The next morning despite a hangover I collected all the newspapers and booked my flight for the final and Steve called to say that he had booked a coach and arranged a a pub stopover prior to the final where the landlady was putting on free food for us. The pub is only 15 minutes from Wembley by tube. I can't wait!

A few days later, with me back in Abu Dhabi, Blues were again in Cup action this time against Coventry City at St. Andrews in the 4th round of the FA Cup. Alex McLeish made 9 changes from the team that played in the semi final and it showed. Championship side Coventry went 2-0 up before

Bentley pulled a goal back for Blues in the 35th minute. Parnaby levelled the score on 67 minutes and super Kevin Phillips scored the winner in the 73rd minute to make the final score 3-2 and Blues were in the 5th round. What an incredible Cup run Blues are having this season. It's brilliant. I watched it live and had Blues scarves and flags all around my apartment and afterwards I celebrated with a cold cider in my Birmingham City pint glass. Class!

The next day I started work on yet another new ward - Ward A, which meant I had now worked in every department at the Corniche hospital. When I got home I watched the FA Cup 5th round draw live and was pleased to be drawn at home against Sheffield Wednesday.

A couple of days later I had to take my car in for its vehicle test (Middle East version of an MOT) and it failed because the roof needed a polish and paint! I couldn't believe it and when I went to the dealers I discovered it would cost over £100 and take 2 and a half days. They were actually a worried about the weather as it had rained a bit today (rain is extremely rare in Abu Dhabi) and I don't think they have indoor work shops! Hopefully the evening game against Manchester City would cheer me up

It was back to League action and Manchester City were the next visitors to St. Andrews which had been moved to the Wednesday night at short notice because of Manchester City having played their Cup tie on the Sunday. It was a really entertaining game that saw a Manchester City player knocked out in a collision with one of his own teammates. Kevin Phillips scored a deserved equaliser from the penalty spot which gave Blues a 2-2 draw in front of nearly 25,000 inside St. Andrews. Blues remain 17th in the league.

It was off to West Ham's Upton Park again only this time Blues were victorious as we came away with a great 1-0 win with a goal from Zigic which took Blues up to 16th place.

Once again Blues we're back in FA Cup action as we took on Sheffield Wednesday at St. Andrews. Disappointingly there was only 14,607 inside St. Andrews for the occasion. It was a much stronger team that took on League One side Sheffield Wednesday and it took a only 6 minutes for Blues to take a 1-0 lead and we were 2-0 up on 17 minutes when Obafemi Martins scored his first goal for the club. A good 3-0 win was completed when Murphy got the 3rd which took Blues into the quarterfinals for the second year running. Fantastic times! The following days saw Blues drawn at home again in the 6th round against Bolton which was pleasing.

Zigic was on the scoresheet in the next game against Stoke City and he left it late to score in the 93rd minute as Blues again won 1-0 and moved up to 14th place. Obafemi Martins made his Blues debut in this game.

Blues were poor in their next game as they lost 2-0 at home to Newcastle and although we remain in 14th place Blues are only 3 points off the relegation places. Alex McLeish blamed the flat performance on fatigue. I wasn't too despondent as we were off to Wembley next week in the Carling Cup Final.

Chapter Three - League Cup Final

I was so excited to be heading home for the League Cup Final despite having to embark on a night flight back to the UK after a 12 hour shift at work. Hence I arrived knackered but happy. I had ordered loads of Blues Wembley memorabilia and on day of the match me, Annette and Stephen (my nephew) donned jester hats, giant hands, scarves and flags and made our way to Harborne to get the coach. I had a blue 'bob' wig on and Steve's brother Eddie fell about laughing when he saw me. I thought I looked cool! I had even painted my nails blue! It was a great trip up to London with music playing - mostly Blues related, and singing and chatting. Stephen had commented on his Facebook status that he was 'just off to London to pick up a cup'. His girlfriends (she's from London) brother is an Arsenal fan so that could be fun!

We arrived at the pub 'Wards' at 11.15 am and it was already full of Bluenoses as word had gotten around that this was where we were headed. It was fantastic and there was Blues flags everywhere. The landlady had put on hot food (free) for us and it was lovely. Everyone was singing Blues songs and the atmosphere was brilliant. I painted a few faces and James even painted his nose blue. I was chatting to Snowy who had travelled down with us despite not having a match ticket. He was planning on watching the game in The Greenman pub near Wembley. Word and photos reached us via social media showing a large flag which had been put up on the gates at

Villa park which said 'while we're at Wembley the City is yours - KRO'. Class!

We set off for Wembley with plenty of time as we wanted to enjoy the pre match atmosphere. There had already been quite a few drinks consumed at this point though as we headed to the nearby tube station. It was fun on the tube as it was mostly Bluenoses with only a couple of Arsenal fans. We sang 'we'll be running round the bullring with the Cup!' Although none of us actually thought we would win the cup with Arsenal being overwhelming favourites. We were here to enjoy our day out. They were under the impression that they only had to turn up though. There was talk of this being their first trophy of the season.

So we arrived on Wembley way in the rain but in very good voice. I was interviewed by TV presenters about the game and I bravely predicted blues would win with a goal in the last minute. I think it was the blue wig that attracted them and I'm not sure the interview made it to the telly as I was probably a little tipsy at this point. Then it was into Wembley stadium as we joined the amazing blue army that were already singing their hearts out and I immediately joined in. We were up in the third tier at the corner and had an amazing view.

The teams had already arrived with the Blues players in really nice suits for the occasion whereas the high and mighty Arsenal arrived in track suits to pick up 'their cup'. That was immediately picked up by the pundits who commented on Blues looking the part but Arsenal being a bit disrespectful. The media had been focused on the fact that this would be the first of a possible quadruple for Arsenal and they were overwhelming favourites with the bookies.

When the players came out for kick off the noise was tremendous and it was the loudest version of Keep Right On that I had ever heard and it took the roof off the new Wembley stadium! Even the pundits remarked that the Blues fans were the loudest ever at Wembley! There were 88,851 in attendance and the Blue end was well and truly enjoying the occasion. Although we dreamed of a win we were realistic and were here to enjoy ourselves and the occasion.

With only 2 minutes gone Bowyer ran through and was brought down by the Arsenal goalkeeper and it should have been a penalty and a red card but the linesman's flag was up for offside so Arsenal were saved. Replays showed the decision to be incorrect as Bowyer was indeed onside! The noise from the Bluenoses at this injustice was immense.

On 28 minutes Blues won a corner which was put into the area by Larsson to Roger Johnson who's header towards goal was headed into the net by Zigic and the Blues end exploded in celebration. We all went absolutely crazy, Stephen picked me up in the air and we were all jumping on each other. We couldn't believe we were 1-0 up against the mighty Arsenal in a Cup Final at Wembley. Incredible!

Of course Arsenal threw everything at us and disappointingly they equalised just before half time with a goal from Van Persie and the red half of the stadium woke up for the first time. Blues fans responded with another very loud rendition of Keep Right On to spur our players on. We were still in this game. Halftime came with the score still at 1-1. In the second half Blues were unlucky when Keith Fahey's shot came back off the inside of the post and as the game went on Blues started to tire and Arsenal threw everything at us but Ben Foster in goal, had a great game which culminated in him winning man of the match for the second time in 3 years at Wembley.

With 7 minutes remaining Obafemi Martins came on to make his debut as he replaced Keith Fahey. It looked to be going to extra time as we entered the 89th minute as Ben Foster made a long clearance which was flicked on by Zigic and as an Arsenal defender and the goalkeeper got in each other's way the ball fell to Obafemi Martin who swept the ball into an empty net. I went absolutely mental as did the entire Blues end as we all jumped on each other amongst unbelievable scenes like I have never seen before. Most of us had tears in our eyes as we realised we may just win the cup! Obafemi Martins ran off and did a string of somersaults whilst the other Blues players tried to catch up with him without getting kicked in the face. The noise was unbelievable as we celebrated.

Blues then defended well for the last few minutes but we could have gone further ahead when Obafemi Martins rounded the keeper but the angle proved to be too tight. Jerome and Ferguson were booked for time wasting before the referee blew and Wembley erupted in celebrations like nothing ever seen before and Birmingham City were the Carling Cup winners 2011 beating Arsenal 2-1. Our first major trophy for 50 years. I couldn't believe it and was so happy. We were all hugging and singing and crying with happiness. It was a lifelong dream. We all stayed behind for ages as we watched captain Stephen Carr lift that beautiful silver cup with Blue ribbons on it and we watched them parade it before our fans as they popped champagne bottles and drank it from the cup. Such fantastic scenes!

When we eventually headed to the escalators to exit Wembley the noise was incredible as we sang 'we're all going on a European tour!' To the tune of yellow submarine, and 'we won the Cup!' What a fantastic day! It will live long in the memory. We headed back on the tube to the pub where the landlady had laid on more food and the celebrations really began. We drank and sang 'all dance if you won the cup' and 'we're all going on a European tour' for quite a while before climbing back on the coach knackered and headed back to Birmingham. I will never ever forget this day. It will be known as Obafemi Martins Day!

I had found a wedding ring in the stadium as I left and I gave it to Steve to see if he could find out if anyone lost it, which he did and he got the credit for that in the local Mail. A good happy ending. I collected all the newspapers the next day and watched Central Sport and Midlands Today as they showed Blues fans and interviewed Jasper Carrot and Alex McLeish. They showed the Cup coming home to St. Andrews - brilliant!

There was a lot of anger towards Birmingham City council after Blues fantastic cup win as they would not allow us to have a civic reception it Town with an open top bus tour. Disgraceful! It would be different if it was our neighbours Vile who can do no wrong but the football club that bears the name of our mighty city - oh no, not for us! They insisted it be held at St. Andrews over a week later. That's our 'villa' Council for you. I don't know how they get away with it. This meant that I would miss the celebrations as I would be back n Abu Dhabi.

The next day I went to Northfield and bought all the newspapers to read about our fantastic Cup win and there were people in Blues shirts and scarves everywhere. The villa fans must be sick. It all caught up with me on the night though and I was knackered.

I was still in Birmingham for the next game against West Brom at St. Andrews and saw Blues display a cup hangover and a poor performance saw us lose 3-1 in front of over 27,000 and drop to 18th place. The highlight of the day was our pre match drink and catch up in The Cricketers and obtaining scarves with 'Wembley Winners' On it and badges with Cup winners on. I then had to go home and pack ready for tomorrow's flight back to Abu Dhabi and I really don't want to go. I have been to view a house just across from my moms and I am looking into getting a mortgage which is not easy and when you are an expat.

I was back in Abu Dhabi and I watched the Everton game on live TV in as Blues took the lead through Beausejour but Everton equalised and the game ended 1-1 which lifted us to 17th and out of the relegation zone. Blues still have a game in hand but worryingly 7 out of our last 11 games are away from home and with some tough games coming up.

A few days later and it was back to Cup action and as it was the quarterfinal I was beginning to dream of another trip to Wembley. I was off work and able to watch the game live with flags and scarves draped around my apartment. Blues had so many players out injured that they had to give a squad number to a 17 year old defender and were unable to name the full compliment of 7 substitutes.

Bolton then took the lead after 21 minutes before Blues lost another 2 players to injury. Jerome then grabbed an equaliser for Blues but Bolton went ahead again before Kevin Phillips hit the post. Phillips did get his goal though with a cracker that made it 2-2 and Blues went all out for the win. It was looking really good until Bolton snatched an injury time winner to break our hearts and all dreams of a semi final were gone. I was really disappointed. I cheered myself up the next day by going and getting my Wembley photos printed.

Back to League action and Liam Ridgewell scored in the 6th minute to give Blues the lead at Wigan but couldn't hold on as Wigan equalised and then grabbed the winner in injury time which took us down to 19th and into the relegation places. I watched the game live and Blues were awful. There's not much in it though and if we win our game in hand we could be up to 13th!

It was the international break the following weekend so I decked my apartment out in England fans and watched England beat Wales 2-1 in Cardiff to top the group in the Euro 2012 qualifiers.

Bolton then returned to St. Andrews and Blues were out to revenge our recent cup exit at the hands of our visitors. Kevin Phillips gave Blues the lead after only 4 minutes and Gardener scored a 2nd on 59 minutes. Larsson had a goal disallowed before Bolton pulled one back with a spectacular goal from distance. Blues hung on to win the game 2-1 and all was hopeful again. It is still really tight at the bottom of the table though.

Blues then traveled to Blackburn where Lee Bowyer gave Blues the lead but following lengthy treatment for a head injury to Roger Johnson which seemed to distract Liam Ridgewell, Blackburn were allowed to run through and get the equaliser. A bit disappointing but a good away point nonetheless. I thought Blues should have won and I could hear the Blues fans singing throughout the game as I watched it live and on TV.

Next it was Sunderland at St. Andrews and goals from Larsson in the first half and Gardener in the second half saw Blues win 2-0 and we are now 5 points clear of the relegation places with a game in hand over most other teams so it looks good. That is now 7 points from the last 3 games and Blues are up to 14th. It's a really close League this year so it is going to remain nerve wracking until the end of the season. I am always weary of being the surprise team that gets sucked in at the last minute though.

Blues now had two very difficult games against Chelsea and Liverpool, both of them away from home. In the first of theses games Blues played really well at Chelsea but lost 3-1 with Larsson converting a penalty for our consolation goal. I should have known it was going to be a bad week when a Porsche crashed into the front of my apartment building a couple of days before the Chelsea game! I was cheered up by the arrival of my brother and sister-in-law the next morning though as they were visiting for a couple of weeks.

In the St. George's day trip to Anfield Blues were soundly beaten 5-0 but remained safe in 15th place. Goalkeeper Ben Foster had to go off injured and was replaced by Colin Doyle.

The local derby game against Wolves at St. Andrews was a very hot tempered game in which Wolves took the lead before Larsson scored a great goal to make it 1-1 and St. Andrews erupted. Unfortunately Gardener received a second yellow card for diving and was sent off leaving the ten men to hold on for a point. Many Blues fans thought of this as a turning point for Blues as we could and should have gone on to win the game had Gardener remained on the pitch. But he didn't and Blues only got a point.

Another difficult away trip next as Blues traveled to Newcastle and once again Blues were reduced to ten men as Liam Ridgewell saw red for handling on the goal line. Newcastle scored from the resultant penalty before going further ahead. Bowyer pulled a goal back just before half time and Larsson had a great chance to equalise but blasted over and Blues slumped to a 2-1 defeat and were down to 16th place with only 2 games remaining. I was already feeling a bit down anyway as my brother Neil and his Wife Sue had flown home last night. The apartment felt empty although a phone call with my mom cheered me up.

There was a near full house at St. Andrews for the last home game of the season against Fulham and a chance to secure Premier League football again for next season. It was a must win game. Blues looked really nervous and never got going as Fulham scored twice and Blues finished the game with ten men again but this time because we lost 4 players to injury. We were now down to 17th ahead of Blackpool and Wigan on goal difference. The last game would now decided our fate and it was a very difficult away trip to Tottenham. West Ham were relegated.

On the day of the Tottenham game I was so nervous and I couldn't bear the though that if everything went against us and we lost then Blues could be relegated. There were 5 teams in danger of relegation. Blues had to make sure that we didn't do worse than Blackpool and Wigan and with other permutations from the Blackburn v Wolves game.

Blues went 1-0 down and my nerves were shredded. Then on 79 minutes Craig Gardener scored to make it 1-1 which put a Blues above Wolves and safe but then Wolves scored which meant Blues now needed to win. It seemed to take time to get the message to our players but as we threw everything at Tottenham we were caught on the break and Tottenham scored to break our hearts and Blues were relegated to the championship. I was inconsolable. What a heartbreaking way to finish the season in which we had won the League Cup at Wembley. Would I have traded the Cup to stay up? Definitely not!

The Premier League was won by Manchester United with Chelsea as runners up. Blackpool and West Ham were relegated to the Championship with Blues. Qualification for the Champions League was Manchester United, Chelsea, Manchester City and Arsenal. Qualification for Europa League was Tottenham, Birmingham City, Stoke City and Fulham. Yes Blues in Europe! I can't wait! The FA Cup was won by Manchester City and the League Cup by Birmingham City.

Blues top goal scorer was Craig Gardener with 10 goals in all competitions. Manager Alex McLeish resigned on 12th June 2011. I was really upset when McLeish resigned, especially when he they joined our rivals across the city and became a massive Judas! I can only hope he takes them down too! It's becoming a second city war in Birmingham as the Vile fans don't want him and the Blues fans hate him.

Blues appointed Chris Hughton as manager in June and we all really hoped that he would take us back to the Premier League at the first attempt. Hughton led Newcastle to the Championship title in 2010 so I was as hopeful as ever. Then on 29th June Blues owner Carson Yeung was arrested in Hong Kong on charges of money laundering. This meant that Peter Pannu and Carson's son Ryan were appointed to the board of directors which resulted in Michael Wiseman stepping down and sadly ended an 83 year connection between the Wiseman's and the club.

Another hot summer in Abu Dhabi as well as work becoming increasingly stressful meant that I was now strongly considering leaving it all behind and moving back home. I was busy trying to arrange a mortgage but as I was not living in the UK it meant a large deposit which would probably mean that I would realistically have to remain here for a couple more years. Not something that I was relishing at present. Hopefully Blues would be back in the Premier League by then.

Chapter Four - European Tour

The new kit for the 2011-12 season would be a nice all blue kit - shirts, shorts and socks all royal blue and with Blues having ended their sponsorship with F&C Investment from last season, and no deal being agreed for this season the club chose to appoint shirt sponsorship on a match day basis. This meant that the replica shirts went on sale with no sponsorship. The away kit was a black and blue striped shirt, black shorts and blue socks with a black rim and the third kit was a lovely yellow shirt with thin blue strips, blue shorts and white socks with a blue rim. Very nice.

For the first friendly of the 2011-12 season Blues were without Cameron Jerome and Nikola Zigic for the trip to Irish first division club Cork City. The game was settled by a single goal from Adam Rooney in the 30th minute to give Blues a 1-0 win. A few days later in the next friendly away at League Two club Hereford, Blues failed to take their chances and the game ended in a 0-0 draw. It was the same story in the next friendly game at League Two side Oxford as Blues twice hit the bar but lost the game 2-0. Not good really.

I flew back to Birmingham again on 27th July for a nice summer holiday with my family and despite all the unrest at Blues I was looking forward to the friendly game against Everton at St, Andrews. My brother dropped me, Annette and Stephen at St. Andrews where we obtained tickets then headed to the Cricketers pub for a couple of pre match drinks. It was beautiful day and we stood outside in the sun for a while. I bought the Carling Cup shirt in a box for £50 as well as the Made In Brum fanzine and some badges and then it was off to the match.

It was heartbreaking seeing a completely new team after Carson Yeung had sold off all our best players. It was like going back in time to the days of the Kumars! Blues played well though and we were unlucky to lose the game 2-1.

It was great to be home for the opening match of the new season and I had been really looking forward to the trip to Derby. Me, Stephen and Steve traveled to Derby by train and we got off in Burton and headed to a pub to meet some other Bluenoses. The pub was already busy with Bluenoses and we met Fiddler, Hockey, Beksy and others and we enjoyed a few drinks before heading back to the station and getting the train to Derby. We were soon inside the stadium and my seat was next to Brendan and his family who had come straight from Manchester airport after returning from their holiday.

Blues took the lead when Curtis Davies scored in the 19th and we all went wild in celebration. Unfortunately Derby soon equalised and then scored another before half time. Blues battered Derby but just couldn't score and lost the game 2-1. I was optimistic as we played so well and despite the defeat I had a great day out.

After the game it was kicking off everywhere as the Derby fans tried to attack the Blues fans but just ended up getting run all over the place. The police didn't know what to do for the best. As we walked up towards the station a group of Derby fans came out of an alley to ambush us but discovered that there were hundreds of us who then chased them back down their alley. Quite funny really. I headed back to moms and early the next morning I sadly headed back to Abu Dhabi.

A crowd of 19,225 turned up for Blues first home game in the Championship for the local game against Coventry City at St. Andrews. Blues got the win they needed when Keith Fahey shot home from 10 yards on 73 minutes in a

1-0 win. Now that Blues are in the Championship I am unable to watch the games as they are not shown live out here - only the Premier League and I really miss being able to watch them.

I was really excited about Blues first European game away in Madeira against CD Nacional and I knew a lot of Blues fans who were travelling there. Blues were weakened by injuries and gave David Murphy and Nathan Redmond their first starts of the season with Chris Wood the lone striker up front. Blues played really well but despite Chris Wood hitting the crossbar the game finished in a goalless draw.

The Middlesbrough away game was being shown live but I had to work and I was so tired that I forgot to set it to record the game. I didn't miss much though as Blues lost 3-1 despite taking the lead and are 18th in the table. Early days yet though.

The second leg of our Europa League game against CD Nacional was being shown live in Abu Dhabi but was on quite late due to the time difference hence I watched it in bed. My sister Annette had gone to the game with Steve and they got me a scarf which I was delighted with. It was brilliant to watch Blues play in Europe and I was so excited!

For this game Blues had to widen the pitch to comply with UEFA regulations from 66 metres to 68 metres. There was a good attendance of 27,698 and Blues took the lead on 15 minutes when Nathan Redmond scored and the stadium went wild. There were even more celebrations when David Murphy made it 2-0 on 24 minutes and when Chris Wood wrapped it up with a tap in on 86 minutes our joy was complete. Blues qualify for the group stages and I was so happy. Absolutely fantastic!

Blues were drawn in Group H with Braga from Portugal who were last season's finalists, Slovenian Champions Maribor (who had originally been in the Champions League) and Club Brugge from Belgium. Not an easy group by any means.

Back to league action and a 2-2 draw away at Watford saw Blues drop to 21st place but still early days as I keep telling myself. Then it was back to St. Andrews and Chris Wood got a hat trick as Blues won 3-0 in front of 17,901 and Blues made a big jump up to 12th place.

Meanwhile I had found a lovely house back in Birmingham not far from my family and after sending my mom for a viewing I put in an offer and I was absolutely delighted when it was accepted.

Blues were about to continue on their European adventures and we began the Group stage as last years finalists Braga visited St. Andrews under the floodlights as nearly 22,000 watched Blues suffer our first defeat in the competition as Braga beat us 3-1. Blues did play some great football though and most of us remain hopeful.

The disappointment continued into the next game as Blues lost 4-1 away at Southampton which saw our hosts go top of the table. It is a totally different team this season after all our star players jumped ship following relegation. I blame our owner Carson Yeung as this never happened when we got relegated under Sullivan and the Golds who always kept hold of our players and hence quick returns the the premiership.

Just 3 days later and Blues we're away at Premier League side Manchester City, without Chris Wood who was ineligible and despite an admirable performance and a Curtis Davies overhead kick being cleared off the line, Blues suffered a 2-0 defeat and exited the competition. Still lots to play for though.

It was back to League action on the Saturday at St. Andrews as Blues drew 1-1 with Barnsley in which manager Chris Hughton said was as poor as we have played since he has been here.

I was working the day Blues travelled to Slovenia to take on Slovenian champions Maribor with 800 Bluenoses making the long trip. Oh how I wished I could have been there. This is one of the reasons that I am currently putting everything in place to return to the UK permanently in the next few years and I am currently in the process of an ex pat mortgage to buy a wonderful house not far from my family's homes.

I had to make do with listening to the game on my iPhone (radio) and I could hear the Blues fans singing 'Keep Right On'. Maribor took the lead and they had never lost at home in Europe but Chris Burke equalised on 64 minutes and then Wade Elliott scored the winner on 79 minutes as the Bluenoses went totally mental. I was dancing around my room and was so happy. Fantastic!

In the next game Blues were away at Nottingham Forest and were 1-0 down with 15 minutes remaining but pulled of a fantastic comeback by scoring 3 times to win the game 3-1.

I was able to watch the home game against Leicester City at St. Andrews live on TV as I was off work after having surgery to remove a skin cancer from my forehead. I didn't look my best as I had a massive bandage on my head and I hadn't been well due to either the anaesthetic or the painkillers. The first half was a bit boring but in the second half Blues won a penalty which Marlon King scored and then Leicester had a player sent off. Chris Wood scored again and Blues won the game 2-0 to move up to 15th in the table with 2 games in hand.

I had been staying over in Dubai on the day of the Brugge game as my boyfriend had been back onshore for a couple of days but I drove back to Abu Dhabi in plenty of time to watch the match live on TV. There were 5,600 Blues fans inside the stadium in Brugge and a further 13,000 in the city without tickets - amazing! Oh how I wished I could have been there. There had been stories that there would be 5,600 Blues hooligans heading to Brugge but this was not true and after the game the Belgium police thanked the Blues fans on their Twitter account for their friendly behaviour.

It was an amazing game to watch although Brugge took an early lead but after 25 minutes David Murphy scored to make it 1-1 and the away end exploded in celebration. Towards the end of normal time a clash of heads saw Blues Pablo Ibáñez unconscious for quite some time and it looked really bad. So much so that his teammate Guirane N'Daw was in tears. Pablo was carried off on a spinal stretcher and there was ten minutes of injury time added. In the last minute of the injury time Marlon King crossed the ball in for Chris Wood to smash home the winner and the Blues end went absolutely mental as I did in my bedroom where I was watching the game (it was really late in Abu Dhabi due to the time difference). This made Blues the first English team to win at Brugge's stadium and took us to the top of group H. What a night and what a brilliant game!

Back to League action on the Sunday and a great 2-0 away win at Bristol City moved Blues up to 14th with 3 games in hand. It's quite exciting at the moment and I'm really wishing I was back in England for this exciting season. I am currently working hard on completing my mortgage for a lovely house back in Weoley Castle in Birmingham that is near to all my family which I am really excited about. It's the first step towards coming home to England to live in the next few years.

Attendances are starting to increase at St. Andrews and 21,426 were there for the Leeds game as a goal from Nikola Zigic gave Blues a good 1-0 win which moved us up to 8th place, only 1 point off the play offs with 2 games in hand now. The next game against Brighton at St. Andrews was a game of very few chances that ended in a 0-0 draw.

On the day Blues played Brugge at St. Andrews in the Europa League I was at the British Club in Abu Dhabi for the annual bonfire night, which was fantastic as always and I was also looking forward to my mom and sister visiting the next day. I was home in time to watch the game though in which Blues went 2-0 down before making a triple substitution and scoring twice to draw the game 2-2.

In the next game away at Reading Blues had many chances but Reading did a smash and grab as they scored the only goal of the game and inflicted a rare defeat and Blues dropped to 13th. The crowd dropped to 18,000 for the visit of Peterborough as a 1-1 draw took Blues up to 12th. Marlon King said Blues need to be more clinical.

There was 16,253 inside St. Andrews to see Blues take the lead against Burnley after only 2 minutes but Burnley equalised before halftime. Happily Chris Burke scored the winner in the 91st minute taking Blues up to 8th again. Blues again left it late at Blackpool when Nikola Zigic scored an 85th minute equaliser in a 2-2 draw as Blues remain in 8th place. The next day came the awful news that footballer and Wales manager Gary Speed had died. He was only 42 and had been found hanged, how very sad.

I was really excited as I was heading home to Birmingham again even though I had to work a 12 hour day shift then catch the night flight later. The flight did go okay but on the flight from Paris to Birmingham we were warned to expect delays due to industrial action by the border control. Happily I had no problems and was I straight through, probably because my flight arrived so early in the morning.

I headed to my moms and grabbed a couple of hours sleep before heading to the Kings Arms in Harborne to watch the Europa League game against Braga which was being played in Portugal. My nephew Stephen came with us and we watched as Blues played really well but there were groans all around the pub when Nikola Zigic stepped up to take a penalty for Blues only for the keeper to save it.

This proved to be the turning point as Braga went on to win the game with a goal from a very lucky deflection when Blues were clearly the better team. To make matters worse Maribor - who were leading 3-0 with about 20 minutes remaining but then lost 4-3 which means that barring a miracle Blues Europa adventure is all but over. The next day I went to view my new house for the first time and I was delighted with it and we agreed a date of 13th December to exchange contracts. I'm so excited.

I was up early on the Saturday to head to Cardiff for the away game and Steve picked me up in a taxi to take us to St. Andrews to get the coach. We persuaded the taxi to go through McDonalds so that we could obtain breakfast and drinks. I took some plastic 'Halloween' glasses with me so when we stopped at the services we had a nice vodka and coke in them. Once we arrived at Cardiff the 7 coaches were escorted straight to the ground where we met up with Craig, Graham, Mark, Ron, Brendan and Liam inside the stadium and had a nice pint of cider before the game.

It was my first time to Cardiff's new stadium and I thought it was quite nice for a new ground. We had some great banter with the home fans, which can be quite rare these days, and I particularly liked "Swansea are shit but they're better than you!" It was slightly amusing when Cardiff sang '1-0 to the sheep shaggers' when they took the lead. Somewhat disappointingly Blues lost 1-0 and we headed back to Birmingham where I met my sister Annette in the Kings Arms for a post match pint before heading back to moms for a lovely Sunday roast. Unfortunately I lost my beautiful gold Blues ball and world necklace that I had been given for my 18th Birthday so I was really sad about that. It had been made specially for me in the jewellery quarter.

A few days later and I was headed to another away game with Blues only this time it was off to Hull. I met up with Brendan and Ron at The Old Crown in Bartley Green where Dave, our lift, picked us up just as it was getting cold and dark. The motorway near Hull was closed to high sided vehicles due to the weather as we arrived. Once we had parked up we headed to the nearby social club (the Walton) where we enjoyed a pre match drink.

It was a really windy and cold night as we headed back to the ground. It was another new ground for me and it was quite a nice stadium. We had some good banter with the home fans and there was about 600-700 of us Bluenoses. We were loud though and I enjoyed it when we sang "we came in a taxi and we're louder than you!" Blues went 1-0 up and we all celebrated but after a goalkeeper error we ended up losing 2-1. Very disappointing and we didn't get out of Hull till 10pm meaning that we got home at 1am and it was freezing cold. Blues were now down to 14th.

A few days later on the Friday night me, mom, Annette and Jean headed to St. Andrews for the Grease tribute night and what a fantastic night it was. There were loads of girls in pink ladies jackets with SOTV on the back - classic! After telling the organiser that I had traveled 3,500 mile to be there and would love to hold the Carling Cup (Blues were the current holders) she arranged for security to get the key for the trophy cabinet and I was taken to see the Cup. I was so excited and when I held the cup in my hands and got photos taken with it I was overwhelmed. I was getting comments like 'put it on your head' (which I didn't as it was too heavy) and 'kiss the cup' (which I did and got a great photo) and it was the best Christmas present ever! What a fantastic night.

The next day I went back to St. Andrews for the game against Doncaster Rovers and I headed into the Cricketers pub to meet Brendan, Eddie and the lads for a pre match drink and I proudly showed them my photos with the Carling Cup and they were suitably impressed. Then it was off to the match where Blues went 1-0 down before coming back to win the game 2-1. Great win and I was happy.

A few days later and I finally got the keys to my new home and me, mom and Neil (my brother) headed straight over to it to look around it and we opened a bottle of bubbly to celebrate. What a wonderful feeling to open my front door and go inside my new house. It had been left clean and immaculate and Neil set my central heating and alarm. It was lovely to be inside my house and I am so happy as everything is starting to fall into place.

The last Europa League game was a bit nerve wracking as Blues had to beat Maribor and hope that Braga, who had already qualified, win in Brugge. Stephen had traveled down from Manchester (on the Megabus!) where he was currently living and we went with Steve to the Cricketers before the game where we met up with the lads again.

It was a good game and a Blues were outstanding and took the lead when Adam Rooney scored after 24 minutes and despite several chances that was how it stayed as Blues won 1-0. It was a bit subdued though as Braga were 1-1 at Brugge which meant that somewhat unusually 10 points was not enough to see Blues qualify and our wonderful European adventures were at an end. Not to be too downhearted Blues fans sang "we've all been on a European tour!" which was tinged with sadness but a fitting tribute. We headed home sad but grateful for our European adventure.

Chapter Five - Play Offs

I flew back to Abu Dhabi very early on Sunday morning and I have to admit to being quite sad about leaving Birmingham behind and I am already looking forward to the time when I will be able to return.

On the Monday night Blues traveled to Crystal Palace and lost 1-0 and I felt sorry for our fans on what would have been a very cold night. Blues are 14th in the league.

I was back at work for 3 long days and before I knew it Christmas Eve was here and I was off to the British Club for the party on the beach and this year Santa arrived on a Camel which I missed as I arrived late. Christmas Day was spent at a friends massive house with a bunch of us who had a lovely time and Christmas dinner was accompanied by Moët champagne. Lovely, although I did miss my family.

The Boxing Day game saw Blues take on West Ham at St. Andrews and despite falling behind early on Blues came back to equalise and share the points in a 1-1 draw. Blues finished the year with a fantastic 3-0 home win over Blackpool which means that so far Blues are unbeaten at St. Andrews this season and it moves us up to 12th with 2 games in hand.

The first match of 2012 was away at Peterborough and there was a minutes silence for ex Blues player Gary Ablett who has sadly died the day before from blood cancer. Very sad. It took only 29 seconds for Peterborough to take the lead but Blues did manage to salvage a draw with a penalty converted by Marlon King.

It was FA Cup action next as Blues were drawn away at Premier League side Wolverhampton Wanderers. It turned out to be a bit of a boring 0-0 draw which meant a replay at St. Andrews in a couple of weeks time.

The first home game of the year saw Blues get our first win of 2012 in a 2-1 win over Ipswich in which Zigic scored in the 9th and 91st minute to move Blues up to 9th in the table.

Blues were then away at Millwall in a game that was to become legendary. Blues took a 1-0 lead in the first half against 10 men Millwall who had a man sent off but when Millwall had a second player sent off in the second half Blues ran riot and scored another 5 goals. A fantastic 6-0 win which inspired the chant 'who put the ball in the Millwall net? Half the fucking team did!'

It was back to the FA Cup next as Wolves came to town for a place in the 4th round. Both sides fielded weakened sides but Blues came out winners as Wade Elliott scored in the 74th minute and it finished 1-0 and Blues now have a 4th round tie at League One side Sheffield United to look forward to.

In the next game two goals from Davies and one from Burke saw Blues beat Watford 3-0 and move up to 6th and into the play off places.

Then it was FA Cup action again and Blues comfortably progressed to the 5th round with a very good 4-0 away win. Next up will be Premier League side Chelsea. My mom and sister were here in Abu Dhabi to celebrate my birthday with me and we had a great time but I was really lonely when they left. I seem to be longing for home at lot these days.

Back to league action and Nikola Zigic ran riot scoring 4 goals in the away trip to Leeds as Blues won 4-1 to move up to 4th place and only 5 points off an automatic place with a game in hand. It was freezing cold with thick snow when Blues entertained Southampton at St. Andrews in a game that ended in a 0-0 draw. No goals to warm up the cold Bluenoses.

Blues game in hand came against Portsmouth at home, a club who were facing liquidation and had not paid their players wages. It was decided by an 86th minute goal from Nathan Redmond that won it for Blues and took us up to 3rd in the table. The following week it was again at St. Andrews with Hull City the visitors and the game ended in a goalless draw.

I watched the FA Cup match at Chelsea live on TV in Abu Dhabi and despite King and Zigic being out and Carr gong off injured, Blues played really well. I was jumping around the living room when Murphy scored for Blues after only 12 minutes and again when Doyle saved a Chelsea penalty just 2 minutes later. Could it be our day and could Blues pull off a great FA Cup upset? Well no, Chelsea pinched an undeserved equaliser in the second half and despite missing a couple of good chances in the last few minutes the game ended 1-1 and a reply at St. Andrews.

Then it was back to League action as Blues travelled to Barnsley and returned with a very good 3-1 win. Sadly Blues unbeaten run came to an end a few days later as we lost 2-1 at home against Nottingham Forest. The League then imposed a transfer embargo on Blues for not submitting their accounts by the due date but not before Blues brought in 3 loan signings of Andros Townsend, Erik Huseklepp and Peter Ramage.

It was Huseklepp who scored the first goal in the next game against Derby at St. Andrews as Blues went 2-0 up before conceding 2 goals through poor defending to draw the game 2-2. Two points dropped.

As I was planning on leaving Abu Dhabi in a couple of years I decided to have a bit of a clear out and have a stall at the Flea Market at the Sheraton hotel with one of my friends. Although I was nervous about it we had a fabulous day and I had sold all my stuff by 13.20 and made nearly £300. Great day!

Nearly 22,000 were at St. Andrews for the FA Cup 5th round replay as a weakened Blues side took on Premier League side Chelsea. Despite putting up a strong fight Blues went down to two second half Chelsea goals although Doyle again saved a Chelsea penalty from Mata to keep the score at 2-0 as Blues exited the Cup. What a fantastic run it had been though.

Back to League action and a trip to Coventry City where both Gary McSheffrey and Marlon King scored against their old clubs in a 1-1 draw. Jordan Mutch was sent off for Blues against relegation threatened Coventry. The second away game if a matter of days saw Blues head to Leicester as 2 late goals from Leicester condemned Blues to a rare defeat as Leicester won 3-1 and Blues dropped to 8th place.

Once again I was heading back to England for a well earned break and I was looking forward to seeing my family and Blues. My sister Annette and I headed for St. Andrews by bus for a change and walked from town just like the old days. It was great. We stopped off at The Old Crown which was full of Irish celebrating St. Patrick's day as well as loads of Bluenoses. Then we got a taxi to the Cricketers and met up with Brendan, Ron, Eddie, Steve and Ray and had a pie and a pint before speed walking to the stadium.

What a great match as Blues got back to winning ways with a 3-0 home win over Middlesbrough in Blues 50th game of the season which took us up to 4th place. I had a great day and we saw my 'brick' outside the KOP which says 'Truly Blue' (after my book of the same name) which Annette had bought me for my birthday.

Then came the shocking news that over at White Hart Lane ex Blues player Fabrice Muamba had suffered a cardiac arrest on the pitch whilst playing for Bolton against Tottenham in the FA Cup. It was a live televised game as Muamba received CPR as his heart stopped for 78 minutes before it was restarted. Happily he did recover after lengthy hospital treatment but sadly had to retire from from football. He is only 23 and was a great player at Blues and we were all praying for him. Of course their game was abandoned. Thank god there was a consultant cardiologist in the crowd who made his way to the pitch.

On the Tuesday me, Brendan and Ron got a taxi to the Cricketers for a pre match drink before boarding the coaches for the trip to Portsmouth. Hockey was the steward on our coach so that was great. Once we arrived at Portsmouth we headed for the nearest pub called Pickwick and had a couple of drinks before heading to the ground.

The game saw some shockingly bad refereeing that resulted in Blues being down to 10 men and losing 4-1 and it was painful to watch. The trip back was long and tiring and we arrived back in town at 01.20 and it's off to

Bournemouth for me tomorrow for a little break. Manager Chris Houghton was seething as he said afterwards that he has not been as angry with a refereeing performance this season.

The Cardiff game was an early kick off on the Sunday morning and although it was 12.00 the clocks had gone forward so in reality it was 11am in our heads! I think early kick offs spoil the atmosphere and today was no different. We had been to the Cricketers before the game but it was painful watching a poor Blues display as the players looked sluggish. King had a penalty saved but Huseklepp scored a brilliant goal in a 1-1 draw as Blues gave away a soft goal and we remain in 6th place.

The next day me and Annette headed to the travel agent to book a surprise holiday for moms 70th birthday in August. It took 3 hours of planning as we wanted fulfil moms dream of visiting Graceland as well as visiting Los Angeles and Las Vegas. It was so exciting. We decided to tell mom as she would need to prepare for the trip and she was totally overwhelmed. She so deserves this trip.

The trip home got even better a few days later when we went to see the Osmonds at the NIA. They were brilliant and I got a lovely silk retro scarf which I waved in the air prompting Merrill to point at me, put his thumb up and then wave at me as he was singing. To top it off we bumped into Jimmy Osmond in the foyer of the Hyatt Hotel afterward as we waited for a taxi. He said "Hi Honey" and put his arm round me for a photo. Excellent!

The next day I was off to Doncaster for the Friday night game and the lads had hired a 7 seater which Mark was driving. I met up with them at the Crown Pub in Bartley Green and Graham had brought a bag of booze with him so I had a vodka and coke in a can! We arrived early in Doncaster and went to the Beefeater near the ground. When it got packed we headed into Doncaster's bar in one of the stands and then headed into the ground to watch the game.

The home end was almost empty and Doncaster went 1-0 ahead after only 4 minutes but Blues were playing well and we came back to win 3-1. Both King and Zigic hit the woodwork and Blues were back up to 4th place. It was non stop singing from the Blues fans and I had a great night. It was spoilt somewhat by having to stop off at a pub in Worksop and then stopping in Stourbridge which meant we got back at 2am and I had to be up at 3am to head to the airport for my flight back to Abu Dhabi.

On the bright side my brother and sister in law were travelling back with me for a holiday and I had complimentary vouchers for the business class lounge in Amsterdam which was brilliant and was all inclusive food and drinks. We all had Buck's Fizz and Neil even had a Jack Daniels!

Blues repeated their 3-1 score line in the next 2 games as they defeated Burnley away with goals from King, Mutch and Murphy and then winning at St. Andrews against Crystal Palace with Burke, Fahey and Murphy scoring as Blues went 3-0 up after 32 minutes in a game that was never in any doubt. Blues again scored 3 on their visit to West Ham in which Blues were 3-1 up at half time but West Ham were awarded a penalty for handball in the 89th minute as the ball hit Burke's hand from close proximity and the Hammers levelled the score as it finished 3-3.

Crowds were on the increase at St. Andrews as the business end of the season approached and over 23,000 were in attendance for the home game against Bristol City. Blues came back from 2-0 down but were unable to get a 3rd and had to settle for a 2-2 draw.

Another draw at Ipswich 1-1 was followed by an identical 1-1 draw at home against Brighton which, although Blues dropped to 5th place, it confirmed our place in the playoffs barring some exceptional results (which would involve Blues losing our last game and Middlesbrough winning by 23 goals). This meant that manager Chris Houghton rested King and Burke for the last match of the season at home to champions Reading.

Adam Rooney replaced the injured Zigic and scored Blues first goal on 24 minutes in an entertaining game which saw Blues hit the post before Doyle saved a Reading penalty. Elliott scored Blues second from the penalty spot before having a second penalty saved as Blues ran out 2-0 winners in front of 25,516. The win moved Blues up to 4th which meant home advantage in the second leg the play off semi final against Blackpool who finished in 5th place. A good day all round especially as Villa look odds on for relegation.

I stayed up late to watch Blues lose the first leg of the playoff semifinal at Blackpool by a single goal from a cruel deflect and we were poor but I was sure that we could overcome them at St. Andrews in the return leg. I watched the second leg live as a sellout St. Andrews saw Blackpool score twice to take an aggregate 3-0 lead before Blues began our fight back. Nikola Zigic and Davis scored in the 64th and 73rd minutes but we just couldn't manage to get the 3rd and it was heartbreak once again as we were condemned to another season in the Championship. It would take some time for our wounds to heal but overall it had been a fantastic season in which we enjoyed a European tour, a great FA Cup run and a 4th place finish. I wonder when we will ever have a season this good again?

Blues played 62 games this season and Chris Burke was voted player of the season. What a brilliant season it has been! Blues average home attendance was 19,126 with the highest being 28,483 against Reading and the lowest was 14,494 against Wolves in the FA Cup.

Reading were promoted to the Premier League as champions as well as 2nd place Southampton and were joined by West Ham who beat Blackpool in the playoff final. Joining us is the Championship from League One was Charlton as Champions, Sheffield Wednesday 2nd place and Huddersfield as playoff winners.

Champions of the Premier League were Manchester City while Chelsea won the FA Cup, Liverpool the League Cup and Manchester United the Community Shield. Relegated from the Premier League were Blackburn, Bolton and Wolves.

In May Birmingham City Ladies won the FA Cup by beating Chelsea on penalties after the Final finished 2-2. As a Bluenose and ex-Birmingham City player I was absolutely delighted! Blues Ladies are certainly doing us proud at the moment.

During the summer I became even more homesick as events such as the Queens Diamond Jubilee and the London Olympic's were broadcast around the globe and I looked on with pride and envy. I would have loved to have been at home for it all. It was extremely draining at work too as many midwives were leaving due to the staffing levels and I was shattered every night when I got home. I did get to watch Euro 2012 though so not all bad and my family visiting regularly cheered me up.

England won their group and were up against Italy in the quarterfinals and so I was optimistic and hoping for a place in the semifinals. It meant a late night for me to watch the England v Italy game which went to penalties with England losing out once again. Very disappointing. Italy went on to reach the Final where they were beaten by Spain 4-0 as Spain won Euro 2012.

In July Great Britain Ladies won their first match in the Olympics as they beat New Zealand 1-0 with 3 Blues players in the squad, 2 of whom played. Three days later Team GB Ladies won their second game as they defeated Cameroon 3-0 and it was a very enjoyable game to watch. In the last group game GB Ladies beat Brazil 1-0 at Wembley to progress to the quarterfinals with a 100% record and without conceding a goal.

On the 1st of August I was headed back to England ready to head off on our big American adventure and I was so excited. Unfortunately the day after I got home GB Ladies lost 2-0 to Canada to exit the Olympics but they had done us proud. The men's team also exited in the quarterfinals going out on penalties.

Before I knew it me, mom and Annette were on our way to Los Angeles via an overnight stay in London because of the early flight. We arrived jet lagged in LA, picked up our hire car and checked in to our fabulous hotel in Hollywood. Our room was on the 12th floor with a fantastic view of Hollywood, downtown LA and the Hollywood sign could be seen in the distance. We were all knackered due to the long flight and the time difference so it was an early night for us.

On our first day we decided to take the open top bus tour which probably wasn't our best decision as it was a really hot day. We got to explore Santa Monica Pier and the Chinese Theatre where we admired all the hand prints of the stars and we saw Captain Jack Sparrow, Dark Vador, Cat Woman and the Joker strolling about. We also passed by the Chateau Marmont, Johnny Depp's bar The Viper Room and other interesting places. We arrived back at our hotel burnt but happy.

The following day it was off to Venice Beach where we saw lots of interesting shops, stalls and characters. The next morning we were up early and off to Disneyland for the day. We had tickets for both Disneyland Park and California World. It was unbelievably hot but it was fabulous inside Disneyland and we were all thrilled. Toon Town was fab and we took loads of photos. We went over to California World just in time to see the fabulous parade by characters and floats from Toy Story, Monsters Inc, Bugs Land etc. It was a fabulous day out and we picked up some wine for the night.

The next day we visited the Chinese Theatre walk of fame, Madam Tuesards waxworks and the Hollywood museum. We also did the tour of the movie stars houses and saw the houses of David Beckham, Elton John, Katy Perry, Jennifer Anniston, Justin Timberlake, Lyndsey Lohan, Cameron Diaz and many more. Great day.

On the Friday we drove to Universal Studios on yet another hot day. There were lots of 'cool zones' with fans and cold mist. It was absolutely brilliant and the studio tour was fantastic although mm found the skull island 3D King Kong experience terrifying which left me crying with laughter. We all loved it.

We had a shopping/ chilling day on our last day in LA and I was a bit tired from all the driving and excitement. The next day I drove us to Las Vegas which took nearly 5 hours and I was knackered when we arrived on the strip with the car engine sounding very much like a helicopter! We checked in to the Luxor which was fantastic and very much like a mini City inside. Our room was a delux room in the pyramid itself and on the 11th floor. The elevator or'inclinator' to get to our floor was brilliant and travelled sideway!

We spent 5 days in Vegas and saw lots of the strip and visited the Titanic museum which was conveniently located in our hotel. I wanted to get tickets for the Donny and Marie show as I had wanted to see Donny Osmond ever since I was young but unbelievably they were away on a 2 week holiday. I was really disappointed. It was great to see the dancing water at the Bellagio though. There was a spectacular storm on the Tuesday which was interesting to see but still plenty to do in our mini city. The next day we bumped into Batman, Homer Simpson and a couple of the Transformers as we walked on the strip. Did lots of shopping, had champagne and had a great time.

It was soon time for the last part of our adventures as we returned our hire car and flew to Memphis and checked into the Marriott Downtown hotel. Everyone here was so friendly and they had a real drawl to their accents. Once again we had a great view with a room on the 14th floor with a fantastic bathroom. We also had the best steak/ribs that we have ever had here. The pizza was unbelievable too.

On the Saturday we headed to Graceland and we had booked VIP passes for us all. Graceland was amazing and each room still has all its original fixtures and fittings. The graves of Elvis, his twin, his mother and his father are all in the Meditation Garden and we passed by each grave.We also went on Elvis's private Jet and saw all his cars in the automobile museum. It was all fantastic. At the end we called into the Heartbreak Hotel which was very nice. There was an Elvis tribute singing on the complex with lots going on due to the anniversary and it being 'Elvis Week'. Last night Prescilla and Lisa Marie had held a candlelight vigil with 90,000 people.

Sadly the next day we had to head to the airport to catch our flight to Dallas to get our connection to London. It had been an absolutely fantastic holiday, the trip of a lifetime where we had seen and done so much together and although we were sad to be leaving we were all happy.

Chapter Six - Lee Clarke

As Blues fans we knew we would be in for a difficult season at the start of the 2012-13 season as soon as Chris Houghton left to join Premier League

Norwich City and Lee Clarke took his place, plus we still had a transfer embargo in place. A new season so ever the optimist though.

Blues began their training in Austria in July and played a friendly against Borussia Monchengladbach in which they drew 2-2. Blues returned to England and played a friendly at Shrewsbury Town winning 2-1 with goals from Hancox and Zigic. The next friendly saw a 1-0 loss to Cheltenham before getting back to winning ways with a 5-1 defeat of Bury. This was followed by a trip to Plymouth and a good 5-0 win before a final preseason friendly at St. Andrews as Royal Antwerp beat us 3-1.

Whilst I was still in America Blues began the season with a League Cup game against Barnet at home as Blues entered at the 1st round this season. Just under 10,000 turned up to witness a good 5-1 win with 2 of the goals in injury time.

The first League game of the season saw newly promoted Charlton visit St. Andrews as Jack Butland made his debut a few days after making his England debut. The game ended in a 1-1 draw with Nikola Zigic rescuing a point with a goal in the 94th minute.

Although I had only got back from America the day before and was feeling really fed lagged Me and Annette got the coach to head to Sheffield Wednesday. I had to take travel sickness tablets to deal with the jet lag before I got on the coach though. We survived the journey but Blues played awful in the first half and our young keeper made a couple of errors and we were 2-0 down by half time. Blues played better in the second half but lost the game 3-1. Over 2,000 Bluenoses made the trip and the atmosphere was fantastic and we sang throughout the game. Then we had more travel sickness tablets as we got back on the coach to head home. Boss Lee Clarke blamed his use of the 4-3-3 system and Blues were 19th in the table.

Another defeat followed in the next match at Watford as Blues conceded a penalty after 3 minutes and a second goal after 17 minutes to lose 2-0 and down to 22nd. It was League Cup action next as Blues travelled to League One Coventry City who had just sacked their manager. It ended in defeat again as Blues lost 3-2 to a last minute goal and exited the competition at the second round. I'm already thinking that Blues may struggle this season.

Paul Caddis made his debut at home to Peterborough as Blues got their first win of the season 1-0 to move up a place and hopefully kick start our season. Blues had 5 teenagers on the bench due to injuries. The following week was the international break as England started our 2014 World Cup campaign with a good 5-0 away win at Moldova. A few days later England drew 1-1 with Ukraine as Stephen Gerrard was sent off leaving England with 10 men.

Blues got their first away point of the season with a 2-2 draw at Nottingham Forest but after being 2-0 up it was a cruel deflection 4 minutes from time which rescued a point for Forest. A few days later Blues won again this time at home to Bolton 2-1 which took them up 10 places to 11th but the crowd of 14,693 was the lowest for a league game for 15 years.

The next game at home to Barnsley saw an even lower attendance of only 13,893 as Blues lost 5-0 - their worst home defeat for 25 years after which Lee Clarke issued and apology for that embarrassing performance. As Stephen Carr (out for 6 months), Paul Caddis, Murphy and Pablo are out injured Blues were reduced to only 2 senior defenders and so Paul Robinson was brought in as a free agent. Blues were down to 19th.

Blues bounced back in the next game as they surprised everyone by winning 1-0 away at league leaders Brighton where the match was held up for 25 minutes due to floodlight failure.

The roller coaster continued as Blues then lost the next 2 games, 2-1 at Cardiff after taking the lead and 1-0 at home to Huddersfield as Zigic was sent off for a high tackle and Lee Clarke accused his players of failing to take responsibility and that they can't hide behind him all the time. At least the attendance rose to 18,000 due to half price tickets but Blues were down to 21st.

It was the international break again but the Poland v England game was postponed due to a waterlogged pitch in a multimillion pound stadium with a roof which was left open despite the forecast of heavy rain! I don't know what was going on there but I felt sorry for the thousands of England fans who had traveled to Poland for the game. It was the first England game to be postponed due to weather since 1979.

St. Andrews again saw over 18,000 for the visit of League leaders Leicester City as an improved Blues performance resulted in a 1-1 draw but Blues were unlucky not to get the win. Away to Millwall Blues went 3-0 down in a 7 minute spell in the first half but a hat trick from Marlon King rescued a point in a 3-3 draw. This was followed by a great 1-0 away win at Leeds but lost the next game 1-0 at home to Ipswich in a dull game as Blues sit 18th in the table. I had some good banter with my mate Tracey who is a Leeds fan.

Only 14,380 turned up to see Blues beat Bristol City 2-0 at St. Andrews as Burke and King scored and Peter Løvenkrands missed a penalty in the last minute after insisting on taking it much to the annoyance of Zigic. Away to Blackburn Blues went 1-0 down but rescued a point when King equalised after Zigic hit the post. Blues then went 3-0 down for the third time this season at home to Hull City and although they fought back they lost the game 3-2. The next match was an identical score line away at Derby as Blues again lost 3-2 and are 19th in the table.

Blues travelled to Blackpool and returned with a 1-1 draw which was followed a few days later by an exciting game against Middlesbrough at St. Andrews which was televised live and saw Blues win 3-2. The away game at Wolves was decided by an own goal from King who sliced the ball into his own net as Blues lost 1-0. A real rollercoaster ride this season.

The next game against Crystal Palace at home saw Blues draw 2-2 and the score was again identical in the next game against Burnley again at St. Andrews as Blues started the game with 7 teenagers and Zigic as the lone striker as Løvenkrands was injured in the warm up. Blues remain 19th in the table.

I spent yet another Christmas is Abu Dhabi but hopefully not many more and it was great to see my family on skype as they opened their presents. Blues then won 2-1 away at Barnsley on Boxing Day which saw us 7 points clear of the relegation places but in the next game away at Bolton Zigic scored after 11 minutes before getting sent off after being booked twice and Blues went on to lose the game 3-1. Not a good way to end the year.

The new year began as badly as the old one finished as Blues had no senior striker due to injury and lost at home 1-0 to league leaders Cardiff City. Blues are 20th in the table and it's looking dismal.

Blues had been drawn away to Leeds in the 3rd round of the FA Cup and several youngsters were given squad numbers ahead of the game. Blues dominated and went ahead with a stunning long range shot from Elliott but this was undone in the second half when Curtis Davies was robbed of the ball and Leeds equalised. Will Packwood suffered a broken leg as he fell awkwardly and broke both his fibula and tibia.

In the next game Lee Clarke returned to the club that sacked him as Blues drew 1-1 with Huddersfield. The next game against Brighton at St. Andrews was also drawn as Zigic scored in the 92nd minute to secure a 2-2 draw.

Elliott scored again in the FA Cup 3rd round replay at St. Andrews but it wasn't enough as Leeds equalised and they were then given a helping hand when the referee adjudged that Paul Robinson handled in the area and awarded Leeds a penalty. This meant that Blues lost the tie 2-1 and were now out of both Cup competitions. A couple of days later I watched the Gulf Cup Final as the UAE beat Iraq 2-1 and the whole of Abu Dhabi were out celebrating which involves traffic at a standstill, flags and the honking of car horns which went on late into the night!

Blues again scored a 90th minute goal in the away trip to Burnley which took us up to 17th place. I'm worried that we could go down this season. Chris Burke was the hero at home against Nottingham Forest as he scored twice to give a Blues another 2-1 win. The Queen Mary 2 Liner was docked in Abu Dhabi so I went to see it. It was massive and was double the size of the Liner next to it. Apparently it's the biggest and most expensive in the world. A few days later and I had my mom, sister and cousin Bernadette out visiting so that was great.

Charlton took the lead in the 88th minute in the away fixture at the Valley but another late goal, this time in the 94th minute, by Elliott secured a point in a 1-1 draw. Lee Clarke dropped Zigic for the home match against Watford and Blues lost heavily 4-0. He was reinstated for the next game - a goalless draw against Sheffield Wednesday at home in which he failed to take several chances.

The last game of February saw Blues travel to Peterborough and return with a good 2-0 win which moved Blues up to 16th. The feel good factor lasted up to the next game away at Hull when Blues conceded five goals to lose the game 5-2 through bad defending. Blues scored their 2 goals in the last 7 minutes. At home to Blackpool it should really have been a win but Elliott made a bad miss and the game ended 1-1 sending Blues down to 18th in the table.

Nathan Redmonds first goal and 2 from Wes Thomas helped Blues beat Derby 3-1 at St. Andrews which moved us above Derby and 7 points clear of the relegation places. This was followed by a good 1-0 win over Middlesbrough also at St. Andrews with a goal from Zigic which put Blues into the top half of the table. Blues then had an amazing and totally unexpected 4-0 away win at Crystal Palace as Redmond scored and played exceptionally well to command the game.

Once again Blues went 3 goals down in the first half at St. Andrews against Wolves then Elliott scored 2 late goals before running out of time and losing 3-2. Lee Clarke said Blues were rubbish in the first half without the ball. Blues drew the next two games - 1-1 at home against Millwall and 2-2 away at Leicester as Burke scored a 91st minute penalty. Blues were now 13th in the league.

It was away to Bristol City next and Blues won 1-0 to confirm relegation for the Robins. The following day I was on my back to Birmingham and I was upgraded to business class on the flight from Abu Dhabi. It was absolutely brilliant!

Then a few days later Blues entertained Leeds at St. Andrews and me and Annette headed to the ground. Frank Worthington was drinking in the George Pub so we headed there but it was packed and we didn't get to see him. Blues gained revenge for the Cup defeat by beating Leeds 1-0 which moved Blues up to 10th place and finally safe from relegation. We were also still mathematically in with a chance of a play off place. In the evening we went to watch Celebrities on Ice at the NIA which ran late due to a hole in the ice!

On the Saturday I went to Ipswich with Stephen by coach for the last away game of the season and there were loads of Bluenoses in fancy dress and it looked fantastic. I saw Shrek, Bill and Ben the flowerpot men, Batman, Robin, Beetlejuice, Mr Blobby, the Blues brothers, a horse, Mickey Mouse, Superman, Super Mario and loads of others.

The last Away game of the season saw a poor display from Blues at Ipswich as they scored 3 goals and had 2 disallowed although Blues got a 90th minute consolation goal the game ended in a 3-1 defeat. Lee Clarke said afterwards "I'm 3 stone overweight and even I could have gone out and played at that tempo" which just about summed it up.

It was an early kick off on the Sunday and Stephen and I headed to the Cricketers to meet the others for a pre match drink. There were big queues to get into the ground and just under 19,000 were inside St. Andrews for the last match of the season against Blackburn with nothing to play for but that didn't deter Blues who attacked from the start.

Blues scored after 42 minutes but Blackburn equalised through Jordan Rhodes and despite having greater possession and number of shots Blues had to settle for a 1-1 draw and a 12th place final position Blues lowest placed position since 1995-6. The players came back out with Stephen Carr for a lap of honour. It was tinged with sadness as Stephen Carr has announced his retirement and he will be greatly missed.

Blues top goalscorer was Marlon King with a total of 14 and the average attendance was 16,702. The highest was 19,630 against Wolves and the lowest was 8,962 against Leeds in the FA Cup 3rd round replay.

In the Championship Cardiff were crowned Champions and Hull City and Crystal Palace were promoted to the Premier League with them. Relegated to League One were Peterborough, Wolves and Bristol City.

Manchester United were Premier League Champions, Wigan Athletic won the FA Cup, Swansea won the League Cup and Manchester City won the Community Shield.

I spent yet another hot summer in Abu Dhabi and I took my family to visit Ferrari World on Yas Island. It was fabulous and we went on a few rides and I got a lovely red Ferrari designer handbag. I had found a tenant for my house in order to keep it maintained till I got back and had a reputable agency overseeing it so hopefully no problems. All was well with the world and I was still looking to move home at some point.

Chapter Seven - The Great Escape

Back at Blues with all the turmoil in the club it looked to be a difficult season ahead with Lee Clarke needing to sell players before he could bring any in. Worrying times indeed especially with owner Carson Yeung in jail in Hong Kong.

Blues home kit this season is a Penguin style shirt - royal blue shirt with a wide white stripe at the front, white shorts and royal blue socks with the away shirt being yellow with blue trim and navy shorts and socks. It was decided that Blues would close the Gil Merrick Upper Stand for the 2013-14 season as it would not be viable to open it.

Blues played a lot of pre season friendlies beginning away at Alfreton Town with a 3-1 win. Two days later it was away at Shamrock Rovers and a 4-0 win followed by a surprise 4-1 defeat at MKDons. Back to winning ways in the next game away at Swindon Town as Novak got 2 in a 3-0 win. The away trips continued as Blues drew 1-1 at Oxford then lost 4-2 at Shrewsbury. The final pre season friendly was at St. Andrews as 5,252 saw Blues beat Hull City 2-1 with goals from Green and Shinnie.

The 2013-14 season began with a home game against last season's play off finalists Watford. There was a minutes silence before the game for Christian Benítez who had sadly died a few days before in a hospital in Qatar at the age of 27. Both teams played well with the difference being Troy Deeney scoring the only goal of the game as Blues missed their chances and lost the game 1-0. Not a good start.

Blues began their League Cup campaign in the first round at home against League Two side Plymouth and despite Burke missing an open goal and Novak having a penalty saved Blues twice took the lead only to be pegged back and the game went to extra time. It took only 2 minutes into extra time for Bartley to score what proved to be the winner for Blues as the game finished 3-2 after extra time and we go into the next round of the competition.

Away at Yeovil and it was their first ever home match in the second tier and it was Blues 2000th. The game was settled by and own goal as Blues got their first win of the season 1-0. A few days later I watched the England v Scotland game at Wembley as England won 3-2. Brilliant!

Only 14,885 were inside St. Andrews to see Blues lose at home to Brighton 1-0 after Andy Shinnie and Lee Novak had both hit the crossbar. This was followed by another defeat away at Leicester City 3-2 which sees Blues in 18th place but early days yet.

Blues travelled to Yeovil again but this time in the 2nd round of the League Cup in what turned into a very controversial game. With Blues leading 2-1 going into the last minute and having put the ball out of play for an injury, Yeovil failed to return the ball and instead they passed to another Yeovil player who ran on to score. The Blues players went mad and there was a confrontation between both sets of players. Yeovil then took the lead in extra time and then bizarrely allowed Blues Lee Novak to walk the ball into the goal unchallenged to equalise. The match finished 3-3 and Blues won the penalty shootout to progress to the 3rd round.

Once again there was just over 14,000 at St. Andrews this time for the visit of Ipswich which saw Blues grab a 1-1 draw. I was then heading back to England again and my second flight from Amsterdam to Birmingham was packed with England fans returning from the game at Ukraine the previous night.

On the Saturday there were 14 of us who got the train to London and then tube to Wetherspoons in Shepherds Bush before walking to QPR's ground for the game. It was a great atmosphere in the packed Blues end and lots of singing despite losing 1-0. Blues fans threw a smoke bomb on the pitch which held up play for 5 minutes. We all went back to Wetherspoons before heading back to Euston to get the train back home.

The following Tuesday we were on our travels again as mom dropped me in Harborne where I met Brendan and the lads in the Stores Pub for the trip to Burnley. I was in a nice comfortable Volvo with Dave, Jordan and Brendan whilst Graham and the others were in a Ka. We set off for Burnley at 4pm and the journey took over 3 hours as there was an accident on the M6 involving 2 lorries and a car so the traffic was horrendous.

On arrival we parked at the cricket ground next to the stadium with only 20 minutes to spare. Brendan headed for a pint and me, Dave and Jordan headed into the ground. I didn't have a ticket so I paid on the gate. It was a cold night and Blues were poor and lost 3-0 (it could have been 6). It was depressing and Blues were down to 21st. The journey back was much quicker and I was back at my moms by 00.15.

A day later and I headed off on holiday with mom, Annette & Steve and Jean (my aunt) to Tenerife for a week. We had a nice time but my sister was taken into hospital the night before we were due to fly home. This meant that Steve and Jean would fly back as planned and I had to get new flights for me, mom and Annette a day later. To top it off when I got back to Birmingham our cases were missing and I was due to fly back to Abu Dhabi at 6am the next morning. I had to go home without my case which was found in Bristol the next day and delivered to my moms as I didn't trust them to get it to Abu Dhabi.

In the next game at home to fellow strugglers Sheffield Wednesday Blues gave a debut to new loan signing Jessie Lingard from Manchester United. Jessie went straight into the starting eleven wearing number 9 and scored after 20 minutes, completed his hat trick 13 minutes later and added a 4th in the 2nd half as Blues won 4-1. What a debut!

There was only 7,470 at St. Andrews to see Blues play the holders Swansea City in the 3rd round on the League Cup. Swansea hit the crossbar in the first half but Blues outplayed them in the 2nd half to win 3-1 and we were into the 4th round.

Blues then lost the following game a few days later in the league away at Reading 2-0 with both goals coming from free kicks. The referee admitted afterwards that maybe he made the wrong decision for the second in which Dan Burn had claimed that the player dived. Only 13,133 saw Blues entertain Millwall at St. Andrews at the beginning of October as Lingard missed an early penalty but scored on the 89th minute to complete a good 4-0 win.

The rollercoaster ride continued as Blues then lost the next game at home to Bolton 2-1 which I watched live as Blues had 11 shots and a blatant penalty turned down and then lost away at Leeds 4-0 and Blues were 20th.

The next weekend was the international break and England beat Montenegro 4-1 at Wembley in a World Cup qualifier. This meant that England now needed a win against Poland at Wembley to qualify for the World Cup in Brazil in 2014. A few days later at Wembley England duly beat Poland 2-0 and qualified for Brazil! Fantastic!

Back to the Championship and in a game of many chances at Derby Lee Novak came on to score with his first touch on 66 minutes to equalise for Blues and the game ended 1-1.

A break from League action saw Blues take on Premier League Stoke City at St. Andrews in the 4th round of the League Cup. It was 1-1 just before Wade Elliott got sent off but then Stoke led 3-1 with 5 minutes remaining. Peter Løvenkrands then scored twice to take the game into extra time and after falling behind again Olly Lee scored for Blues to make it 4-4 and take the game to penalties. Hancox and Reilly missed Blues first 2 penalties as Blues lost 4-2 to go out of the competition.

Damari Gray made his first start in the home match against Charlton but despite Blues having a goal disallowed they lost the game 1-0 and fell into the relegation zone for the first time this season.

The rollercoaster continued as Blues achieved a very good away win at Huddersfield although goalscorer Kyle Bartley jumped the advertising boards after scoring his 2nd and Blues 3rd in the 81st minute to celebrate with the fans and was sent off after receiving a 2nd yellow card.

My mom and sister had been out to visit me in Abu Dhabi for 2 weeks and I was flying back with them for my holiday in England. On the Saturday me and Stephen headed to the match and called in at the Cricketers for a pint and a catch up with the others. Then it was into the ground and a 1-1 draw against Blackpool which was spoilt by dire defending at times and the referee was awful. Our players were being pushed off the ball all the time and we had 2 shots cleared off the line plus hitting the woodwork. We really should have won.

We were going to the next game at Barnsley by train and mom dropped me at Selly Oak station to meet Brendan and the others to get the train to New Street and then Barnsley via a change at Sheffield. When we arrived in Barnsley we got a taxi to the 'Dove Inn' where we enjoyed a few pre match drinks. They were serving freshly made pork and stuffing sandwiches and homemade pie and mushy peas. They were even selling matchday programmes in the pub.

We all had a nice time (there was 9 of us) and the pub was full of Bluenoses. We then walked to the ground. It was brilliant. Inside the ground the Blues fans (920 of us) sang throughout entire match and Blues were 3-0 up after only 37 minutes. The game finished 4-0 and we were all celebrating like mad and a few new songs were born too, I loved the new Caddis song and the Wade Elliott song. Jack Butland was in goal for Barnsley and he got some stick which was a shame really as he didn't want to leave. The Bluenoses did sing 'there's only one Jack Butland' at the end though and he applauded us and gave his gloves to a young Bluenose. Then we were off to a pub by the station before getting the trains back to Birmingham.

It was a cold night when Stephen and I headed to St. Andrews as Blues took on Doncaster Rovers which saw the lowest league attendance of the season at 12,663. I was well wrapped up and had a drink with Stephen in the bar at the back of the KOP/Tilton corner. It was a frustrating game with Blues leading 1-0 and playing well and then throwing it away with 10 minutes to go by conceding the equaliser. Despite 5 minutes of frantic injury time with Blues sending in crosses left right and centre we just couldn't get the winner. It was disappointing but at least we didn't lose.

I was off to St. Andrews again on the Saturday as Middlesbrough came to town. It was me and Stephen again and we headed into the Cricketers for a drink and met up with the others. The match was really frustrating and finished 2-2 with Blues getting the equaliser in the 94th minute and we all went mental.

A few days later and I was heading back to Abu Dhabi for what I vowed would be my last Christmas there as I was missing home so much. I was really sad heading back and leaving England behind.

Next up Blues notched up another good away win at Bournemouth with a 2-0 win with goals from Shinnie and Zigic in the first half which took Blues up to 14th. This was followed by a goalless draw at home against Nottingham Forest before travelling to Wigan on Boxing Day and repeating the score line as Jessie Lingard was sent off.

Back in Abu Dhabi I spent Christmas Eve at the Christmas beach party at the British Club and this year Santa arrive by speed boat. I was off work on Christmas Day but all of my 'friends' had plans and my good friends had left so I had my Christmas dinner at Ikea on Yas Island. It was really nice though!

Blues good form on the road continued as they retuned from Blackburn with a great 3-2 win after being 3-0 up at half time which meant that Blues finished 2013 on a 9 match unbeaten run. Fantastic.

The new year started with a 1-1 draw at home to Barnsley before Blues went on a run of 3 defeats starting with a 1-0 League loss at Brighton followed by home defeats to Yeovil 2-0 and league leaders Leicester City 2-1. Blues were having a torrid time at home in the league and were win less for 4 months at St. Andrews.

It was different in the FA Cup though as Blues cruised into the 4th round with a 3-0 home win over Bristol Rovers which set up a home tie with Premier League Swansea City. Blues took the lead against Swansea but failed to hold on as Swansea scored twice to win 2-1 and Blues were out of the competition.

Back in Abu Dhabi I had decided that the time was right to return home to Birmingham and on the 29th January 2014 I handed my notice in. After 16 years at the Corniche Hospital I did expect more of a reaction from the management but at the end of the day I am just a number. My work colleagues were really upset though and that was hard to see. My last working day will be 2nd of May and I am so excited.

Back to League action and an exciting game at St. Andrews as Blues took on Derby and took the lead in the 2nd half only fo fall 3-1 behind. Blues got a goal back and then Blues debutant Federica Macheda scored in injury time to make it 3-3. Macheda scored 2 more goals in the next Away game at Charlton which saw Blues win 2-0. Disappointingly this was followed by defeats in the next 2 games as Blues lost 1-0 at Watford and 2-1 at home to Huddersfield as Lee got a 95th minute consolation for Blues. It really is grim at St. Andrews this season.

There was more cheer in the next game as Blues travelled to the seaside town of Blackpool and enjoyed a great day out as Blues won 2-1 and returned with all 3 points which moved Blues up to 16th place for a week before falling back down to 17th after losing at Ipswich 1-0. Over in Hong Kong Blues owner Carson Yeung was found guilty of money laundering and could face up to 14 years in jail.

Blues lost at home again in the next game to QPR 2-0 which took Blues non winning streak to a record 12 matches. A few days later Blues were again at St. Andrews against Burnley and came from behind to draw 3-3 with the equaliser coming on 94 minutes from Macheda.

The next 2 games ended in defeat. The first game away at Sheffield Wednesday saw Blues put in a poor performance, with Robinson going off with concussion and a 4-1 defeat. The second defeat was a contrast to the last game as Reading scored twice on the break at St. Andrews as Blues played well but lost narrowly 2-1 after having a goal disallowed when a corner was adjudged to have gone out of play. Blues were down to 20th. I'm starting to worry that we could get relegated. On a positive note Blues Ladies beat Arsenal 1-0 at St. Andrews in the first leg of the Champions League quarterfinal.

Blues then had a good trip to London as they scored 3 times to beat Millwall 3-2 at the Den. The high of a win was then met by the low of another defeat at St. Andrews as Blues were 3-0 down by half time to Bournemouth before conceding a 4th just after half time. Blues did pull 2 back but the 4-2 defeat meant that Blues had not won at home for 6 months. Down in London Blues Ladies were busy beating Arsenal 2-0 on their own patch for an aggregate 3-

0 win which sees Blues Ladies into the Champions League Semi Finals! What an achievement!

April began well with another away win, this time at Doncaster Rovers by 3 goals to 1 as Macheda got 2 and Novak got the 3rd taking Blues up to 18th and above Doncaster on goal difference. The rest of April saw 5 defeats which condemned Blues to 22nd place going into the last game. The first 2 defeats were both away at Middlesbrough 3-1 and Nottingham Forest 1-0. This was followed by 3 home defeats to Blackburn 4-2, Leeds Utd 3-1 and the last home game of the season to Wigan 1-0 where 20,427 turned up hoping to witness the great escape. This left Blues needing at least a point away at Bolton and with other results favouring them. It can't help feeling that it will be League One for us next season which is typical now that I am coming home.

On the 2nd May I worked my last ever shift at the Corniche hospital and I was on an early shift. I went round saying goodbye to everyone some of whom I have known for 16 years and so many people were crying that I was in tears at times too. Two of the staff on my ward were inconsolable and I had to just walk away in the end. It was very sad but I am hoping to see many of them at the leaving party that they have organised for me in a few weeks time. From some of the lovely comments I received I hadn't realised how many lives I had touched. It was a very emotional day.

The last game of the season away at Bolton was massive and Blues fans filled the away end and were in great voice. In Abu Dhabi there was no live coverage of the game and I had to make do with live commentary and Twitter updates. It was a very stressful afternoon as I wished I was there and I vowed that I would never miss a big game again now that I was leaving Abu Dhabi for good.

The first half finished 0-0 but just before the hour Bolton went ahead. My heart sank. Just a minute later and Doncaster went a goal down at Leicester which would mean that Blues only needed a draw to stay up. Then Bolton scored a second to make it 2-0 and I was devastated. It was extremely stressful especially as Nikola Zigic pulled a goal back with 12 minutes to go. It was all out attack from then on from Blues and in the 93rd minute Zigic had a header cleared off the line but up popped little Paul Caddis to head home from 4 yards and there was absolute bedlam as the away end erupted in a noise so loud it took the roof off. The players mobbed Caddis as he ran to the away end to celebrate with the fans. Caddis said afterwards that when Bolton got their second all he could hear was our fans singing and that gave the team extra motivation.

When the final whistle sounded not long after the goal the away end erupted and all the Blues players and staff headed to the fans to celebrate. Lee Clarke sprinted to the Blues fans and dived into the away end in scenes not seen for a long time. Blues were safe and boy were we celebrating. I had to make do with running around my apartment in hysterics. What a game! I was so looking forward to another season in the Championship with me there to follow Blues. I headed off to Etihad Towers to celebrate with champagne.

One Bolton fan and season ticket holder was so impressed with the 3,800 travelling Blues fans that he wrote a letter to Birmingham City:

"Thought I would write a few lines to you. Firstly, an explanation. I am a Bolton supporter and have been going to watch my team for at least 50 years now. We have seen all the so called big teams at Bolton during that time, and have been lucky enough to beat a few of them as well. As I'm getting on a bit now I can say I've been to a good few away grounds and I have been to St. Andrews on more than one occasion.

I have also been to Villa Park frequently as well. Man U, Arsenal, Liverpool, you name it I have been there at some point. I feel the main difference between Birmingham and Villa is the people. By that I mean Birmingham supporters on the whole come from within the City and are working class and that shows in the type of atmosphere they create. Villa supporters tend to come from outside the region as well because of their history.

It's so easy to support teams with a successful past like Man U up my way and Villa down yours. So when it was written in the stars that Birmingham needed to beat us or draw and rely on Leicester to beat Doncaster. It was no surprise to me the kind of delirium Birmingham fans would bring to our stadium.

But I have to say the support we witnessed that day was far above anything I had seen before. To be two nil down and still passionately singing for your team is something else entirely. The noise and the famous anthem they sang was simply superb and I must admit it made me shiver a little. Absolutely fantastic what a set of fans exist at Birmingham, they certainly do not deserve to be in the position they were last Saturday.

Normally I would not care a jot if we were playing a side and it meant if we beat them they got relegated, because you normally finish where you deserve to be. The table never lies. But Saturday when Birmingham got the first I found myself inexplicably hoping the equaliser would come and we all knew the roof would come of the stadium if it did. I have to say you did leave it a little late.

The noise generated when that goal went in was something else and it will stay with me for a very long time. Because it is very rare you see fans in the position Birmingham were in giving their side the kind of backing they provided on Saturday. It took us ages to get to the motorway and we had a great time with Blues fans on the way. It was as if they had won the league, and I dread to think what they would be like if that ever happened.

I remember watching the League Cup Final between Birmingham and Arsenal and they said Blues fans were among the noisiest ever to visit the new Wembley stadium. Well by the evidence of last Saturday you can see why. It leaves me only to wish you all the best for the future and say the Championship would be worse off without Birmingham and it's exceptional supporters. They of all sets of fans deserve a winning team and investment in their famous club. That club really is a sleeping giant in the true sense f the word. I think we kid ourselves at Bolton that we could be a future Giant. But at Birmingham you really do possess one of the leagues true potential giants.

All the best

A Bolton season ticket holder for many years"

Brings a tear to your eye and your heart swell with pride doesn't it!

In the Championship Leicester City were crowned champions while Burnley and QPR were promoted to the Premier League with them. Relegated from the Championship were Doncaster Rovers, Barnsley and Yeovil Town. Manchester City were champions of the Premier League while Norwich City, Fulham and Cardiff City were relegated to the Championship. Manchester City also won the League Cup defeating Sunderland 3-1 and Arsenal won the FA Cup beating Hull City 3-2.

At St. Andrews when my book 'Truly Blue' was published

Me and Mom with Blues Manager Alex McLeish at Wast Hills when I was about to be interviewed for the Blues Programme about my new book.

Pre- season friendly away at Kidderminster as we turned their town blue.

On the way to Wembley for the Carling Cup Final

Pre Match drink in London ahead of the Final – the City is blue!

Wembley Way! Stephen, Me, Annette and Eddie

Stephen and Me inside Wembley 2011

Annette and James celebrating Blues Carling Cup win in London!

Stephen and myself a bit the worse for wear celebrating Blues Cup Victory

Paul Fidler and myself after the Cup Final – The celebrations continue!

Chapter Eight - I'm Coming Home!

I was really excited at the thought of moving back to England and the 'green green grass of home'. I now had 3 weeks to sort out everything for my move and mom and Annette would be here for all of that time and would also fly home with me. My sisters partner Steve would also be here for the first 2 weeks and I would have the last week with just me and my family. There was loads to do and it was really stressful. I had to sell my car, close phone lines, cable etc and arrange the shipping of my furniture and belongings. I had sold some of my things at the Sheraton Flea Market a few weeks earlier and that had been fun.

In the midst of all this I had a health scare that involved numerous hospital visits, CT Scans and MRI and would require major surgery when I got back to the UK. A worrying time indeed. Thank god mom and Annette were here to see my through it all. We did have some great times too though which included spending our last two nights in a Suite at the Sofitel on the corniche with a fantastic view over the sea and Abu Dhabi. It was lovely and a wonderful end to my 17 years in the United Arab Emirates. Everything had been done by now and my furniture was packed away in a container awaiting shipping to the UK. My tenant in my house in Birmingham had been given lots of notice and should be out by the time I got home, although recent emails from from my agents seemed to suggest that she was dragging her feet. That was worrying.

The day of my departure arrived and a company car was sent to the hotel to pick us up and transfer us to Abu Dhabi airport for us to get our flight home and it was an emotional experience. Once onboard our Etihad flight I was perhaps a bit subdued as I pondered my 17 years away and when the flight attendants approached me with champagne and a card they had made and all signed wishing me good luck after my long UAE residency it all became a bit much and I was a bit tearful. It was a long time to be away from home.

Once the plane touched down in Birmingham I was so happy to be home again and planned to stay at moms for a couple of months whilst I got my house as I wanted it. I was in no rush to get back to work as I had worked solidly since I left school and a few months break would be wonderful, although I would be keeping an eye out should any midwife posts come up at my nearby hospital the Birmingham Women's hospital which is where I really hoped to work.

My first and biggest problem was getting my tenant to move out as she had lied about moving out dates and was now refusing to move. I found this quite puzzling as she had been recommended by my agents Dixons and she was a professional person as an agency nurse at the nearby Queen Elizabeth hospital and had two children. It just goes to show. So now I had to go through legal channels with a solicitor although many of my relatives wanted to go round and have a word. I had to decline because of course it wouldn't help my case. Hence it was costing me a lot of money and I was concerned that my belongings would be arriving in the UK in the next 6 weeks.

The six weeks passed as I awaited a court date and my container arrived at Southampton. The shipping company very kindly agreed to a months storage without any charge and I was desperate to get her out as I was planning on getting my house painted, carpeted and a new bathroom put in before I had to put the furniture in. I was given an eviction date just before the months grace on my container and happily this horrible tenant moved out the night before the eviction and put my keys through the letterbox of the estate agent, thereby not giving a forwarding address. This meant I would get my house back but would not be able to recover the court costs that she had been ordered to pay me.

I was so happy to get my house back despite the mould in the back bedrooms, the ants in the kitchen, stains on the carpet and six foot weeds and grass in my garden. This did break my heart a little as I love my garden and seeing it in such a state was hard. I got to work on cleaning up and organising the painting etc. I also had to get the electrics done as it was 1970s wiring and an old fuse box. Unfortunately the carpet fitter was going on holiday which meant that the upstairs carpets would have to be fitted after my furniture arrived, which included two king sized beds and a wardrobe.

My container arrived and I set about emptying all the boxes with the help of my mom whilst some of the work was being carried out. Amidst this time I had to prepare for an interview at the Birmingham women's hospital and happily I got the job and it would take a couple of months to get clearance etc which suited perfectly. Me and mom had some fantastic times during this lovely summer shopping for things for the house and watching all the work being completed. As well as the new bathroom with a walk in shower, I also had an ensuite put in upstairs and had a brand new white gloss modern kitchen fitted. I also had work done on my garden to try to restore it to its former glory and improve upon it. Once everything was completed it looked wonderful and I fell in love with my house and garden again.

In June my sister Annette asked me to go to a UB40 tribute with her at the Weoley Castle Working Men's club and when I arrived there it was a surprise welcome home party with loads of family shouting 'surprise'. They had 'welcome home' playing and my cousin John started singing 'Keep Right On' as I entered and everyone joined in and it brought a tear to my eye. What a wonderful surprise and a lovely evening where I got to catch up with everyone and it made me so happy to be home.

I was due to start my new job at the end of September which meant I could get to the first few games of the new season before I would have the hassle of trying to plan shifts (that are usually done 2-3 months in advance) to enable me to get to the rest of the games. The World Cup in Brazil began but England didn't do very well in their first group game as we lost 2-1 to Italy although England were a bit unlucky to be honest.

Next up for England was Uruguay and they were really dirty and Luis Suarez was a disgrace as England lost 2-1 and our World Cup is more or less over barring a miracle. In the last game against Costa Rica Roy Hodgson basically played our reserves as we were already eliminated and the game finished 0-0. Costa Rica won the group and Uruguay also went through after beating Italy 1-0 and Suarez bit an opponent again (that's his 3rd bite!). So England were on their way home and our World Cup was over at the group stages.

On the last Sunday in June I went over to Solihull Moors to watch Blues Ladies play Manchester City Ladies and it was really strange as it was the first time I had watched them play since I actually played for them many years ago. I just wanted to be out on the pitch playing so it was really hard. Blues won 2-0 to go top of the Women's Super League and I had a fantastic day. A few days later I went to Weston Super Mare for a break with my mom and sister and we had lovely time by the seaside.

I was still watching some of the World Cup games although the interest had gone and I was amazed by the semi final where Germany beat hosts Brazil 7-1. Their fans and players were crying and I felt so sorry for their fans. What a result. Germany went on to win the World Cup beating Argentina 1-0 in the final.

For the 2014-15 season the home kit would be blue shirts, white shorts and blue socks, and the away kit is a red and white penguin shirt with the middle being red and each side and sleeve being white with red shorts and socks, with a third kit of orange shirt with white strips on the sleeves, blue shorts and socks. I must admit that I treated myself to all three of them.

The pre season friendlies began with a trip to Cork City which Blues won 3-0 with goals from Robinson, Caddis and Novak. This was followed by an away trip to Forest Green which I was unable to make and Blues won 1-0 with a goal from Clayton Donaldson. Then the Mansfield away game was suddenly cancelled for fear of the amount of Bluenoses rumoured to be traveling. Next it was Kidderminster away and I drove to this game as it was close and it would be my first Blues game since moving back to England and I was really excited.

It was a lovely sunny day when I arrived with Steve, my sisters boyfriend, in Kidderminster and I parked up in the railway station car park and walked to the nearby pub which was full of Bluenoses already. Everywhere I looked there were Bluenoses and for today Kidderminster was blue! We walked to the ground and it was a new ground for me and I thought it was really nice. There were nearly 4,000 inside the ground and the majority were from Birmingham. It was buzzing with loads of new blues shirts on display. Everyone was in a good mood and I saw lots of people I knew.

The game got underway and I soon spotted a large spider on the back of the Blues shirt worn by the fan in front and although I was too terrified to inform him or move, I still managed to get a cracking photo of it and have a little giggle. Blues were totally dominant in the game and went in at half time 1-0 ahead with a goal from Wes Thomas, which was loudly celebrated by us traveling Bluenoses. After the break Blues got a second and from Clayton Donaldson and then another from Wes Thomas to round off a good 3-0 win and we headed back to the pub for Steve to have a drink before heading to the car to head home. There were Blues fans celebrating everywhere.

A few days later Blues traveled to Notts County for another friendly and Blues won 4-0 with a brace from Clayton Donaldson and the others from Shinnie and Grounds. It was a good build up to the new season. There was one last friendly which would be played at St. Andrews against a team from Scotland, Inverness Caledonian Thistle. There was 4,444 inside St. Andrews on a lovely day to see Blues win 3-1 which meant a 100% win record in our pre season. Is this a good omen? I'm not sure as I often find that we do better after a bad pre season but I'm ever hopeful that it will be a good season.

I had a short break at the seaside before the start of the new season as we went to Torquay for a few days. We went into Paignton for the day as well and also visited 'Greenways' Agatha Christie's house and it was a really lovely break.

The season began with an long away trip to Middlesbrough but at least it was on a Saturday and 1,044 Bluenoses made the trip. I was on coach 4 with Hockey as the steward and when we arrived we went into Boro's pub 'The Red Lion'. Once inside the ground I saw all the lads including Snowy! It was a poor display as Blues lost the game 2-0 and we didn't even have a shot. Manager Lee Clarke said after the game "the stat of no shots on target tells the story". Still a long season ahead though. We watched Blues Carling Cup Final win on the way back.

Due to my recent health problems I was required to undergo a venesection at the QE hospital just a day before the Cup game against Cambridge at St. Andrews. I had been diagnosed with polycythemia, which is high haemoglobin levels in the blood, and it was suspected that it was caused by a massive fibroid that had also just been diagnosed as a result of my blood diagnosis. Because of all this I needed major surgery but my haemoglobin levels were so high that it was not safe to do so and required me to undergo venesections (removing blood from me) to reduce the levels. If these worked then I was scheduled to have the surgery in the January to remove the fibroid and hope that this corrected the polycythemia.

I underwent the procedure on the Monday and they seemed to take a lot of blood from me and I did feel a bit unsteady afterwards. The next day although I didn't feel well I thought I should be fine and headed to St. Andrews for the League Cup first round match. On arrival one of my friends told me I looked grey and I did begin to feel awful as I took my seat. Blue were playing a Cambridge team that had just been promoted to the Football League and were starting their first season in league two. Should be an easy game then? Well no, of course not. Blues played several fringe players and it wasn't the best atmosphere with only 9,816 inside St. Andrews and 1,064 were in the away end.

Blues took the lead when Clayton Donaldson scored but his namesake Ryan Donaldson equalised for Cambridge. I was mortified that this now meant extra time as I was now not feeling well at all. Unbelievable Blues scored just 5 minutes into extra time - why couldn't we have scored 5 minutes before and prevented the extra 30 minutes of suffering for me? Mind you, I was just pleased we had scored and celebrated accordingly! Not long afterwards Mark Duffy made it 3-1 and we celebrated again as Blues progressed to the second round and I headed home to my bed.

The first home league game of the season saw just 15,000 in attendance, which was disappointing but perhaps it was due to the fact that Blues were currently winless at home in the league since October 2013, a record for the second tier of 18 matches without a win. Could we get that win today over Brighton? I am always optimistic and a goal from Wes Thomas from a David Cotteril cross just after half time gave Blues a 1-0 win that ended our winless run at St. Andrews and Blues were 16th.

There were even less in attendance at the next home game, although it was a night game, as 14,022 saw Blues gain a point in an entertaining 2-2 draw against Ipswich Town. It was disappointing that Blues conceded in stoppage time but the point means that we move up to 15th in the table. Early days yet though.

Next it was a nice trip to Brentford a trip I always enjoy. I enjoyed the game too, although Blues really should have won, especially when Brentford had a player sent off after only 15 minutes. Blues scored through a Paul Caddis penalty but only managed a 1-1 draw and it was back down to 16th place.

Premier league Sunderland visited St. Andrews in the second round of the League Cup and 11,248 were in attendance to see Blues dominate. Despite being a league apart Blues were the better side and had many chances including a David Cotteril shot which hit the woodwork. Blues dominance continued but in the 77th minute Sunderland caught Blues on the counter and scored. To make matters worse they then repeated this twice more and a 3-0 defeat in no way reflected the game as Blues outplayed their premier league opponents throughout. So Blues were out of the Cup but although we left St. Andrews disappointed we could at least be happy with our performance.

There was a good away following to Wigan of 1,386 but it wasn't a good day to be honest as Blues fell apart and lost the game 4-0 and Blues were down to 20th place. Not a good start to the season so far.

It was another 2 weeks before Blues were in action again due to the international break and it was Leeds who came to St. Andrews for an early kick off game that was being shown live on Sky TV. There were just over 15,000 of which over 2,000 traveled from Leeds and the atmosphere was good. Wes Thomas put Blues ahead and his shot was so powerful that it broke the Stanchion of the goal and the game was delayed for 9 minutes while it got fixed. Brilliant! Unfortunately Leeds came back to grab a point and Blues remained 20th.

A few days later and Blues were at home again with Sheffield Wednesday coming to town. Blues played well in the first half but failed to score and then conceded 2 goals in the second half to lose the game 2-0. I'm starting to think that this is not going to be a great season.

A long trip to Norwich saw 762 of us hardy Bluenoses make the trip but at least it was on a Saturday. It was a really entertaining game as a deflected Callum Reilly shot put Blues 1-0 up and then Demari Gray scored to make it 2-0 against top of the table Norwich at halftime. Blues should have had a penalty too but in the second half ex Blues Cameron Jerome scored twice to rob us of what would have been a deserved win.

In the next game at home to Fulham, Blues again wasted chances but at least David Cotteril managed to score from one of them and put Blues 1-0 ahead. Again though, Blues managed to throw it away as Fulham scored twice to inflict another defeat and Blue are down to 21st with the fans getting restless.

I couldn't make the Millwall away game as I had started my new job at the Birmingham Women's Hospital on the Monday and my first week was induction and study days. It seems really nice here but it meant that I couldn't travel to Millwall. It sounds like I missed a good game too as Donaldson, Cotteril and Thomas all scored in a great 3-0 away win which took Blues up to 19th place. Koby Arthur has been recalled from his loan at Cheltenham.

It was a good trip to Charlton as 1,500 of us made the trip. Blues fell behind early on but Davis's first goal for Blues meant that we came away with a point. It should have been two though as Koby Arthur had a goal disallowed for Donaldson being offside despite not interfering with play.

The home game against Bolton turned into a bit of a nightmare as Blues lost 1-0 which meant that we have only won at home once in a year. Goalkeeper Darren Randolph was sent off when he conceded a penalty because of Paul Caddis's poor back pass. Blues had already used all three of our substitutes and so Lee Novak had to go in goal. Happily Bolton missed the penalty but the loss sends Blues down to 21st in the league. Worrying times indeed.

Just hours after the manager had made his pre match press conference on the day before the trip to Blackburn Lee Clarke and his assistant were sacked. Perhaps it was better now rather than later? We also had keeper Darren Randolph suspended so Colin Doyle took his place. Only 510 traveled up north to watch Blues fall to yet another 1-0 defeat and remain firmly in 21st spot. Neal Eardley was sent off for Blues and Andy Shinnie hit the post in stoppage time.

I had to work on the day of the Bournemouth game but it will stay long in my memory as I'm sure it will for all Bluenoses even though I (luckily) wasn't there. I was working on the ward but many people know I'm an ardent Bluenose and kept informing me every time Bournemouth scored a goal - and there were a lot of them! Eight to be exact! For me this was the lowest point in Blues history and I was devastated. To lose 8-0 at home was horrendous even if it was to the team at the top of the table. Shocking! I don't think any of us have ever got over that one.

Blues were a goal down after only 3 minutes then down to ten men after only 6 minutes! Caddis missed a penalty on 53 minutes which would have made it 3-1 and perhaps changed the course of the game but it was not to be our day. It became our record home defeat and Paul Robinson apologised afterwards for 'that shambles of a game' and promised that he and the rest of the players would take responsibility for putting things right. Blues slipped to 23rd and into the relegation places.

Blues were still looking for a new manager and MK Dons had refused permission for them to talk to Karl Robinson and it was rumoured that Chris Houghton may return. However, the shortlist now consisted of Owen Coyle, Mike Phelan (former assistant manager of Sir Alex Ferguson at Manchester Utd) and Burton Albion's Gary Rowett. Gary Rowett was appointed on 27th October 2014 on a one year rollover contract and brought his Burton back room staff with him - all former Blues players. Rowett called it 'the job I just couldn't turn down'.

Rowett's first game in charge was a really difficult one away at Wolves who were level on points at the top of the table. Blues took 2,500 to Wolverhampton and we were in good voice from the off. Throughout the game we sang our hearts out and got behind the team who put in a much more defensive performance than the disaster against Bournemouth. Gary Rowett had brought in Michael Morrison on loan and he went straight into defence and we played with a lone striker, Clayton Donaldson up front. It paid off as we came away with a good point from a 0-0 draw. Blues moved up a place to 22nd and we headed back to Birmingham much happier than we had been. Perhaps Gary Rowett will be the man to turn things around.

A few days later and Blues were to take on another difficult game as Watford came to St. Andrews and were currently sitting on the top of the table. New manager and renewed hope attracted a bigger crowd to St. Andrews of 18,300 which was the biggest crowd of the season so far and we were in great voice as Keep Right On resounded around the stadium. It took only 2 minutes for Blues to take the lead with a goal from Clayton Donaldson which was Blues first goal for a month. St. Andrews exploded in celebration but it wasn't long before Watford grabbed an equaliser. Blues continued to press with the crowd spurring them on and with about 5 minutes remaining Donaldson got his second and sent the Bluenoses into raptures. Blues won the game 2-1 and I had hope in my heart once again. Blues were up to 21st.

Blues were at home again the following Saturday as Cardiff came to town but we couldn't break them down despite having a goal by Wes Thomas disallowed. Thomas was sent off late on for striking a Cardiff player and the game ended 0-0 which dropped Blues back into the relegation places.

It was off to Rotherham next, another trip that I enjoy and Blues took over 2,500 and were in excellent voice. Although Blues looked poor at times we did hit the post twice before Donaldson scored the winner in the 67th minute to take Blues out of the relegation places. I must admit though, I don't like playing the lone striker game, I prefer a more attacking style of play but I guess this is what we will have to get used to under Gary Rowett. Rowett described the game as "the most complete performance we've had since taking over. We played with really good control and good composure". The Rotherham manager thought that "it looked like two poor teams out there".

The last game of November saw Nottingham Forest visit St. Andrews and they brought a large following of 2,900 which swelled the attendance to 18,592 and the ground was buzzing. Blues took the lead with a brilliant curling 20 yard shot from David Cotteril and St. Andrews went mental. I celebrated like mad - we haven't had much to cheer this season. Forest were lucky to get an equaliser just before the end when Brit Assombalonga scored - he always seems to score against us. As many fans headed for the exits I said 'they will miss the winner' as I always said to be honest.

In the 89th minute Blues had a shot that was goal bound until the hand of Assombalonga turned it wide. It was clear as day but the referee and linesman signaled for a corner. The players were going mad and eventually the referee spoke to the fourth official who confirmed that it had been a handball and therefore the referee awarded Blues a penalty and sent off Assombalonga. After the game Forest manager Stuart Pearce admitted that he had seen the handball. Up stepped Paul Caddis to score and give Blues a 2-1 win and the celebrations began. This means that Blues are unbeaten in November and are up to 17th.

Blues old manager Lee Clarke had taken over at Blackpool who were struggling and had so far not won a game under Clarke. This did not bode well for Blues as records are normally broken against us! I was proved correct as Blackpool snatched a very lucky 1-0 win (only their second the season) as the Blues players did not perform as well as they have of late. Gary Rowett said afterwards that 'a lot of his players were playing against their old manager and I think a lot of them expended a lot of nervous energy in getting up for the game and I don't think that helped them'.

Only 15,240 were inside St. Andrews for what turned out to be the best game of the season against Reading. Those that stayed away missed a treat! It took only 4 minutes for Blues to take the lead as Caddis powered in a shot to make it 1-0. With just 11 minutes gone Damari Gray scored and it was 2-0. On 24 minutes it was 3-0 as Gray scored again with a clinical finish. In first half injury time Damari Gray completed his hat trick and St. Andrews went mental as Blues went into the halftime break with a 4-0 lead. Amazing.

Blues continued in the same vein in the second half as Andy Shinnie dribbled and hit a low shot into the net to score a 5th goal in the first minute of the second half and we celebrated. David Cotteril scored from a free kick from wide on the left to make a final score of 6-1. Nikola Zigic came on as a late substitute having re signed for Blues on a much lower wage than he had been on previously. What a fantastic day inside St. Andrews and I was so happy as I headed home.

It was off to Huddersfield next and a great goal from a David Cotteril free kick put Blues ahead and some great defending ensured that we came away with the 3 points and a 1-0 win which took us up to 15th in the table. Over 1,200 Bluenoses made the trip.

I had a lovely first Christmas back home with family. It was really nice and then on Boxing Day it was back to football. The biggest crowd of the season, 23,851, which included 2,900 away fans, were inside St. Andrews for the Boxing Day clash with 5th place Derby. What a disappointment it turned out to be as a poor Blues display resulted in a heavy 4-0 defeat. Very embarrassing.

A few days after the Derby hammering we set off for the early kick off game at Nottingham Forest on a freezing cold day. At least it turned out to be very worthwhile and enjoyable as Blues scored 3 goals in a ten minute spell just before half time which put us 3-0 up. Forest did pull a goal back but Blues held on for a great 3-1 win and a double over Forest that took us up to 14th in the table.

The FA Cup draw saw Blues away at Blyth Spartans of the seventh tier Northern Premier League and the lowest ranked team left in the competition. This would be a new ground for most Bluenoses but I was unable to travel due to my new job being shift work and with shifts done almost 3 months in advance I had been unable to request this day off. I was gutted believe me. Gary Rowett made 10 changes to the team, which I was really unhappy about. I have always loved the FA Cup, as do most football fans and to disrespect it in this manner does not sit well with me. Besides, we pay good money to travel to the games and deserve to have a fighting chance in the competition.

It nearly went tits up too as Blues were 2-0 down at half time and looking odds on for a Cup upset. Rowett made changes and thanks to 3 goals in a 7 minute spell after half time we came away with a 3-2 win and progressed to the next round and breathed a sigh of relief as we avoided an upset. The draw gave Blues a home tie against Premier League West Bromwich Albion on my birthday. I would be undergoing major surgery very soon but got a ticket in the hope that I would be well enough to go by then.

The home game against Wigan would be my last for a while due to my pending surgery and I was hoping for some revenge for the heavy defeat up at their place. My wish was granted with a hat trick from Clayton Donaldson that began in the 2nd minute with the second goal on 14 minutes and he completed his hat trick on 64 minutes. Wigan pulled a goal back but Blues took the points with a 3-1 win which saw us in the top half of the table for the first time since to 2012-13 season.

By the time the Leeds game came around I has just come out of hospital after my surgery which had been more complicated than first thought although I came through it well my recovery looked to be much longer than I first anticipated. Obviously I couldn't travel to Leeds as I could barley walk around the house and was still in a lot of pain when I moved. I was staying at my moms for several weeks as I made my recovery.

Blues took the lead at Elland Road with a penalty scored by Caddis but when our defence failed to clear a cross Leeds grabbed the equaliser with only 6 minutes remaining and the game finished 1-1 but the point took Blues up to 11th. Gary Rowett certainly seems to be turning things around so far and everyone has been singing his name.

The FA Cup game against West Brom was a sell out with the away side bringing 5,487 across the city and I knew it would be a fantastic atmosphere. However, I was still very early in my recovery and could hardy walk let alone make it to the match and I had to concede defeat the day before the game and gave my ticket (very reluctantly) away to a friend and fellow Bluenose to go in my place. I was heart broken to be missing it, especially as it was my birthday too. It would take me 3 months off work to get anywhere near normal again and even then I needed a phased return to work,

The day of the game came and I was a bag of nerves listening to it on the radio. Once again I was disappointed with Rowett's decision to rest our striker and top scorer Donaldson and Demari Gray who had just been awarded the Football Leagues Young player of the month for December. In came Lee Novak and Lloyd Dyer and Blues were soon 2-0 down but in first half stoppage time Jonathan Grounds scored to make it 2-1. Blues played much better in the second half and Demari Gray came on as substitute but despite our dominance we just couldn't score and went out of the FA Cup in a narrow 2-1 defeat to our Premier League opponents. No disgrace in that to be honest.

Next up was a trip to Sheffield as Blues took on Sheffield Wednesday and it was still too soon for me to travel. By all accounts it wasn't exactly a thriller and the game ended in a goalless draw in front of the 689 Bluenoses who made the midweek trek.

I decided to make the trip to St. Andrews for the Norwich game as my friend Michael took me and parked close to the ground so that I didn't have far to walk. It was a real struggle walking to the ground though and I was constantly worried that people may knock into me as my wound/ abdomen was really sore when I walked. I had to walk really slowly. I made it to my season ticket seat. It was nice to see everyone again and we discussed the £5 million bid for Demari Gray from Bournemouth that had been turned down by Blues. We really need him to stay at Blues at the moment. The game ended in a 0-0 draw and I had a very slow walk back to the car feeling very sore.

I was slowly getting better and decided to make the trip to Fulham with my friends on the train and we met up with my nephew Stephen in the Rocket pub across the bridge. We enjoyed a lovely breakfast amongst the Bluenoses in the pub then took a slow walk across the park to Craven Cottage. I had to keep asking Stephen to slow down as he is tall and walks fast whereas I was struggling due to my surgery. It was great once we were inside amongst the 3,209 Bluenoses who were in great voice as usual. Fulham scored first but David Cotteril equalised from a free kick and the away end went mental. My celebrations were a bit subdued due to my discomfort and I still had to be careful and couldn't jump about but I still enjoyed the moment. The game ended in a 1-1 draw and we headed home happy.

A few days later and Millwall came to town along with just 289 traveling fans. I was able to get there okay as Michael took me again but it was a really disappointing night as Millwall won 1-0 to get their first win over us at

St. Andrews since 1968. Blues remain in 11th place but we are certainly having some ups and downs this season.

Top of the table Middlesbrough were the next visitors to St. Andrews for another midweek night game. Blues were awarded a penalty in second half stoppage time and their goalkeeper was sent off. Paul Caddis scored from the spot to put Blues ahead and the stadium exploded in celebration. Unfortunately Blues couldn't hold onto our lead and Middlesbrough rescued a point. Clayton Donaldson came close to snatching a win when he headed over from 6 yards in the 94th minute. It wasn't to be though and we had to settle for a 1-1 draw.

The next game away at Brighton was a truly amazing game with Blues playing much better football apart from the moment that Randolph let the ball squirm under him and into the net to give Brighton the lead. Clayton Donaldson equalised for Blues and it was a game of many changes. Blues won a penalty in first half stoppage time but Caddis shot was saved and it proved to be the turning point as Brighton went 3-1 ahead in the second half. Blues then changed to 4-4-2 and brought on Novak and Thomas and they both scored but so did Brighton again and we lost an exciting game 4-3.

The next game away at Ipswich was a bit of a strange one as David Davis was back to strengthen the defence but he went on to score 2 goals and Blues conceded 4 goals to lose the game 4-2 and drop to 17th place.

The last match of February saw Blues get back to winning ways at St. Andrews with a 1-0 win over Brentford which saw us back up to 13th place. Somewhat worryingly Blues holding company went into receivership and it was rumoured that we could be facing a 10 point deduction, it's never dull being a Bluenose.

Yet another midweek game saw Lee Clarke return to St. Andrews with his new team Blackpool and we were keen to get revenge for our defeat up at their place. New loan signing Robert Tesche played and it was his cross that Shinnie headed home for the winner. Great result me thinks.

Against Rowett's old team Derby he dropped Donaldson for the first time and started with Lee Novak and Blues were poor. Derby went 2-0 up and Blues didn't have a shot as we approached stoppage time. Rowett had a heated exchange with Derby personal over them deliberately taking time to return the ball at throw ins. Quite a few Bluenoses had given up and left when Blues were awarded a penalty in the 93rd minute but those of us that remained celebrated as Caddis made it 2-1. In the 96th minute Blues won a corner which was scrambled into the net by Donaldson and the away end went completely mental. I forgot my recent surgery and ended up clutching my stomach after jumping in the air in delight. Painful but oh so worth it! After a poor performance with no shots in normal time Blues managed to grab a fantastic 2-2 draw and boy did we taunt the Derby fans on the way out.

Only 14,747 (747 being the away fans) saw the home game against Huddersfield as David Cotteril's 10th minute goal gave Blues a 1-1 draw and we were 15th in the table. It doesn't feel like this season will be another relegation battle now that Gary Rowett has the reins and that makes a nice change.

The trip to Cardiff wasn't much fun for the 1,582 of us that traveled to Wales, apart from winding up the Cardiff fans, as Blues put in a poor performance that saw Gary Rowett sent to the stands for throwing the ball to the ground over a disputed throw in and Blues lost the game 2-0. It's been a funny season so far, it's never boring being a Bluenose. Then it was the International break and I watched England beat Lithuania 4-0 at Wembley to top our group with a 100% record.

Good Friday and Rotherham came to St. Andrews and Blues put in a good performance and won the game 2-1 to make it a happy Easter for us noses.

On a lovely sunny Easter Monday we headed to Bournemouth on the official coaches which involved a nice stop on the way down where we could all sit outside in the sunshine with our drinks and lunch before setting off again. We arrived early enough to head into the Wetherspoon's in town where we met Brendan and co and enjoyed a lovely cold pre match drink. Then it was back through the park to Bournemouth's nice little ground and into the away section which was baking in the direct sunlight. No wonder they give this section to the away fans as we roasted throughout the game and the refreshment stalls ran out of water!

Blues began the game well and played the best attacking football that I have seen all season to race into a 2 goal lead against the table toppers and the away end went mental each time and sang we want eight! It could have been 3 had it not been for a missed chance before we allowed Bournemouth to score 2 to go in at halftime all,square at 2-2. Unbelievably Blues conceded 2 more in the second half and ended up losing the game 4-2. Paul Robinson had conceded the penalty for Bournemouth's 3rd and was sent off just after they got their 4th goal. Rowett admitted it may have been a mistake resting Rob Kiernan and playing Robinson instead. You just couldn't make it up. We headed home sunburnt and disappointed.

Wolves were a team on form when they came to St. Andrews with their 4,000 traveling army and they took the lead when their prolific scored Benik Afobe scored. Diego Fabrini had come in on loan and played with a protective face mask due to a broken nose. Blues levelled the game when Rob Kiernan headed home after Jonathan Grounds shot had crossed the line unnoticed by the officials and had been palmed back out. Demari Gray then scored the winner after going on a run and St. Andrews exploded. 'Always shit on the old gold and black' rang out. Gray's goal later won goal of the season. This gave us a fantastic 2-1 win over our local rivals and took us up to 14th.

Blues were at home again a few days later On a Tuesday night as we took on Blackburn who twice took the lead against us. Both times Blues equalised though as Grounds and Gray scored in a 2-2 draw.

We had a nice trip to Watford by coach and went to a nice pub just up the road called 'Odd Fellows' which was already full of Blues fans. It was another lovely sunny day and when we got in the away end we saw Chris Kamara in the outdoor commentary box. This resulted in loads of songs being aimed at him - especially when he was reporting back on sky news live - 'Chris Kamara is a Blue! He hates Villa!' was greeted with a smile and a finger to his lips. 'Kammy, Kammy give us a wave' was also directed at him. Great fun. The match wasn't as good as Blues lost 1-0 to a good Watford side on their way to the Premier League. Their fans created a good atmosphere too with all their yellow and black flags.

A midweek trip to play a a Reading side that had just lost in extra time to Arsenal in the FA Cup semi final saw Blues put in a poor performance. Diego Fabrini had to be substituted when his face mask was split by what Gary Rowett said was a punch from a Reading player. Clayton Donaldson headed in an 83rd minute winner that sent the Blues fans into raptures and gave us a 1-0 away win. Blues were now 13th and no relegation worries at all this season!

The last home game of the season attracted an attendance of 17,775 and saw Blues dominate against Watford but we only scored once when Lloyd Dyer grabbed the winner in the 82nd minute. I was happy with the 1-0 win which took Blues up to 11th and it was great to see Blues finishing the season strongly. Gary Rowett has been brilliant since he arrive at at time when Blues were second from bottom and awful but now we are as high as 11th with a much better record.

The last game of the season was away at Bolton and Blues fans were planning an inflatables party as well as the traditional fancy dress. Blues had been given the entire stand behind the goal and the atmosphere was brilliant. There was loads of fancy dress costumes and loads had gone as manager Gary Rowett in his traditional jumper and Gary masks. The best bit was all the inflatables being bounced around - there was lilo's, sharks, bananas, beach balls etc and it looked fantastic. Many found their way onto the pitch and those that weren't returned to the fans were confiscated behind the hoardings by the miserable stewards. The singing was brilliant too.

Thankfully the match was way less dramatic than last years end of season match and when Tesche scored after Gray's shot was blocked on the goal line, the away end went bonkers and the celebrations began. The 1-0 win moved Blues up to 10th place and our highest position of the season. What an amazing season it had been and we all headed home happy and looking forward to the next season under new manager Gary Rowett with a pre season behind him. We would dare to dream again no doubt.

Clayton Donaldson was Blues top scorer with 16 goals and the average attendances were 16,111 some of which were up by 4%. Bournemouth won the league and were promoted to the Premier League along with Watford in second place and Norwich in the playoffs. Hull City, Burnley and QPR (bottom) were relegated to the Championship with Vile escaping relegation by 3 points. Millwall, Wigan and Blackpool (bottom) were relegated to League One and were replaced by Bristol City (Champions), MK Dons (2nd) and Preston (play offs). Cheltenham and Tranmere Rovers dropped out of the football league.

The FA Cup was won by Arsenal who battered Villa 4-0 - great stuff and the League Cup was won by Chelsea who beat Tottenham 2-0. In the Premier League Chelsea won the title and Manchester City finished runners up.

I had a lovely summer which included a family holiday to Los Cristianos in Tenerife in May and then me, mom and Annette went to Murcia in Spain to visit my cousin Bernadette at her Spanish house in June. I also watched the Women's World Cup in Canada as England won bronze.

Chapter Nine - Gary Rowett

As the 2015 - 16 season was Blues 140 year anniversary the home kit was a reproduction of the original shirt from 1875 - blue with a white sash, white shorts and blue socks and supporters could pay to have their name woven into the shirts. The away kit is the 'German flag' kit that was worn in the 1970s with a bright yellow right side and sleeve, red middle and black left side and sleeve, black shorts and yellow socks with black tops. Both shirts had the 140 year anniversary logo instead of the club badge.

The pre season began with an away friendly at Nuneaton on 14th July which I couldn't attend due to work and Blues won 3-0 with goals from Novak, Shinnie and Davies. Four days later it was away to Kidderminster which again I couldn't attend due to work and it ended in a disappointing 1-1 draw.

On the 21st July the squad split into two teams who traveled to both Shrewsbury Town and Northampton Town and I was again working. We won 2-0 at Shrewsbury and drew 2-2 at Northampton. Then it was Burton Albion away and a disappointing 2-0 defeat.

The final friendly was at St. Andrews as Blues faced Premier League Leicester City and would be a stern test of our team. It was a really good game which I enjoyed immensely amongst the 7,026 inside St. Andrews. Blues played really well against a good Leicester side and were unfortunate to lose the game 3-2 with goals from David Cotterill and Demari Grey. I'm really looking forward to the new season.

I was really looking forward to the Reading game as I love the first home match of a new season whereby everything starts from scratch again and every team is on a level pegging. There is usually a good bit of optimism flying around amongst the fans and a real hope of seeing good football played by our boys in blue and perhaps even achieving something come the end of the season.

Due to work commitments the only pre season friendly I had been able to get to was last Saturday's game against premier league Leicester City at St.Andrews. I wasn't too concerned about missing the friendlies at Kidderminster, Shrewsbury, Northampton and Burton as I don't think they count for much these days with managers chopping and changing players, formats etc. Rarely will you get to see the team that will start/play regularly throughout the coming season. I had already been informed that Blues were crap at Burton from fellow Bluenoses who made the trip. Mind you, I would have liked to have gone to get in a new ground but I was working.

The game against Leicester had been entertaining and Blues didn't do too bad considering it was against premier league opposition but it was a little disappointing to let a 2 goal lead slip and end up losing 3-2. On the positive side David Cotterill's free kick was a cracker for the first goal and Damari Gray's goal 2 minutes later to make it 2-0 was a screamer. So lots of hope for the forthcoming season?

On the negative side I don't think our defence has improved at all and the new goalkeeper looked a bit dodgy at times. The 3 goals conceded were somewhat sloppy. However, friendlies are a learning curve so hopefully Blues will take this forward to today's opener against Reading.

I had woken with a sore throat this morning so I decided to give the pub a miss and headed straight to Boots chemist near the ground to get some strepsils and orange juice. It was lovely to be outside St. Andrews again surrounded by a sea of blue and white on a lovely sunny day.

The Blues superstore was packed but unfortunately the new replica shirts were still not available. I find this shocking and disturbing that the club does not have the replica shirt available for the start of a new season. We must be the only football club in the league to do this.

The start of the new season brings a real buzz of excitement around St. Andrews. 'You can smell the hot dogs' as they say. The sellers with their fanzines, badges and scarves were doing a roaring trade as the Bluenoses flooded into the stadium. I was so excited as I went through the turnstiles and up the steps to the refreshment area at the back of the Kop/Tilton corner.

It was great to see old friends again and hear the buzz of expectation. As I walked down the steps to my seat I breathed in the familiar smell and sounds of St. Andrews on match day. I took in the scene around me, the massive stadium already filling with supporters, the beautiful green of the new pitch, the players warming up, the photographers setting up their equipment and taking occasional snaps of the stands as they fill up and that wonderful sense of new hope all around the ground.

I sat in my seat watching the stands fill up whilst reading my match day programme. The Tilton was filling up quite quickly and was looking very impressive. The away section was also starting to fill with blue and white stripped Reading fans.

As the match kicked off the Tilton looked full and was in good voice, belting out 'Keep Right On'. Blues played well and were soon 1-0 ahead with another great free kick from David Cotterill who celebrated in front of the somewhat subdued Reading fans, before racing to the Kop. And that was how the first half finished.

The second half was soon underway and Blues went further ahead when a fabulous cross from the hardworking Clayton Donaldson was headed home by our new loanee Jon Toral. He looks a great player and a real addition to the team. Reading then seemed to up their game and were causing us problems at the back. I was getting worried as our defence can be a bit suspect at times and sure enough they pulled a goal back from a set piece. The Blues fans were in good voice though and were behind the team the whole way.

The board went up with 5 minutes of added time. Blues were defending as fans headed for the exits and in the 96th minute (some state 97th minute) a somewhat soft penalty was awarded to Reading. I was gutted. I couldn't believe we're were to be robbed of 3 precious points with the last kick of the game. The fans already in the aisles froze and everyone was transfixed as the Reading player placed the ball on the penalty spot as the boos rang out around the stadium. He took his run up and hit a low shot to the goalkeepers left and to our delight Kuzac dived the right way and saved it. The loose ball was then hit across goal and wide as the stadium erupted. All around the Blues fans were celebrating including wild celebrations in the aisles where the fans had been stopped in their tracks.

I left the stadium overjoyed. What a great start to a new season. Yet another Blues goalkeeper saving a penalty on his debut for Blues (remember Tony Cotton and Jim Montgomery). The last time Blues won the first game of the season they were promoted. Here's hoping! A look at the league table shows Blues in 5th place.

On the Tuesday night the 11th August Blues set off to Bristol to commence their League Cup campaign against Bristol Rovers at the memorial ground. I had previously visited this ground on 9/11, the day of the twin towers attack when Blues beat Bristol Rovers 3-0 in the same tournament. On this occasion though, I was I was unable to attend due to work. My sisters boyfriend Steve was able to go though, so he got me a programme.

I love our manager Gary Rowett but my only concern is his wholesale changes in the cup competitions like many other top flight managers currently do. To myself and perhaps many others, this is disrespecting the competition that offers our best chance of a trophy. Every football fan wants to visit Wembley and see their team lift the cup – no matter how their team does in the league. Our trip to Wembley in 2011 when Birmingham City lifted the League Cup is one of the most memorable days in Blues history and one we will never forget or would have swapped for anything in the world.

Tonight Gary Rowett 'only' made eight changes! Again disappointing, but Blues did manage to progress to the next round with a 2-1win in our new red/ yellow/ black away shirts (which I like). Another goal from our Spanish loanee Jon Toral put Blues 1-0 up only for Bristol Rovers to equalise. However, a few minutes later and a great shot from Andy Shinnie restored parity and the sold out Blues end celebrated being 2-1 ahead. The draw set up a home tie against Gillingham in the next round and keeps alive our hopes of another trip to our beloved Wembley.

Next up was the first away trip of the new season at Burnley's Turf Moor on the Saturday. Unfortunately these days, television rights dictate what time and when a lot of our games are to be played and because our match was being shown live it will be an early kick off at 12.30. For me this meant leaving the house at 7am to get the coach from St. Andrews that departs at 8am.

It was a cool overcast morning as I queued for the coach but I was excited about the day ahead and it was good to catch up with friends on the way as we took over the back seat. With our lively banter (Baz in particular). And a stop at the services we were soon arriving in a somewhat gloomy Burnley. Perhaps it was just the weather? Some of the Blues crew went for a drink in the nearby cricket club, but as it was just under an hour to kick off we made our way into Turf Moor. Once inside we got our drinks and made our way to the back of the seats as the away end began filling up.

Burnley were only relegated from the Premier League last season so I thought this could be a bit of a difficult match for us and I wasn't really expecting much of a result for us. Ever hopeful though I stood at the back amongst the singing throng and cheered as the Blues players came onto the pitch for kick off. I must admit I was pleasantly surprised by how well Blues were playing and the Bluenoses were in full voice, belting out song after song. The locals certainly knew Blues were in town! It wasn't long before Jon Toral hit a fabulous shot that flew into the bottom corner of the net from the edge of the penalty area. The away end exploded and I was amused at the sight of a large crowd of Bluenoses in a pile on the ground as they jumped on each other in celebration. It was wild!

At half time the score was 1-0 to Blues and I made my way down to the toilets and found the lads I know having a drink – Brendan, Craig and Graham etc. So I had a chat with them. In the second half Burnley equalised with a headed goal from a free kick given away on the left side of the penalty area. I didn't think it was a free kick and neither did David Cotterill who was adjudged to have committed the offence.

Blues hit back with a counter attack that saw Clayton Donaldson brought down in the box and a penalty awarded to Blues. We were delighted in the away end and celebrated accordingly. Up stepped Paul Caddis and he smashed it into the net before sprinting to the celebrating Blues fans – 2-1! As we were jumping around someone set off a blue flare right in the middle of the main Blues section about 10 feet from us and we were engulfed in blue smoke! It did look amazing but did cause a bit of coughing and choking. The stewards and police didn't really know what to do so nobody moved. Usually people scatter – but not us Bluenoses! They did eventually locate the canister once most of the blue smoke had blown away.

However, Blues managed to throw away their advantage, conceding from yet another soft free kick. Admittedly it was a cracking goal that went in off the crossbar but we really have to stop giving away these free kicks. So the game ended in a 2-2 draw and we had to settle for a point – which we probably would have been happy with before kick off. Now though, we were a little dissappointed as we headed back to the coaches. Blues remain 5th in the league.

A week after the Burnley game Blues had our second live game of the season and our first Friday night game as they took on Derby at St. Andrews. I do love night games at St. Andrews under the glare of the floodlights. There is something magical about it somehow. It would be a tough game as Derby have a good team and beat us 4-0 in the same match last season and that was during the period when Blues were doing well.

The match turned out to be a cracker for the neutrals watching on live TV. It was end to end football and really exciting. Blues played great and hit the post a couple of times. There were 18,134 inside the stadium who enjoyed a thoroughly entertaining game. Blues deservedly went ahead with a thunderbolt from Stephen Gleeson from long range and he ran towards the Railway End to celebrate. Derby hit back in the second half with an equaliser in the 61st minute to force a draw. Once again we were slightly disappointed with the 1-1 draw but ended up going home having witnessed a great game of football. In Rowett we trust. What a difference to last season.

A few days later on the Tuesday night I was heading back to St. Andrews as Blues took on Gillingham in the Capital One Cup (League Cup). Gillingham were currently flying high in League One and would be hoping for a cup upset. Gary Rowett again made wholesale changes to the team which, as you already know by now, I am not happy about. Hence the game was not as entertaining as the last match against Derby but Blues still managed to win the game with some ease. Two goals from Wes Thomas gave Blues a 2-0 win to send us home somewhat happy and into the draw for the next round.

I sat watching the draw for the next round – OMG! It's the Vile away! That will be interesting and the talk of the city for the next couple of weeks. Villa are not doing very well these days (great, I know!) and they are the ones in fear of this draw. Bring it on. Blues are presently in 6th place in the Championship table - only 8 points behind leaders Brighton.

I had been looking forward to the trip to Milton Keynes since the fixture list came out as it will be a new ground for me. I was traveling on the official Blues coaches and I was looking forward to the trip. It was a good job I set out early because my journey to St. Andrews takes me past the Edgbaston

Cricket ground and there was a Twenty/Twenty Semi Final being played there today. Luckily most of the traffic was from the opposite direction and it was fun seeing the fans in various fancy dress costumes and with amusing head gear such as large traffic cones.

There were seven coaches traveling from St. Andrews and we finally got underway about 11.15 am. I was at the back with June, Barry and the lads and we had a somewhat entertaining trip which passed quickly.

We arrived at Stadium MK at 1pm and it looked a really impressive Stadium. Right opposite the away end was a strip of restaurants/ bars with outdoor seating. These included TGI Fridays, Bella Pisa and Frankie & Bennies plus others that I can't remember the names of. Perfect! All the restaurants were already filling with Bluenoses. We all headed into TGI Fridays where Barry got the drinks in and set up a 'tab'. We had a look around and managed to find a table. It was a lovely restaurant/bar and was full of Birmingham fans enjoying the occasion. Lots of people I knew passed by and said hello.

At about 2.45pm we headed across the road and into the Stadium MK. Our seats were in the upper tier and I have to say it was really impressive. Great view and the atmosphere among the 4,500 Birmingham fans was amazing! This is definitely my favourite away ground to date.

The Blues fans were in full voice and due to a lack of banter with the home supporters (who were scattered around the stadium), were enjoying an exchange of "we hate villa more that you" chant between the upper and lower tiers. This was really loud and went on for quite a while. There were also renditions of 'Keep Right On' and 'shit on the villa' and then the teams came out onto the pitch.

The first half was forgettable and looked like a Sunday league game. Birmingham just didn't seem to be trying and it looked like a kick about. Gary Rowett later said that it was the angriest he had ever been at half time. I went looking for my other friends at half time and bumped into Brendan and co near the bar. The away section and bar is really quite impressive as it is quite large and has full length tinted windows with a great view outside. Very nice indeed. I saw Barry enjoying a pint with the others and there were some good songs being sang in the bar too.

The second half was a big improvement and Birmingham took the lead with a fabulous goal from ex-Don Stephen Gleeson against his old team. He paused for a moment before sprinting to the away end to celebrate. The stewards were friendly and sensible (yes I know that's a rarity) especially when a Birmingham fan made a run for the pitch and was tackled and returned the the Blues end despite him stripping his top off and waving it around in the process. This prompted a chant of "we're Birmingham City. We'll do what we want!" from the Bluenoses.

Stephen Gleeson was then on the receiving end of a tackle that saw him crash into the advertising boards and following lengthy treatment which involved gas and air and a leg splint, he was carried off on a stretcher to applause from both sets of supporters.

Maghoma added a second goal when he was put through by Clayton Donaldson and ran to the Birmingham fans to celebrate. Bluenoses rushed to the front and burst through the barrier gates, passed the stunned stewards to join the celebrating Blues player. It was great! We were all jumping around in delight up in the top tier (as they were also doing in the lower tier). When the final whistle sounded to cheers from the Blues contingent 'Keep Right On' was belted out at full volume and the players and manager came over to applaud us. What a top day as our unbeaten run continues.

Once back on the coaches we watched as loads of Bluenoses headed into the bars of TGI Fridays etc. Then we were escorted out, passed waving MK Dons fans that were obviously impressed by our support. I did wave back as they seemed a friendly lot and then we enjoyed a bit of banter on the way back, including a 'back seat selfie' for facebook. Another great day out watching our heroes. Birmingham are currently seventh in the Championship but with a game in hand due to the postponement of the Brentford game.

Still on a high from our win at MK Dons I headed to St. Andrews for our home clash with newly promoted Bristol City. Once again over 18,000 were inside St. Andrews to witness another entertaining game of football. Birmingham played well and Clayton Donaldson was on fire, bagging two goals with only twenty minutes on the clock.

Bristol City pulled a goal back in the 32nd minute but Donaldson claimed his hat trick just before half time when Blues were awarded a penalty. Birmingham's usual penalty taker Paul Caddis very kindly handed the ball to Donaldson thereby giving him the opportunity to complete his hat trick which he took with a cheeky shot down the middle. In the second half Bristol City pulled another goal back with a somewhat sloppy goal to concede. It me a little nervous for a while but Jonathan Grounds put the game beyond doubt with a goal in the 77th minute which ensured a 4-2 win for Blues. Birmingham remain unbeaten home and away so far this season.

On Monday I drove down to Weymouth for a four night stay with my family therefore I missed the Tuesday night game against Nottingham Forest at St. Andrews and it turned out to be Blues first defeat of the season. I was informed that Blues didn't play badly but Forest snatched a goal in the second half to take the points with a 1-0 win.

Still a long way to go though and I remain optimistic. In the meantime I has a lovely relaxing break in Weymouth, staying in a lovely guesthouse right on the seafront. I even enjoyed a trip to the lighthouse at Portland Bill. It was fab. Before I knew it we were heading back to Birmingham on Thursday, just in time to travel to Ipswich for the live Friday night match.

We got back from Weymouth on Thursday afternoon after a fabulous time and on Friday it was time for more traveling, this time to Ipswich with the Blues. Steve was coming with me this time and it was down to his insistence that we were about to travel on what can only be described as the 'pub on wheels ' or as it is affectionately known as the 'party bus'. It was with some trepidation that I boarded the coach at 3.30pm and we met the others. The coach was a bit late setting off and I was a bit concerned due to it being 'poets day' (Piss Off Early Tomorrow's Saturday for those of who don't know it) and the rush hour traffic.

However, the magical mystery tour and its driver set off at speed on a somewhat unusual route. I almost expected us to do a 'Harry Potter' and fly over the land below. To say the music was loud was an understatement, it was impossible to hold a conversation. The music was too heavy but it got better when it was changed to UB40. I really enjoyed the next change of music which was very 70's and 80's reggae etc and the lads seemed to know every word as they all joined in the singing! Very entertaining. Of course there was a constant queue for the toilet at the back!

It was getting close to kick off and about five minutes away from Ipswich the coach pulled into a lay-by and was suddenly cleaned up, cans and bottles put in rubbish bags and left by the side of the road and the previously boisterous interior became a coach load of quiet football fans heading to the game.

We arrived about 7.15pm and set off from the car park to the nearby Portman Road for the match. Once programmes were obtained we headed up to our seats. Considering it was Friday night and a long distance, there was still a good following of Bluenoses. We stood up at the back of the stand and I joined in the singing as the players came out and applauded our away following. It is great having so much hope this season rather than the despair we had at the beginning of last season.

Birmingham looked good and David Cotterill, our Welsh wizard, put us ahead in the 22nd minute. The away end erupted as we danced around in celebration. This was a tough away game and live on TVso to be 1-0 ahead was brilliant. The referee however had other ideas and in the 32nd minute he awarded a very dodgy penalty to Ipswich following a routine move into our penalty area where NOTHING occurred! Why did he give a penalty? No idea, neither had anyone else in the stadium. In fact none of the Ipswich players or fans appealed for anything. It was nothing other than a goal kick. Gary Rowett was incensed on the touch line- as was I in the away end!

The Ipswich player calmly dispatched the penalty and it was all square at 1-1. Birmingham played really well in a game that we really should have won, so although it was a result we may have been happy with before the game, we went away slightly disappointed not to have taken all three points. Although looking on the bright side Birmingham are still in the top half of the Championship table and doing much better than this time last season.

Back on the magical mystery tour bus and a very very noisy trip home. How most of the contingent on the coach managed to sleep I will never know! I was really glad to get back to Birmingham at 0130am although we then had to wait almost an hour for the taxi home, but that's another story. Another great away trip and a good result under our belt.

I was originally working a night duty on the day of the Cup game but I took a annual leave day so that I could be at Villa Park instead. We travelled across to the dark side by coach from St. Andrews and me, June and James were soon in the queue to get into the Witton Arms along with loads of Bluenoses singing 'shit on the Villa'

The police had allocated the Witton Arms for Blues fans only and the landlord was capitalising on the occasion by charging a £2 entrance fee. Once inside we obtained drinks and headed into the large marquee that had been set up at the back of the pub and already a couple of hundred Birmingham fans were in full voice – brilliant!

Loads of songs were being sang loudly, most of them being detrimental to the Villa. There were the usual renditions of 'shit on the Villa' as well as the Tim Sherwood song (villa's current manager) which I will refrain from repeating. There were some massive Birmingham City flags hanging on the walls and the place was rocking. The singing was brilliant – 'the Witton is ours! The Witton is ours! We're Birmingham City, the Witton is ours!' Rang out. It was well worth the entrance fee. I particularly liked 'we've taken your pub! We've taken your pub! We're Birmingham City, we've taken your pub!'

At one point a blue flare went off and the marquee was filled with blue smoke as the Bluenoses continued to sing. It was brilliant. It was only thirty minutes to kick off now so we reluctantly left the pub and headed to the ground. There was no real organisation or segregation outside the ground and it was already getting heated as both sets of fans chanted at each other.

As the Birmingham fans were queuing at the away section the police allowed the villa fans to pass behind us and a few bottles and missiles were thrown at us. The police looked in a panic and I saw that someone in the crowd had blood pouring from his head. Disgraceful.

Once inside the away section was buzzing as 'Keep Right On' was belted out. Birmingham had only been given 2,900 tickets despite the League Cup regulations entitling away clubs to 10% of the capacity and to add to that villa couldn't even sell their own end out and empty seats were noticeable. Blues fans sang 'empty seats my lord, empty seats, oh lord empty seats!'

Blues played really well in the first half as Gary Rowett fielded a strong team in the competition for a change, realising the importance of this game to the fans. It was Premier League v Championship, so we knew we had little to lose and really went for it. Blues really should have been ahead at half time but went in 0-0 as villa's fickle supporters booed their team off the pitch. The second half got underway and villa's only good move produced a goal. We held our heads high though and belted out 'Keep Right On'. Birmingham had a great chance as Maghoma raced into the penalty area in a One on one with the goalkeeper but lashed at his shot and the opportunity went begging.

Although Blues lost the game 1-0 we lost with pride and could hold our heads high. Unlike the vile fans who had booed their team off at half time when they were drawing the game, in contrast the Bluenoses applauded their heroes off at the end singing 'Keep Right On' despite our loss. Now that's proper support for you!

It was a war zone when we left the ground. The police had erected a massive steel fence to our right which separated us from the villa fans (something they should have done before the game) and the vile fans could be heard banging on it from the other side. On the left hand side there was a convoy of police vans between us and the villa fans coming out of the north stand (which they should have given us as they have done in the past). They could be seen gesticulating to us as we wished them well in return. A few cans were lobbed over but it was mostly uneventful as we were led to the coaches and the others to the station.

We were then kept on the coaches for nearly an hour on the car park as the police kept us inside. I was tired and just wanted to get away from the dark side and back home. Knocked out of the Cup but flying high in the League unlike our Premiership opponents who are currently sitting third from bottom.

Following the villa game bottom club Rotherham travelled to St. Andrews and we were all hoping for a good win to give us a boost after the last couple of games. Over 17,000 packed into St. Andrews but it was a disappointing afternoon as the Birmingham players appeared to have a hangover from the villa match and never got going. Defensive errors and a poor performance resulted in Rotherham nicking a goal in each half and a surprise 2-0 defeat for us. We all went home stunned! Amazingly Rotherham then sacked their manager after the game. Football eh. So it was off home to watch the football league show and then match of the day. Blues were now 9th in the League nine points behind leaders Brighton and five points behind second place Middlesbrough.

I had been looking forward to this trip even before it had to be rearranged to enable Brentford to re-lay their pitch following their 4-1 defeat by Oxford on what they deemed a 'poor surface'. I do like Brentford's small ground because of the away terrace section. It was a midweek game and I had booked the day off so I could catch the coach at 3.30pm. It was a pleasant trip down to London, although the M25 was as busy as ever.

The only negative aspect of traveling on the coaches is the lack of a car park at Brentford, meaning we were dropped off on a main road and had to negotiate our way through side streets and across a narrow bridge (with no lighting) over the railway. Really easy to get lost. It was much easier years ago when you just looked for floodlights wherever you went.

As we were making our way to the ground we passed a group of locals selling tea and cakes from a table with a big urn on their driveway. Great idea on a cold night and they were a friendly bunch. Once we arrived at the ground we decided to head inside once we had obtained our match program and had to endure a thorough body search on the way in.

It was great to stand on the terrace and we made our way down to the very front to lean on the barrier. It was quite cold really and I was glad that I had wrapped up. Over 1,200 Bluenoses had made the journey and were in good voice as usual. Brentford's ground is quite small and has terraced area behind both goals. The away end has a seated section above the terrace (also for away fans) and made for a good atmosphere.

The game got underway and Blues were doing okay. At half time it was 0-0 and I jogged about a bit to keep warm. The second half got underway and the Bluenoses were having a bit of fun at the expense of the Brentford goalkeeper who was now positioned right in front of us and his name read 'BUTTON' on the back of his shirt.

There were shouts of 'Jenson!' and 'hey! Cadbury!' It took me a while to get the Cadbury one but when I did I was reduced to giggles. However, the comment that I found the most amusing was from a posh voice that kept shouting 'Benjamin! Benjamin!' He was then shouting 'Benjamin, stand there on the Penalty spot Benjamin!' 'Let it in Benjamin! Let this one in Benjamin!' It was really funny. I should point out though, the goalkeepers name was not Benjamin, it was a reference to Benjamin Button – the character who aged rapidly.

On 71 minutes Birmingham won a corner which was swung into the area and Morrison rose high to head the ball home – 1-0 and we celebrated wildly (as you do on the terraces). Brentford then came back at us and forced a couple of corners. I had to smile when I heard a lone cry of 'why does it always have to be this way! Why can't we just win?' I think we all understood the anguish in that statement.

The ninety minutes were up and the board went up with five minutes of injury time. We all felt extremely nervous when on 94 minutes Brentford won a corner. They took the corner which was then cleared up field to Clayton Donaldson to run onto it and he smashed the ball into the Brentford net right in front of us. The away end exploded! Relief and ecstasy washed over us as we jumped around whilst Donaldson was mobbed by the rest of the Birmingham team. The Clayton Donaldson song rang out loudly. 2-0!

A few seconds later the final whistle blew and Blues were 2-0 winners. We were now 5th in the League. 'Gary Rowett's Blue and White Army!' Echoed around the ground as the players came over to applaud us, this was followed by 'Keep Right On'. Gary applauded our supporters and pumped his fist in celebration. Then it was back down the dark side streets to find our way back to the coaches and I was in full voice as we boarded. What a great night. It is so much fun watching Blues away when we win. Next up is Leeds a Utd. Bring it on.

Following Blues midweek win at Brentford I was really looking forward to the trip to Leeds. Last time I visited Leeds was for the League Cup Semi Final back in 1996. I was going on the official Blues coaches again with June but this time our other friend was going by train and would be in corporate hospitality at Leeds with his 'connections' (yes Baz, that's you!).

The trip up north was enjoyable and we were soon pulling into the car park next to Elland Road. I couldn't believe how run down Elland Road has become. It looked really old and worn. We were right outside the away end and I headed to the programme booth to purchase my match day program. I got chatting to a Leeds fan who said he liked what we have done with our badge (club crest) for this season. It's to celebrate 140 years. I agreed with him that it is very impressive but that I hope it really is only for this season as we all love our ball and world club crest. In fact it was placed in a list of the top twenty most easily recognised football club crests.

The football federation supporters trust has planned a national protest today about away ticket prices. It is known as 'Twenty's Plenty' in a bid to make all clubs charge a maximum of twenty pounds for away fans. This is because of the extra cost incurred traveling to away games and the increasing cost of the Match ticket. In fact today's ticket had cost £35!

Linda (from the Birmingham City supporters club) had been sent a massive banner from the federation which read 'BCFC FANS SAY TWENTY'S PLENTY' and we were due to meet Leeds fans by the Billy Bremner statue for the protest.

We arrived early clad in our Blues shirts and I obtained a Leeds badge for my collection whilst we waited for the Leeds fans and their banner, who were currently in the pub while we waited for them, it was soon retrieved though and we all United for the protest as loads of people took photos of us. The press had arranged to be there although amazingly there was no mention of the protest afterwards. With all the money involved in the Premier League and Championship I suppose it's not surprising the football clubs wanted it kept quiet. In fact Leeds would not allow the banners to be taken into the stadium and Linda had to return it to the coach before we headed into the ground for the game.

The atmosphere in the Birmingham section was loud and proud and we were all in good voice as usual. There was some great banter with the Leeds fans. There was the usual 'Keep Right On' and also 'we all hate Leeds, Leeds, we all hate Leeds, Leeds'.

The Jimmy Saville song was a new song for me though as the Bluenoses sang 'he's one of your own, he's one of your own, Jimmy Saville, he's one of your own!' I had to laugh a bit later when the Leeds fans sang 'he's coming for you, Jimmy Saville, he's coming for you'. Demari Gray then scored a cracker to put Birmingham 1-0 up and the celebrations in the Blues end were chaotic. 'We're Birmingham, we're Birmingham' rang out loudly.

The Bluenoses were on form and when they sang 'you're not famous anymore!' the Leeds fans looked extremely unhappy.

As the game headed into the 90th minute Leeds were desperate to get an equaliser but Blues got the ball to Maghoma who smashed the ball into the Leeds net. 2-0! Mayhem broke out in the away end as the celebrations began in earnest. Meanwhile Maghoma had ran to the Blues end only for the Leeds fans to throw missiles at the celebrating Blues players. To the players credit though they ignored this and continued their celebrations. What a great away win! At the end of the game the players came over to applaud the Blues fans and we sang our hearts out in response. Back to the coaches and a pretty enjoyable trip home. Birmingham now sitting in fourth place in the League table. Happy times.

Then it was the international break and I watched as England won away in Lithuania 3-0 to finish top of the group with a 100% record. Brilliant! Then it was back to St. Andrews again to take on one of last season's relegated premier league teams – Queens Park Rangers. It would be a tough game as QPR would be expecting a quick return to the Premier League as most relegated teams do.

It was another good attendance inside St. Andrews of 19,161. It is great to see good crowds again and this season and our attendances are on the rise. The average attendance is already up by over 3,000 this season. We were treated to another great game too. Despite falling 1-0 behind in the 17th minute, Paul (Robbo) Robinson grabbed his first goal for Blues in the 24th minute to restore parity. "Robbo! Robbo!" rang out as he ran back to the half way line and saluted the fans singing his name.

The second half got underway and Blues were awarded a penalty in the 63rd minute in front of the Tilton End. Up stepped Paul Caddis and he smashed the ball into the back of the net. Goal! 2-1 to Blues which is how it remained to the final whistle. Great win yet again and we all left St. Andrews happy, except the cockney contingent of course. Blues remained in fourth place in the table (joint second) on 21 points, 4 points behind leaders Brighton.

I couldn't get to the Bolton game as I was working but my friends kept me informed of their adventures and got me a programme. I was told there were around 900 Bluenoses there, which is good for a midweek game. No doubt they would have been in good voice as always. Another fantastic result was gained against bottom club Bolton as Blues chalked up another great away win with yet another goal from Paul Robinson (Robbo) in the 20th minute.

Blues have remained unbeaten away from home in the League this season. Great times indeed. We are now second in the table! Two points clear of third placed Reading and 4 points behind leaders Brighton.

It was an early start for the trip to Hull and we were traveling on the official coaches again. This time Steve had decided that he was coming as well, so we were on coach three this time whereas the others were on coach one. We arrived at the services in good time only to see that the party bus was already there and had two coaches this time. This meant six coach loads descended on the motorway services at the same time. It was blue and white as far as the eye could see. As we headed into the services we bumped into Graham, Phil and a couple of the others. Because the services were now so busy with all the Bluenoses we headed over the bridge and picked up a KFC to take back on the coach with us. It was lovely.

The coach got underway again and it didn't seem too long before we were coming into Hull and we could see the massive Humberside bridge. 'There's the Golden Gate bridge' I said to Steve pointing to the bridge. Not long later we saw the KC Stadium, home of Hull City. I had been to this ground before but it was a new ground for Steve. Once in the car park we headed onto coach one where June and Jake were sheltering from the torrential rain as the turnstiles were not open yet. We persuaded them to join us on a trek to the pub and I led them across the car park to a social club that I went to last time I came to Hull.

I picked up a badge for my collection on the way to the club. It's a nice club called the Walton Social Club and well worth the £1 entrance fee. 'Do you think it will be okay for away fans?' Someone asked as we approached. I pointed to a very large Birmingham City flag on display outside and said 'I'd say so yes'.

Inside it's really big and there were loads of Blues fans already drinking in there. We had a couple of drinks and a catch up then headed back across the car park and into the away end. There were around 1,500 Bluenoses that had made the trip and were in good voice inside the stadium. Hull City's stadium was like most new 'flat pack' stadiums, lacking character but with good unobstructed views.

As usual the Blues contingent stood up throughout and lots of songs were sang. I always love to hear our anthem 'Keep Right On' belted out. My favourite song today (apart from Keep Right On) was 'you know who you are, you know who you are – Hull City Tigers! You know who you are!'. The Hull fans didn't take too kindly to that one.

Blues started well but when Hull hit two goals past us in two minutes in the 36th and 38th minutes we looked shell shocked and never really recovered. When the first goal went in we responded with 'Keep Right On' in defiance but two minutes later we were fearing the worse. The referee was awful again and even though we sang 'we're Birmingham City we'll fight to the end!' the game ended in defeat. The players came over to applaud us are we sang 'Keep Right On', then we trudged back through the puddles to our coaches. Our first away defeat this season. Hull moved up to replace Blues in second place as we dropped to 6th, five points behind leaders Brighton.

It was an early kick off for the Wolves game in front of the Sky cameras so I had to set off early for St. Andrews. Like most Blues fans I don't really like Wolves and dread the thought of losing to them, especially as they play us on the back of three heavy defeats. They couldn't even sell their ticket allocation which says it all really.

The crowd was 18,946 which is a drop from the last home attendance but I suppose it is because of the early kick off and the live TV broadcast. It is still much better than last season though. Because of the early kick off time I had chips with chilli sauce inside the stadium as I made my way to my seat. Just before kick off a canon was heard and there was a minutes silence for remembrance. It was really haunting as the last post was sounded on the bugle.

Then the game got underway. Blues started well but Wolves took advantage of a Robbo blunder in the 11th minute and snatched a early lead. As the Wolves fans celebrated 'Keep Right On' rang out loudly around the stadium in a bid to lift our players. In the 19th minute there was a minutes applause for a Bluenoses named Josh who had sadly died aged only 19. It was observed by the entire stadium including the Wolves fans so respect to them for their part.

However, the game never got any better and Birmingham continued to make mistakes and send wayward passes directly to the feet of the Wolves players. If anything we looked even worse in the second half and it was no surprise when we conceded another sloppy goal where everyone seemed to stand still, including our goalkeeper, as the ball was almost 'passed' into the net from a Wolves player on the edge of the penalty area.

Our hopes sank as Blues looked inept today and never really looked like scoring. It was not an inspiring performance. However, I still cannot understand the 'fans' who streamed out of the stadium with ten minutes still to play. Do they not remember Derby away last season when Blues were losing 2-0 in the 90th minute and despite never looking like scoring all game, managed to score 2 in injury time and draw 2-2? I could give many more examples over the years too.

It's embarrassing to think that all those watching on TV saw our ground empty with 10 minutes to go and to witness how fickle some of our fans are. I thought our fans were better than that. Yes, I felt despondent and couldn't see us getting anything from the game but I have never left before the end of a game. What happened to 'we're Birmingham City we'll fight to the end'?

Never one to be down for long though I trust Gary Rowett to pick the players up and get that fighting spirit back for the next game. Gary has performed miracles with the team he has. Blues remain in 6th place, 6 points behind leaders Brighton and 4 points behind second placed Hull City.

I could not make the next game which was against Blackburn Rovers at St. Andrews as I was working a night duty. I had tried everything to swap my shift but was unable to do so and I was gutted that I would have to miss it. It was a cold rainy night and apparently I didn't miss much in what was reportedly a rather dull 0-0 draw. Although after two defeats at least it was an improvement. This meant that Blues remain 6th and Hull City take top spot from Brighton with 31 points. Blues are now on 25 points just 6 points behind the leaders.

Chapter Ten - London Calling

On Thursday I texted my nephew Stephen, who lives in London, to see if he is going to the Fulham game on Saturday. He said he wasn't planning to but if I am going he will try to get a ticket. He did manage to get a ticket in the mixed fan section next to the away end as Blues had sold out our 4,000 allocation. Great news, so I will meet him in London when we head to Fulham this Saturday.

I was up early and really looking forward to the trip to Fulham as we were traveling by train. Steve got the bus to mine and the June and James picked us up in a taxi which took us to Snow Hill station to catch the train to London. We met Barry at the station and boarded the 09.50 train to London Marlybone. It was a nice journey as we all chatted and enjoyed food and drinks and I texted Stephen to let him know what time I thought we would arrive.

Once we arrived at Marlybone we went on a London Underground adventure that involved four trains and culminated in our arrival at Putney Bridge about an hour later. Stephen was waiting for us outside Putney Bridge station and it was great to see him again. We then had a lovely walk through the park along the riverbank as we headed towards the stadium. We saw boats and rowers in the river and stopped for photos with Putney Bridge in the background. It was damp and overcast but it was still lovely.

After passing a couple of pubs packed with Blues fans we picked up programmes near the ground and I popped into the club shop to get a badge for my collection. Then we followed Baz, for what seemed like ages, to a pub called 'The Crabtree' which, although full of Bluenoses,it wasn't as packed as the others pubs we had passed.

I was really hot when we got in the pub after that walk so once we had our drinks we headed to the covered patio area outside. There were Bluenoses there already enjoying their drinks, a few of who I already knew and I had a bit of a catch up. It was great having a catch up with Stephen too and before long the singing began. It started with 'Keep Right On' and we all joined in. It was loud and proud and we all had a great time as we enjoyed our pre match drinks.

Then it was time to head back to the stadium and amazingly the walk appeared shorter than before. Once inside the ground it was swarming with Bluenoses. As everybody stands at away games we managed to get Stephen in with us in the away end so that we could enjoy the game together. The atmosphere was amazing amongst the 4,000 Birmingham fans and song after song rang out.

Craven Cottage, the home of Fulham, is a nice ground with character (sadly lacking from most new stadiums) and we had an amazing view of the Thames from our vantage point in the away end. Blues started the game well and totally dominated. Stephen Gleeson scored a cracker in the 18th minute and the Blues end went wild. Everyone started singing and bouncing and I could feel the stand moving.

Three minutes later cheers broke out again as Clayton Donaldson was upended in the penalty area and the referee pointed to the spot. Up stepped Paul Caddis to smash the ball in the net leading to more wild scenes amongst the 4,000 Birmingham fans plus those in the neutral section. Once again the stand rocked under our feet as the fans bounced in celebration. We were in heaven when Jon Toral scored a fantastic third goal in the 31st minute. Unbelievable celebrations broke out in the away end. The stand was literally shaking. 'Easy! Easy!' broke out and then 'you may as well go home' was sang to the Fulham fans who were looking extremely despondent at this point.

There were cheers at halftime as Blues went into the break with a 3-0 lead. Brilliant! It would have proved too difficult to get halftime refreshments as it was absolutely packed below the stand. It was hard enough getting to the toilets and back. I did see several people that I knew in the process though. Blues were just as good in the second half and Fulham had a player sent off for a second yellow card (in a matter of minutes) in the 49th minute. Fulham did rally a bit though and pulled a goal back in the 66th minute.

This was definitely not a fair reflection of the game though but parity was restored when Clayton Donaldson got our fourth goal in the 82nd minute. The Blues end erupted and Stephen and I jumped around together as the stand shook again. 'All bounce if you love the Blues' rang out. 'Gary Rowett's Blue and white army' followed. Somewhat fortunately Fulham then got a second goal when a lucky deflected pass fell nicely into the path of a Fulham player in injury time. Once again I didn't think that 4-2 was a fair reflection of our dominance but then Solomon-Otabor scored a fantastic solo goal in the 95th minute to make it 5-2 to Blues.

Amazing celebrations broke out in the away end as we celebrated. We had all thoroughly enjoyed this win. Especially as we had been passing the ball about in such style. The Blues fans had been singing 'we're taking the piss, we're taking the piss, we're Birmingham City- we're taking the piss!'

This has definitely been the performance of the season for me. Blues dominated the game and were loudly applauded at the final whistle. The players came over to the away end to applaud the Blues fans and as 'there's only one Gary Rowett' rang out, the man himself turned to wave back and applaud us.

As we all headed back through the park we decided to have a couple of drinks across the river with Stephen before we had to head back to get our train. We crossed Putney Bridge and went into a Wetherspoon's pub called The Rocket, overlooking the Thames. There were several Bluenoses already in there that we knew such as Fidler and Becksy. We took our drinks outside to cool down and watched a fireworks display across the river in the general direction of Fulham's stadium.

Stephen had to head off to meet his friends at a firework display on the other side of London so he headed off to Putney station to get the first of several trains to get him there. We then headed back across Putney Bridge to also get several trains back to Marlybone and our 8.40pm train back to Birmingham. We picked up burgers and pasties etc for the train journey and we were soon on our way home. What a fantastic away day we had enjoyed! Blues stay in 6th peace and Hull City won again to remain top of the table.

The International break weekend saw me jetting off on a holiday with my family for a two week break in my old home town of Abu Dhabi. It was great being able to visit on holiday rather than working there. It would mean that I would miss the next two Blues games against Charlton at St. Andrews and Brighton away.

I had a lovely relaxing week before the Charlton game. We spent the mornings relaxing by the pool of our five star hotel – the Sheraton, in the 28 degree sunshine. The afternoons were spent in the Club Lounge which we had the use of as we were lucky enough to be staying in 'Club rooms'. It was wonderful.

We dined out most evenings at luxury places and also enjoyed a fabulous brunch at the five star Fairmont hotel. It was really lovely. The only cloud on the horizon was Blues home defeat to Charlton 1-0. According to friends who were at the game and Gary Rowett's post match comments, Blues were unlucky to lose. But lose they did, even though they had 20 shots they were unable to make them count. Despite this defeat Blues remained in 6th place.

Our second week in Abu Dhabi seemed to go a bit quicker but was still really enjoyable. I met up with a friend Pam,who was also back visiting, and we went round to our old place of work to visit and see our old work colleagues. The Corniche hospital has changed a lot but still has the same faces and it was lovely to catch up with them all.

We did another brunch on the Friday before the Brighton game. It was in our hotel at Flavours restaurant and was fabulous. The crab and lobster were amazing. We had the bubbly package which included cocktails and we tried an impressive cocktail called a 'melontini' which was inside a massive melon with six 'straw' holes so that you could share the 1 & ½ litre cocktail.

During the week (on Mondays) the Sheraton had an 'American Diner' night in Flavours restaurant. It was great and there was a big 50's style American juke box playing 50's and 60's music. The food selection (buffet) was amazing and included live cooking stations making a selection of burgers and hotdogs. My favourite was the chilli hotdog and there was also the New York hotdog and the New Jersey hotdog. It was all lovely.

Rays Bar was another fabulous place we visited. It is on the 62nd floor in the Etihad Towers and had spectacular views far out over the city and out to sea. Even the bathrooms have to be seen to be believed! Marble floors and sinks that overflow down the sides like fountains and floor to ceiling windows looking out over Abu Dhabi. Fantastic! It's a bit pricey of course with the cheapest vodka being £10. It does come with a fancy selection of nuts and popcorn though. Well worth a visit.

There are several large shopping malls in Abu Dhabi and we visited a few and did a bit of shopping. I got a new blue and white handbag – just the right size to fit a football programme in – you see my thinking. Our last day in Abu Dhabi was the Saturday 28th November and Blues were away at Brighton who were unbeaten. We had spent the morning chilling by the pool, popped in the Club Lounge and then headed to the restaurant at Abu Dhabi City Golf Club where we sat outside and enjoyed an early evening meal. Abu Dhabi is four hours ahead of the UK so by the time we were enjoying free drinks in the Club Lounge in happy hour Blues were about to kick off in Brighton. With one eye on the score updates I enjoyed my (quadruple) vodka and coke whilst willing Blues to win.

From what I was told afterwards Blues played really well. Brighton took the lead early in the first half but our Spanish sensation Jon Toral scored the equaliser not long afterwards. Half time 1-1 but early in the second half Blues went behind again and despite a late resurgence where we were unlucky not to score but Blues lost the game 2-1.

Despite the last two defeats Blues remain in 6th place but the chasing pack are catching up. Not the best way to finish my holiday and I wasn't looking forward to the journey back. It was the Grand Prix weekend in Abu Dhabi too, Lewis Hamilton had already won the drivers championship. On the bright side though Villa are now officially the worse ever Premier League team at this stage of the season. They sit at the foot of the table with only 5 points from a possible 42. And yes, I am smiling at this moment!

After my first week back at work I was really looking forward to Saturday and getting down to St. Andrews again. Blues are entertaining Huddersfield Town who currently sit third from bottom of the Championship. However, with our home form being abysmal of late I was a bit apprehensive.

There has also been a lot of speculation about our manager Gary Rowett over the last week that I have found very unsettling. Following Fulham's 5-2 defeat to Blues they had sacked their manager Kit Simmons and Gary Rowett became the bookies favourite to take the Fulham job. Like a lot of other Championship clubs, Fulham have money to spend, in contrast to Blues.

It was reported that Fulham had approached Blues to speak to Gary. I was worried. There were no denials or statements from Blues. Then QPR threw their hat in the ring too as it was reported that they wanted our manager for their current managerial vacancy. Gary Rowett was said to be flattered by speculation but focused on his job here at Birmingham City. No statement from the Club though and I was nervous. Finally a statement from Blues that they were on contract talks with Gary Rowett who would be staying at Birmingham City. I don't fully trust this but I was relieved. Fulham appointed a new manager and QPR got theirs.

I was now sitting inside St. Andrews on a cold December day awaiting kick off. Whether it is Christmas shopping, the weather or Blues poor home form the attendances seem to be dropping with 15,931 here today. It was good to see everyone after my two week holiday and catch up on the news. However, my day was spoilt after only 32 seconds when Blues conceded another poor goal. It didn't get any better either as we played very poorly. I think we miss Clayton Donaldson who had got injured on international duty for Jamaica, and also David Cotterill.

Blues lack a decent striker at the moment apart from Clayton Donaldson. Brock-Marsden is not really good enough if he is up front alone and even today with Gary Rowett changing our formation to 4-3-3 he didn't look sharp. Damari Gray had a poor game too but most of the team did.

In the second half Blues conceded another poor goal ten minutes from time and the stadium emptied. This I don't understand and never will. We should stand by the team till the end. I know there was no fight in today's team and it was hard to watch but I remained till the referee's whistle signalled a 2-0 home defeat. I have to say that the referee had also been shocking. Due to Cardiff winning at Bolton and Sheffield Wednesday drawing against Derby, Blues drop out of the top six and down to eighth. Things are not looking good.

Gary Rowett is usually positive and supportive in his post match interviews but today he said the players need to start holding their hands up and he will see who he needs to start replacing if they can't do the job. It's the players Christmas party weekend and they were due to have Monday off but Gary said they would now be coming in to work. He said 'I'm gonna have a horrible weekend so they can too!'. Brighton are unbeaten at the top of the table and Middlesbrough are in second place. Blues next game is away at Middlesbrough.

The next evening we had tickets to see Roy Wood's Christmas 'Rockmas' at the NIA. Me, mom Annette and Steve were all going and planned to eat in Coast to Coast first. Steve had said he would pick us up in a taxi and we were amazed when he arrived in a gleaming white Bentley Limousine with chauffeur! It was lovely inside with beautiful ceiling lights, a long curved sofa and a fabulous bar with blue lights glowing and champagne glasses hanging up. The chauffeur then climbed in the back and poured us all a glass of champagne which we then enjoyed on the way to coast to coast.

The Limo pulled up outside the restaurant and we felt like celebrities as we made our way inside. The meal was lovely and then we headed to the NIA for the show. The first part of the show was a bit boring but once Bluenose Roy Wood came on it was fabulous. He sang lots of 'Wizards' songs and his voice was brilliant. A proper rocker! At the end of the show Roy sang 'I wish it could be Christmas every day' with a choir and joined by Chas and Dave. It was great and I had really enjoyed the night. As we came outside after the show there was our gleaming white limo on the bridge waiting to take us home. Once we were on board the chauffeur opened another bottle of champagne and poured us all glasses for the journey home. We felt like stars, it was wonderful.

It was still dark when I headed out to pick up the others to get the coach to Middlesbrough. When we arrived at the car park at St. Andrews it was raining and dull. We had to stand in the rain for a while as we waited to board one of the three coaches to today's game. The coaches got underway and I was relieved that the journey had begun as it will be a long trip today. We all agreed that we would be happy with a point against high flying Middlesbrough who are currently sitting in second place.

The journey was a long one but was broken nicely by a stop at the Services where we all had bacon and egg rolls, which were fabulous. There was also a coach of Watford fans who had stopped off on their journey to Sunderland. As we were nearing Middlesbrough the snow started coming down and the fields started to turn white. I started to worry about the game being called off, especially after traveling all this way.

When we arrived at Middlesbrough's ground it was pouring with rain and the turnstiles were nowhere near opening yet. Nearly everyone stayed on the coaches which were parked right outside the away turnstiles but me being me, I decided to head off in search of the club shop to get a badge for my collection and a match day programme. Steve and Jack decided to brave the conditions and accompany me. Sensibly June and James stayed dry on the coach.

There was no shelter from the elements as we walked around the stadium to the club shop, it was quite a nice shop though, which is more than can be said for their official club badge which was a boring dull silver colour replica of their crest. I got one anyway, for my collection. They had a selection of books also (I love books) and Steve bought the Colin Todd autobiography as he had played for Blues too. I remember him fondly. As we were walking further round the stadium the Blues players coach arrived and we stayed to watch them disembark. Not one of the players bothered to look in our direction or acknowledged us apart from Gary Rowett and we got soaked through in the process.

We headed to the away end and the turnstiles were still closed, despite it now being 13.45. It was cold and raining and Steve now really wanted to go to a pub. I didn't want to go to a pub to be honest as I was wet enough already but I gave in and so we headed down the (flooded) road to the Navigation pub with Jack in tow.

The pub was full of home fans with not a hint of blue anywhere and of course it was now really hot inside. I was boiling because of all my winter layers but I had a Blues top and scarf on under my coat. When I couldn't stand it any longer I took my coat off and of course it did not go down at all well. I soon put my coat back on though and once Steve had finished his drink (I was on coke as I was driving when we got back) we headed back to the ground. By this time the rest of the coach party were still nice and dry inside the away end.

It was still cold inside the away end concourse, although at least it was dry. My coat was soaked through, in fact it was also wet on the inside so I took it off for a while. I was planning to dry it in the toilets but Middlesbrough have the only toilets I have ever been to with no hand dryers! I kid you not. We made our way up to the stand to join the other Bluenoses who had made the trip. There wasn't a lot of us, probably a few hundred or so, possibly because of the weather or the fact that it was the penultimate weekend before Christmas. Anyway, despite the freezing conditions our support was still in good voice.

I thought the crowd of 20,929 was somewhat disappointing for a team like Middlesbrough in second place. The Blues fans sang 'your grounds too big for you!' at all the empty seats around the stadium. The game got underway and although Blues were a little slow to start they grew in confidence as the game went on. Blues looked solid in defence for once and were taking the Middlesbrough defence apart on the counter attack. We really should have scored.

A couple of minutes from time Blues had a corner that was met by the head of Michael Morrison who's header went narrowly wide of goal. Although I was very happy with a point, I felt we could have won the game. A much improved performance from last weekend and much to be pleased with. Then it was back on the coach for the long journey back to Birmingham.

I couldn't make the away trip to Preston, much to my disappointment as this is the only ground in the Championship that I haven't visited. I did manage to listen live to the radio though and watched the highlights the next day. Therefore I saw the very poor goal that Birmingham conceded to go 1-0 behind in the first half. Everyone just stood still – again! I don't know what our goalkeeper was doing. Blues never gave up though and had lots of chances. Eventually Morrison powered in a header in the 67th minute to make it 1-1 and that was the final score. It should have been three points but at least we didn't lose.

The last game before Christmas was a home match against Cardiff City and would be shown live on Sky TV. It was a bit of a six pointer as Cardiff sat one place above Birmingham in 7th place and a win for Blues would mean moving above them on goal difference. It was a cold night and I arrived at St. Andrews in my Woolly hat and blues bar scarf. As it was the last game before Christmas the sellers were out in force with scarves and blue Santa hats on display. I couldn't resist and purchased a blue Santa hat for £2 which promptly replaced my Woolly hat. It looked cool.

The Blues superstore was packed and once inside the ground there were blue Santa hats everywhere. There were also a few traditional red santa's in the Cardiff end. The attendance was disappointing, with only 14,414 making the effort. Perhaps it was due to the close proximity of Christmas festivities, the match being shown live or the fact that we have not been doing well of late at St. Andrews. The game got underway and Blues were playing a bit better than recent home performances. I still think Blues miss David Cotterill, Paul Robinson and in particular Clayton Donaldson. Someone informed me that without Donaldson Blues score on average every four hours but with him in the team Blues score a goal every 68 minutes. I can't wait for him to return.

In the 46th minute, just before half time, Blues were awarded a penalty which Paul Caddis calmly dispatched to ensure that we went into the break 1-0 ahead. And that was how the game finished with a hard fought 1-0 win for Blues and three points that saw us leapfrog Cardiff into 7th place.

I was then working night duties until the morning of Christmas Eve. I went home and slept for a few hours before getting up and going to the early evening (5.15) Pantomime via Wetherspoons with Annette and Steve. It was a brilliant Pantomime (Aladdin) and my favourite part was when Widow Twanky strode across the stage in a Birmingham City top singing Keep Right On! (To cheers) She then turned around to reveal the other half of the shirt to be a Villa shirt and marched back across the stage to a random song (well they don't have an anthem do they) and to a chorus of boo's from the entire audience. Very funny!

Despite being knackered from my nights I had a lovely Christmas with my family and some lovely presents- several being Blues related. However, I was working Boxing Day so I couldn't go to the away game at Sheffield Wednesday. Steve went though and came back with a half/half scarf Birmingham City/ Borussia Dortmund. Really nice. It was one of only thirty brought over from Germany by some German Bluenoses that were over for the game. Apparently Birmingham played poorly and were beaten by a poor Sheffield Wednesday team 3-0. We had a good 10-15 minute spell where we hit the crossbar but apart from that Blues didn't really turn up. So Blues slipped down to 10th as Sheffield Wednesday went above us.

It was lovely to be heading over to St. Andrews again to watch my beloved Blues take on MK Dons. I do admit to being a little anxious due to our home performances/ results this year. I think most teams come here now thinking they can win. Gone are the days we were invincible at 'fortress St. Andrews'.

Anyway, today that buzz was back at St. Andrews. The queue at the ticket collection point was right back past the burger bar. Unfortunately so was the queue for the Women's security check prior to the turnstiles. Pretty bad really especially as the men were going straight in – many not even being searched. Don't get me wrong, I do agree that there is a need for security in these sad times but to have only one woman steward on duty but several male stewards is poor planning.

Luckily I did get there early and had even popped into the Cricketers to say hello to those I knew. Once inside the stadium I could see it was going to be a big crowd. The atmosphere was great and people were still coming in as the game kicked off. There were 19,714 inside St. Andrews, 900 of them from Milton Keynes. Blues had Paul Robinson and Clayton Donaldson back fit and the line up looked to be a really positive one. Demari Gray was on the bench, which I think will do him a bit of good and help make him hungry again.

Blues started well and had a number of chances, none of which were taken but it only looked a matter of time before the goal would come. And come it did, in the second half as Maghoma sidestepped two tackles in the penalty area before smashing the ball into the net as St. Andrews erupted. Blues could have had more as Donaldson and then Gray hit the post after coming on as a substitute. Overall a pretty good display. I thought Robbo and Cadis were great in defence and Donaldson made all the difference but I would personally give Man of the Match to the Spaniard Jon Toral who was outstanding.

So a 1-0 win and Blues up to 9th in the table and level on points with 8th place Brentford and 7th place Sheffield Wednesday all on 36 points. Only goal difference separates us and it's Brentford that are the next visitors to St. Andrews on Saturday. Meanwhile Villa lost again and remain rooted to the bottom of the Premier League with only 8 points! They could be playing Walsall next season as the Saddlers are top of League One. Excellent.

I was unfortunate enough to be working a night duty on New Years Eve (3rd night in a row) so I didn't get to celebrate the New Year but I was really looking forward to the Brentford game. I drove to St. Andrews and picked Steve up from the outskirts of town where he had been to brunch for his dads birthday. It was early when we arrived so I got a parking space quite close to the ground.

Because we were early we went into the Club shop and then round to the Cricketers to meet the others. We didn't stay long and headed back to the ground for chips before going in. There were massive queues for the ticket pick up point but more worryingly there was a massive queue for the women to get searched. As I've said before, having only one woman steward on duty is ridiculous. The men were going straight in, some not even getting searched and yet I had to join a very long queue of women. It took about twenty minutes to reach the turnstiles where we had to queue again. Rubbish!

Once inside though, the stadium was filling rapidly. The atmosphere was great again and the attendance was 17,555. We were treated to a great game too. Blues went ahead when Maghoma scored in the 55th minute to the delight of the fans. Disappointingly though Brentford drew level in the 77th minute and I began to feel disheartened. However, in the 89th minute Blues had a break as Vaughan broke free and his cross cum shot was put in the net by Kieftenbeld as he scored his first Blues goal. Despite six minutes of injury time Blues held on to win 2-1 and moved up to 8th place in the Championship.

Today Demari Gray was noticeably absent and the rumour is that he was at Leicester City having a medical before signing for them. Somewhat disappointingly this turned out to be spot on and he did in fact sign for Premier League Leicester City. Demari's message to the fans was that he is always a blue – yes Leicester are also blue! And where have we heard that before – Wayne Rooney who went on to kiss the red badge of their rivals Manchester United. Loyalty doesn't exist in today's world of football. I'm not too worried though as we have Maghoma, Solomon Ottabor and Cotterill. I hope Gary Rowett spends the money well during the transfer window. He got 3.75 million pounds, much less than he was worth

FA Cup day! I love the FA Cup. Years ago each round of the FA Cup would have produced large attendances of excited fans in love with the dream of seeing their team in the Final at Wembley. Today the competition has been devalued by the Premier League and managers who use the competition to rest their players and play their reserves. It is a insult to the best Cup competition in the world and to the fans.

For some this is the only chance of a trophy, a day of glory that we would forsake all else for. Today we expected a low crowd and to be confronted with Bournemouth's reserves. I was right on both counts as 13,140 saw Blues play against a Premier League Bournemouth team consisting mostly of their reserves. At least Gary Rowett had not made wholesale changes although there were some changes. It was a cold rainy, dark day as the teams ran out at St. Andrews. Blues played really well though and every Blues player put in a shift. David Cotterill played well in the first half and it was his superb free kick that was headed home by Michael Morrison to put Blues 1-0 ahead.

However, Bournemouth were awarded a penalty for what I thought was a dive as did the majority in the stadium as 'you're not fit to referee!' rang out. The referee and the penalty taker were loudly booed as he scored from the spot to make it 1-1. Blues were playing really well and had several chances. Jon Toral came on in the second half and he was superb. Blues were then awarded a penalty and with our usual penalty taker being 'rested' Bluenose Vaughan stepped up to blast it high over the bar. I think he wanted it too much.

He was disconsolate and it affected him for the next 15 minutes or so. He was rocked by the miss. Blues continued to create chance after chance. Maghoma cut inside and hit a great shot which hit the post and the rebound fell to another Blues player who smashed it against the same post and then Toral shot wide. St. Andrews was buzzing but then at the other end our goalkeeper didn't hold the ball and we were mugged as Bournemouth scored to make it 2-1. The last few minutes saw Blues charging forward with attack after attack but just couldn't score. So our Cup dream was over for another year and I was disheartened to lose when we played so well and really should have won. I tried to console myself with the fact that we played so well, but in the pouring rain on the way home it didn't really help.

It's starting to get really cold now so I made sure I wrapped up warm for the trip to Nottingham for the Tuesday night game against Forest. The coaches left St. Andrews at 4.35pm in torrential rain and dark skies and it took forty minutes just to get to spaghetti junction in the rush hour. It was a relatively short journey and there was quite a bit of traffic when we reached Nottingham, which meant that we arrived at the City Ground an hour before kick off. At least the rain had stopped though.

June was chatting on her phone so I walked round to the Club shop with Barry to get a badge. We walked along the bank of the River Trent, it's really close and right next to the ground. The Club shop was rather disappointing and didn't have any badges so I had to walk back and get one from the seller we had passed on the way to the shop. I didn't realise that most Forest fans don't acknowledge their new club crest which they call the 'cloud thing'. I've only known 'the tree' crest, so I was surprised to see all the badges and scarves with the old crest. I was told all this by the seller.

We went into the away end and I saw Brendan, Graham, Phil etc. Then I went into the seats to find June and James again. The game got underway and Blues were on good form. The Blues fans were in good voice too. Jon Toral scored a great diving header in the 24th minute to put Blues 1-0 up and the away end exploded. We jumped around celebrating and singing. Unfortunately Forest scored six minutes later to level the score at 1-1. It was a disappointing goal to concede. Blues came out in the second half and really should have won it. Blues hit the post a couple of times and there were some dodgy tackles and even dodgier decisions by the referee. Why do we keep getting crap referees this season? At one point both the home and away fans were all singing 'your not fit to referee' together! It said it all really.

He should have sent a Forest player off in the first half, he got his card out to book the player then, when the fourth official pointed out that he had already booked the player (hence it should have been a second yellow and a red card) he put his book back into his pocket. Forest were really physical and finally in the 74th minute the referee did send a Forest player off with a straight red for kicking Clayton Donaldson in the face. Blues just couldn't capitalise though and the game finished 1-1. Before the game I would have settled for a draw but after this showing I was disappointed that we didn't win the game. A great atmosphere in the away end though and a really enjoyable trip. Blues remain 8th in the Championship table

I couldn't go to the Derby game as I was working a 12 hour shift. I had tried desperately to swap but to no avail and I was gutted that I was missing such a big game. The Blues end was sold out with over 3,000 making the trip, including my friends.

I did get updates though and watched the highlights on the Football League show when I got home. Blues won 3-0 which was no mean feat at Derby who are currently 3rd in the Championship. All three goals came in the second half, the first was a header by Robbo from a corner. He has scored three now this season. The second was a lovely goal from Stephen Gleeson that looked like it could have been an intended cross but floated over the goalkeeper and into the net. The best of the bunch was saved for last, an absolute screamer from Michael Morrison on the volley from outside the box. The Blues end erupted and Morrison ran to them to celebrate.

What a brilliant away win! Blues remain 8th but are closing in on the play off places. We are now only two points behind Ipswich and Sheffield Wednesday who are just above us. Therefore next weeks meeting with Ipswich will be a big game.

It was my birthday weekend and I was really looking forward to the trip to St. Andrews. We dropped my mom and sister at the Hyatt hotel on the way to the game and I would be dropped back there after the match for our concert and overnight stay (our family Christmas present from Steve).

The atmosphere inside the stadium was as good as ever as over 18,000 were inside and ready for the game. Blues looked good and we were soon ahead when new loanee Will Buckley scored a debut goal in the 23rd minute. The Blues fans were on their feet in celebration. Then just before half time Ipswich had a player sent off after being shown a straight red for a tackle on one of our players. It did look a little harsh from where I was sitting but the referee was near the incident so he must have seen it better that I did.

If anything though I thought it made Ipswich play better in the second half but a wonder strike by our Spaniard Jon Toral killed them off and brought St. Andrews to their feet as he made the score 2-0. The ball had gone from our goalkeeper to Donaldson who passed it to Toral to hit on the volley from way outside the penalty area and the ball flew over the Ipswich keeper and into the net. It was one of the best goals I have ever seen scored by a Blues player. Not to be outdone Michael kieftenbeld also produced a spectacular goal on the volley from the edge of the penalty area in the 70th minute to make it 3-0. The fans were singing and it had been a brilliant afternoon. Blues leapfrogged Ipswich to move up to 7th in the table and just outside the play offs.

I was really happy as I was dropped at the Hyatt after the game and was met with a wonderful room on the 16th floor with a fabulous view of the city through the floor to ceiling windows. I got changed and then it was down to the hotel restaurant for dinner followed by a walk across to the NIA to watch the live Strictly Come Dancing Tour which was fabulous. It was lovely to wake up on my birthday in such a lovely hotel room with my mom and sister. I had a brilliant day and lots of great presents, one of which was a surprise trip to Barcelona with tickets for the Nou Camp tour experience from Steve for all four of us. I was overwhelmed and I would be flying the day after next with mom, Annette and Steve. I was so excited.

Chapter Eleven - Barcelona

We arrived in Barcelona on Tuesday evening and first thing Wednesday morning Steve had obtained tickets for that evening's Spanish Cup Quarterfinal second leg match between Barcelona and Athletico Bilbao at the Nou Camp. I was so excited and really looking forward to the evening. During the day we went on the open top bus tour around Barcelona and we were all impressed with the sights. We stopped at the Olympic Stadium and ventured inside for a closer look and a drink in their café. It was amazing to see.

Our tickets for the match included free transport to and from the game – very impressive I thought. We were staying in a hotel on Las Ramblas and the coachs were leaving from the Hard Rock Café which was just a ten minute walk up the road. The match was a late kick off, 9.30pm, so the coaches were due to depart from the Hard Rock Café at 7.30pm for the Nou Camp. We got there at 7pm and there were already quite a few people already waiting. The coaches arrived at about 7.10pm just after we had arrived. It was really well organised and we boarded quite quickly and we were on our way.

Traffic was heavy and there seemed to be loads of traffic lights, most of them red! There were also scooters and motorbikes parked everywhere, thousands of them. It didn't take long to get to the Nou Camp though and we parked on a car park about two minutes from the stadium. The Nou Camp looked really impressive with all the lights on as we approached. It had a great feel about it. There were lots of stalls selling scarves, flags and memorabilia. I browsed all of them and bought a nice gold stadium badge with the Barcelona crest attached. I wanted a half half Match day scarf but the only one they had that was Barcelona v Athletico Bilbao was dated 30-5-15 from last years final.

We wandered around for a while looking at stalls, taking photos and soaking up the atmosphere. There were lots of tourists about, mostly taking photos on their 'selfie sticks'. I have come to the conclusion that Barcelona is the 'selfie stick' capital of the world! After walking around the stadium to our entrance we headed into the Nou Camp. The first thought that struck me was how much it reminded me of the old Wembley Stadium concourse. I was quite surprised by how old the stadium seemed. I don't really know what I was expecting to be honest.

I was also surprised at the absence of bars as such, although beer could be purchased at any of the many popcorn stalls. Yes, that's right popcorn! There was also hotdogs and crisps available but other than cans of beer no other variety of alcohol was on sale so my craving for a cold cider would not be satisfied. I had to wash my 'Barca' crisps down with a coke instead.

We went up into the stands to look around the stadium and it looked magnificent. There were already quite a few people inside taking photos with the usual selfie sticks! It was quite difficult to find our seats and we had to go down a couple of flights from the turnstiles. When we were in the lower concourse I pointed out a row of seats that were right back inside the concourse and looked awful. As I commented about how bad they were we checked our tickets and it transpired that they were our seats!

I was really disappointed. We sat in them to try them out and the base of the second tier came right over the top of us and went so far down that we could see the pitch but the stand blocked the top/crossbar of the far goal just beneath the stand. A shockingly bad view. This meant we had no view whatsoever of this marvellous stadium so we immediately headed off to find the head steward only to be informed that we couldn't exchange our tickets and could only buy new ones! Therefore we headed back to our crap seats and decided to wait till about ten minutes into the game before moving elsewhere for a better view.

The game kicked off and the Stadium seemed to be buzzing, although there was no real singing like in England. After ten minutes we left our seats and headed up the many stairs to the middle tier and in doing so missed the opening goal scored by Athletico Bilbao. To be honest with you I never heard a sound, no cheer or any noise of note and it was only as I looked at the TV monitor on the second level up that I saw the score line.

At the top of the second tier we found a row of empty seats with a great view of the pitch and the stadium so we sat down to enjoy the rest of the game. We were really high up! I looked around for any away fans but could only see the blue and red of Barcelona everywhere. Behind the far goal was a small section of 'partisan' Barcelona fans who were singing and waving flags. They would bounce and dance every now and then. It was amazing to watch them, they would sing and run from one end of the section to the other end before turning and running back to where they had started and then doing it all again. It looked crazy but funny.

I think my expectations of the Barcelona team were quite high as I was a bit disappointed in their first half performance. Bilbao should have been further ahead in my opinion. I didn't see anything special in Messi, Suarez, Neymar and co and had watched more entertaining Birmingham City performances. Maybe the second half would be better.

I made the mistake of looking for the toilets at half time and despite ending up three floors below I still couldn't locate them and then got lost trying to find my way back to my seat where Steve was. The second half was better and the fans sang the Barcelona football song loudly. Messi was booked for time wasting when Barcelona were leading 2-1 and thousands of white handkerchiefs were waved in the air in disgust. I found this highly amusing as did Steve.

With a couple of minutes to go and Barcelona leading 2-1 (4-2 on aggregate) we decided to head back to the coach before the rush as there were over 69,000 in the stadium. As we were heading out Barcelona scored again to make it 3-1 and we missed it. It is unusual for me to leave early too, as I have never left a Blues game before the final whistle. However, as Barcelona are not my team it wasn't a problem,

The coach was nearby and the walk was nice as I looked back at the stadium with all the floodlights on. There were literally hundreds of coaches from all over Spain and it was so well organised. Our departure was like a military operation as half an hour after the game finished organisers directed one coach after another in a regimented order along roads which had been cordoned off by the Spanish police. We were soon underway and back at the Hard Rock Café in no time at all.

We disembarked and it was an impressive sight as all the 'Barca' fans headed down Las Ramblas. Some, including ourselves, headed into McDonalds which was still open at this late hour. What a wonderful day I had had and I was so looking forward to the Nou Camp stadium experience tour that we were booked on the next day.

I woke early and after breakfast we headed off to the Nou Camp via the underground. It was a lot less stressful than the London Underground and we only had to get one train. I'm not sure if we got off at the nearest station though as we had quite a walk to find the stadium and got lost at one point and had to ask for directions.

Once we were there though we made our way to the tour entrance to join the other visitors. We purchased the 'Nou Camp Experience Tour and Museum' guide but declined the audio headphones, preferring to look around at our leisure and to read the guide book. The museum itself was excellent. There is a massive trophy cabinet of 50 meters with all of Barcelona's football trophies, awards and prizes. There is also a trophy cabinet containing all the trophies won by the Barcelona Ladies team and there were many trophies indeed. There is also several interactive wall displays where visitors can explore the major moments in the clubs history. The second wall is dedicated to the players who left their mark on the history of the club, from Gamper to Messi.

There were many momento's on display such as the first stone, the oldest t-shirt and, of course, the five European Cups. These were won in four capital cities = London 1992, Paris 2006, Rome 2009, London 2011 and lastly Berlin 2015. Very impressive. A photo opportunity not to be missed! Lionel Messi has his own space in the museum and on display are four 'Ballon d'Or trophies' and the three golden boots he was awarded. I had my photo taken by this display too. From the museum we headed to the stands inside the Nou Camp. The tour allows access to a part of the central grandstand where you can see the pitch and the immense FC Barcelona stadium.

We then passed through the press room and on to the changing rooms. The tour grants access to the away dressing room and it is really impressive. From the locker room it was along the players tunnel to the pitch, complete with the sound of the fans in the stands. Half way along the tunnel is the clubs chapel which is truly amazing.

Once out on the pitch it is an extremely impressive view of the stadium. From here it was up to the press box set high up at the top of the stand. Outstanding views. On the way out of the tour there are headphones where you can listen to Barcelona's official anthem. There is then a eight meter long interactive audio visual table that has 200 of the clubs best historical moments. At the end of the tour it is possible to purchase any photos that were taken on the tour with players or trophies. This can be very expensive depending on the package that you choose, and of course, all the photos are pretty tempting!

Then it is on to the Barcelona megastore which has three floors and is the biggest Barca shop in the world. I did pick up a few souvenirs then we headed back to Las Ramblas to meet mom and Annette for lunch. It had been a fabulous experience and obviously I was wearing my Blues home shirt for the tour. Excellent couple of days.

We flew back from Barcelona on the Friday and the next day I was up early to get the coach for Blues away game at Bristol City. The coaches arrived at

Bristol in plenty of time and we headed off around the ground in search of the club shop. Unfortunately they didn't have a official club badge but there was a lovely new sports bar open in the stand next to the shop. It was for home fans only but we soon covered our colours and made our way inside. It was really nice inside with the biggest indoor sports screen in the country. It was full of Bristol City fans and they were given discount at the bar when they produced their season tickets. We spotted some friends, also under cover Bluenoses, and made our way over to join them.

It was quite hot inside and it was hard to refrain from taking my coat off hence revealing my Blues top. Most of the Bristol fans around us had realised we were Birmingham fans but were nice and friendly and we soon got chatting to them. They had been extremely impressed by Clayton Donaldson's hat trick against them when we beat them 4-2 at St. Andrews earlier in the season. They were a bit anxious about playing us and admitted they found the gulf between the Championship and League One (where they played last season) to be massive.

They were all so nice that I hope they manage to avoid relegation back to League One. I had told them about my badge collection and my failed mission to get a official club badge in their club shop and as they left, one of the Bristol fans gave me his Bristol City hat because it had the official crest on it. Very nice of him. I wished them well and we headed round to the away end. Once inside I could see the difference from the last time I visited this stadium. There is a lot of ground improvements ongoing and one side of their ground has a partially built stand which looks like it will be impressive when it is completed. I don't know how they will fill it though if they do get relegated.

Blues had the entire stand behind the goal and the Bluenoses were in full voice. The away end had been sold out for weeks now and I was really hoping Blues could get a win. However, it wasn't the best game ever and ended in a 0-0 draw which was probably a fair result. So we headed back to the coach a little bit disappointed but having enjoyed the trip.

The next game was a big one against high flying Sheffield Wednesday at St. Andrews. Both teams are competing for the 6th place play off spot and Sheffield Wednesday are on a fantastic run of form at the moment. It is a must win game and over 20,000 were inside a buzzing St. Andrews.

Blues played well and Clayton Donaldson put Birmingham 1-0 ahead on 50 minutes and St. Andrews rocked. Blues were great in the second half but unfortunately we were undone in just two minutes as Sheffield Wednesday mugged us with goals in the 77th and 79th minutes. Both goals were poor goals to give away and despite being the better team Blues lost 2-1 and we lost crucial ground in the race for promotion. I headed home deeply disappointed and with a strong sense of injustice.

We went to Rotherham on the coach and I really enjoy the away trip to the New York Stadium, Rotherham's new ground. It has a friendly feel about it. So today I was on good form. The coaches arrived in Rotherham with plenty of time to spare and so after picking up my badge from the club shop we set off into town to find the Wetherspoons that we drank in on our last trip. A random woman stopped us to welcome us to Rotherham and to wish us a good stay. They do seem to be really friendly people up here I must say.

Once in town we soon found the Wetherspoon's, which was already full of Blues fans enjoying a drink. We soon found Brendan, Graham and Co and joined them. By now the Bluenoses were in full voice and 'Keep Right On' was being belted out loudly and I happily joined in, as did June and Jack. I love all the singing and I was having a fabulous time. We didn't want to leave it too late to head to the ground though as it was another sell out in the away end. So it was with some reluctance that I left the singing Bluenoses and headed back to the ground.

As soon as we got inside the stadium the Blues fans were singing loudly in the concourse area. Unfortunately our seats were in separate sections for today's game but as lots of fans go where they want anyway and everyone stands at away games, we managed to stand together. As always recently the Blues end was sold out. The atmosphere was good but the game was somewhat of a disappointment and despite having several chances the game ended in a 0-0 draw. Another two points dropped which could prove important at the end of the season. It had been a good day out though and it was back on the coach and heading home.

It was a cold February night when Bolton visited Birmingham in the next game at St. Andrews. Bolton were bottom of the league and were currently in the middle of a takeover by a consortium and were hopeful of a revival. Almost 16,000 were inside St. Andrews to watch a hard fought game that was won by a single goal from Clayton Donaldson in the 29th minute. I admit to being somewhat apprehensive as Blues don't seem to do well against teams in the bottom half of the table. So I headed home happy that we had avoided another potential banana skin and with our promotion hope still intact.

Up early and an exciting day ahead of me as I was off to London to watch Blues play Queens Park Rangers and meet up with my nephew Stephen who was also coming to the game. We got the train from Moor Street Station about 10.30 and arrived at Marlybone around 12.30 ish. Then it was on to the underground to Shepherds Bush to find a pub. It was busy as we came out of Shepherds Bush Market and we headed to the nearby Wetherspoon's where we had drank last time we were here.

However, this time the bouncers wanted to check our match tickets and would not let us in as we were away fans. This was happening at all of the pubs in the area and we were directed to the away pub which was absolutely heaving with singing Bluenoses. There was no way we would have been able to get to the bar to get a drink. So we headed back to a home pub that we had passed on the way called The Green. I hid my colours (just the Blues crest on my scarf as they are blue and white too) and we managed to get inside possibly because there was only me and Steve. June and Barry had arrived before us on an earlier train and were currently further afield in London looking for a pub.

I text Stephen to let him know where we were and he soon joined us. We managed to get a seat and table by the window and soon enough half the pub broke into a rendition of 'Keep Right On' which the home fans inside the pub were not impressed with. I had to smile. We enjoyed a few drinks then headed off towards to ground. It was really busy as we got closer with police everywhere and it was really confusing for us away fans as the turnstiles for the upper tier was in one road and and the turnstiles for the lower tier where we had tickets, were in another road completely and it wasn't signposted. It was so badly organised and as kick off approached it was chaotic outside with massive queues at the turnstiles.

As we rushed towards our end I bumped into my great mate 'Ballie' who I had played football with at Birmingham City Ladies. We were both delighted and found time for a quick hug before we had to dash off again in different directions as we were in different tiers. It was lovely to see her as I hadn't seen her for years, not since Everton away years ago. The queue for the turnstiles for the lower tier was really big but we managed to get inside with just a few minutes to spare before kick off. There were a few empty seats due to all the chaos and massive queues outside. Quite a few Bluenoses didn't get in until thirty minutes into the game. June got in twenty minutes after kick off.

Despite this the Blues end was buzzing and in full voice from yet another sell out away following. There was a lot of banter between the Bluenoses and the QPR fans close to us. One QPR fan was allowed to run from their end to confront the Blues fans. This inspired a Blues fan to intercept him and he promptly floored him with one punch to the cheers from the Blues end. It took the stewards ages to react and they led the QPR fan away clutching his nose. By now the QPR fans were throwing coins at us and Bluenoses responded by singing 'one punch and he knocked him out!'.

On the pitch Blues were not at our best and some awful defending by Ryan Shotton allowed a QPR player to breeze past him and score, right in front of us. Not good. Things got worse four minutes later when QPR were awarded a penalty as Shotton continued to have a nightmare game. The spot kick was taken right in front of us as we booed and whistled and waved our arms about in the faint hope of putting him off. It didn't work of course and the toe rag ran to the Blues end to celebrate in front of us. Not very nice and not very clever as the Blues response was to hurl coins and missiles in his direction, possibly prompted by similar conduct from QPR fans earlier.

Not all these missiles cleared the Blues fans in the Lower tier though. I was in row three and I saw a half full bottle of water (with no lid on) bounce off the head of a blues fan in the front row on its way to the celebrating QPR player on the pitch. He was okay though and I was in fits of laughter as I found in hilarious and couldn't stop laughing for about thirty minutes afterwards as the tears ran down my face.

It wasn't a laughing matter on the pitch though as Blues went in at half time 2-0 down and the fans singing for Cadis to replace Shotton. Blues did get better in the second half but the damage was done and we just couldn't get back into the game. When the final whistle went to signal a 2-0 defeat we applauded the players off before heading back to Marlybone. There was still plenty of time to spare so we headed into a pub near the station for a drink or two and it was nice to have a bit of extra time with Stephen.

Afterwards we grabbed a Burger King and jumped on the train home. This was to come back to haunt me and Steve as we were both really ill with what was possibly a noravirus from the chicken we ate from Burger King. Never again! Unfortunately I was still really ill on the day of the Hull match so I was unable to go. I had been off work sick all week and felt terrible and it takes a lot for me to miss a Match. It was a massive game too at the top of the table.

Luckily it was being shown live on Sky Sports so I sat at home watching it. Of course it wasn't the same as being there though. I had to have the sound up loud and the atmosphere from the 18,105 inside St. Andrews was fantastic. 'Keep Right On' could be heard really loudly. The players responded and Jon Toral put Blues ahead in the 14th minute as the ground erupted. Toral is having a fantastic season and is my favourite player at the moment. It was a great game and Blues managed to hang on for a fantastic

1-0 win against a top side. This will really help our push for a play off place although we still have a lot to do.

Blackburn away was another game that I couldn't get to due to work commitments. I did manage to listen to the live commentary though and it was disheartening as Blues fell behind in the 20th minute. Blues immediately went on the attack but were hit with a sucker punch three minutes later. Clayton Donaldson was brought down in the box for a certain penalty and the referee ignored it and as Blues players protested Blackburn broke free and scored at the other end. It was a shocker and at 2-0 it effectively killed the game. Blues were broken and we lost 2-0. We never do things the easy way.

The day of the Wolves game was lovely and sunny, perfect for a nice away trip. June, Steve and myself got the train from Selly Oak to town and headed to the old 'Samwellers' bar (now called the Railway I think) to meet the others and enjoy a pre match drink or two. Nearly everyone we knew were in there and so it was great and a real journey back in time for me. I've not been in this pub for over twenty years.

However, it was at this point that disaster struck as June (who usually gets all our tickets together) realised she did not have mine and Steve's match tickets. She had her own and Jack's but she had forgotten to collect ours. I thought she was joking at first but when I realised she was serious I was devastated. It was made worse by the fact that it was a Sunday game and the Blues ticket office was closed. As it was now getting late we dashed off to get a train to Wolverhampton as June rang the Wolves ticket office. They suggested that we go to their ticket office and they will sort it out.

Unfortunately it didn't quite work out like that. They told us that no tickets had been sent over from Blues in our name and that Blues had not sent a seat list either, meaning Wolves could not check our seats. What a nightmare! The manager came out and said the only thing they could do was wait till kick off and then sell us complimentary tickets not used by the Blues players.

This would mean that we paid twice for our tickets but the manager said that we should be able to claim a refund. As June headed off to the away end I paced stressfully till kick off time when we were allowed to purchase our tickets (which had to be paid for in cash – which meant a dash to a nearby cash point!). I am never late into games so I was really upset by this. By the time we had ran around to our end and got our breath back, it was already ten minutes into the game with the score at 0-0. It was a lovely sunny day though and we were basking in the sunshine. The only thing that could cheer me up now would be a Blues win. I was really pleased with the match day badge that Barry had got me though.

It was a really good game and it was being shown live on Sky Sports as Blues dominated. We missed so many chances and I was quite disappointed with the 0-0 draw as I thought we should have won easily. I do worry that all these draws and dropped points could cost Blues a play off place. On that note I headed off to get the train home and enjoy my Sunday roast.

All the games are important now and following the Wolves game Blues were back at St. Andrews to take on a Fulham side that was struggling at the bottom of the table with one of the worst defensive records in the league. They do, however, have one of the best scoring records also. A recipe for disaster? Well, yes, Fulham went ahead in the 38th minute and then defended their lead resolutely. It was really frustrating, as Blues tried desperately to breach one of the leakiest defences in the Championship. Then up popped Michael Morrison to power home a header to equaliser in the 56th minute and St. Andrews exploded. Blues pressed forward for the winner but it just wouldn't come and we had to settle for another draw and another two points dropped.

Another trip to London except this time we travelled on the coach and I had a ticket for Stephen (my nephew living in London) and so we would be meeting up with him in Charlton. It was a pleasant journey which included a nice stop at the services with the usual KFC. I was busy admiring the view of the Olympic Village and West Ham's soon to be new stadium, when my phone beeped to inform me that Stephen was just arriving in Charlton. I told him to head to the pub where the others were planning to go and we would see him there.

There is no place to park the coaches at Charlton (and Blues had a lot of coaches today) so they have to drop us off on the main road just down from the ground. I noticed a pub just across the road from us called the 'Antigalligan', which I thought would be a better option than trying to find the others. Just then my phone rang and it was Stephen saying he was outside a pub called - yes, you've guessed it, the 'Antigalligan' and the bouncers wouldn't let him in as he didn't have a match ticket. "No problem" I said, "look across the road and you will see a load of coaches with Bluenoses getting off – that's us!" He waved and I spotted him and we made our way over to join him.

The bouncers let us in without a problem and although the pub was busy there was a big room at the back with another bar and lots of room so we headed in there. The atmosphere was great inside and the Villa v Chelsea game was being shown live as their game was an early kick off. Villa are currently rooted to the bottom of the Premier League and looking odds on for relegation. I'm sure you are sensing a little smile here, okay a big smile.

It was fabulous catching up with Stephen as we all enjoyed a drink together. The pub erupted as Chelsea scored at villa park and we joined in before returning to our conversation. This happened on three more occasions as Villa went 4-0 down. Blues fans were in good voice as, to the tune of yellow submarine, we sang 'Blues are going up and the villa's going down – we're going up, they're going down, we're going up, they're going down......' it was great. I turned to Stephen and said it couldn't get any better than this but it did as Villa then had a player sent off just as I said it. The Bluenoses sang 'we want five!' As they danced around inside the pub. The game ended with Villa losing 4-0 to Chelsea, much to our delight.

We left the pub with plenty of time to spare and headed towards the ground. There were a lot of Charlton fans giving out a free 'match day programme' which was their protest issue. Charlton currently have issues with their current owners and are also wearing black and white bar scarves as part of their protest. I thought we had turned up at Fulham by mistake.

The Blues end was sold out again and there were already loads of Bluenoses inside, particularly around the bar area. We made our way to our seats and we were chatting away obliviously when a football (hit with some power, I must say) en route from the players warm up, skimmed Stephen's head, sending his hair flying. He made a belated head swerve and exclaimed "what was that?' I had only seen a blur of a football as it shot between us followed by Stephen's reaction and I burst out laughing. In fact I was laughing for ages afterwards as I kept having flashbacks!

The match kicked off and within seconds thousands of mini footballs were thrown on the pitch by the Charlton fans as part of their protests. A few were thrown from the Blues end too! As amusing as it was it did interrupt the game as all the mini balls (really cute they were) had to be cleared from the pitch. In hindsight I think this may have affected our players more than the Charlton players as it disturbed their flow.

This was a big game for Blues in our push for a play off place but also for Charlton who were fighting for their lives at the bottom of the table. Only last week Charlton had managed to beat the current table toppers at The Valley. Blues started the game well and were playing some decent football when Jon Toral gave us the lead in the 32nd minute, sending Blues fans into joyful celebrations. However, the lead only lasted six minutes as Blues failed to clear a ball from a grounded player just outside the penalty area and it fell to a Charlton player who unleashed a powerful shot that beat our keeper.

I was gutted. It was soon half time and we all headed to the bar to join Stephen and Steve who had headed there a few minutes earlier. There was another funny incident when I bumped into Baz. In mid conversation a blue football came out of nowhere and bounced off Barry's head. Cue more tears of laughter from myself.

The second half managed to wipe the smile off my face though. Blues played really well but couldn't get that winning goal that we deserved. Then deep into injury time Charlton snatched a cruel winner. The manner in which Blues lost left me devastated and I was really downhearted on the journey home. I hadn't felt that way for a long time.

After the disappointment of Saturday's defeat at Charlton I wasn't feeling too good about the visit of Brighton to St. Andrews the next Tuesday. Brighton were still in with a chance of automatic promotion, whereas Blues chance of a play off place were now very slim indeed. There were 16,143 inside St. Andrews as Blues started the game well. Our new loan player Kyle Lafferty from Norwich City finished a good move in the 16th minute to give Blues a 1-0 lead. The stadium erupted as hope and optimism flooded the supporters.

Once again though, Blues were undone from a set piece as Brighton drew level following a freekick in the 29th minute. Then three minutes into the second half Brighton scored again and I felt disheartened once again. As hard as Blues tried they couldn't get back into it and once again we lost at home. I left the ground really disappointed again although we did more than match a team in the top six once again.

I couldn't get to the next game away at Reading on the Saturday as I was working night duties. I did get up early and listened to the game live on the radio though and was delighted when Clayton Donaldson scored in the 2nd minute to put Blues 1-0 ahead. Shotton doubled the score in the 27th minute and at 2-0 Blues then cruised for the rest of the game and ran out worthy winners. Game on yet again.

The games were coming thick and fast now that the season was drawing to a close and Blues now had a run of home games at night. The Leeds game was a potential banana skin with the way Blues were playing at home at the moment.

Unfortunately my feelings proved correct. Blues first choice goalkeeper was out and Legzdins was in his place between the sticks and I felt that he could have got to the shot from outside the area in the 11th minute that hit the bottom corner to put Leeds ahead. Blues were the better team by far but were undone by yet another shot from outside the area that doubled Leeds advantage. I was gutted.

Blues were rewarded for our dominance though when Clayton Donaldson reduced the deficit 3 minutes later with a goal. Despite several corners and many attacks, Blues were unable to capitalise on our dominance and the match finished in a 2-1 defeat. Not before Leeds were reduced to 10 men though when they had a player sent off in the 94th minute and deservedly so. I left the ground with a heavy heart once again as Blues again succumbed at home, all be it undeservedly so.

Once again a championship title contestant came to St. Andrews in the shape of Burnley. Due to recent results Blues were again in with an outside chance of making the play offs. Prior to kick off the Vile had been awaiting their fate in the Premier League as Norwich had to win or draw against Sunderland in their early kick off for Villa to have any chance of escaping relegation. Norwich and Sunderland are also in the relegation scrap and were fighting for their Premier League lives.

The outcome was a Sunderland win and the Villa were relegated to the Championship! It was indeed a party atmosphere at St. Andrews with balloons galore and banners with 'The shit are going down' on them. All around the stadium you could hear 'the shit are going down' being sang loudly. Some were even wearing party hats and some were in fancy dress as the villa relegation party got underway.

The atmosphere inside St. Andrews was great as the teams took to the field. Blues started the game well and looked the better side. However, we were hit with a sucker punch again as Burnley took the lead against the run of play just after the half hour mark. Blues ended the first half with several missed chances before heading in for the break. Ten minutes into the second period Blues were back in it as Jacques Maghoma headed into the bottom corner of the net to make it 1-1.

It was now all Blues as we had several corners and attempts on goal before Jonathan Grounds hit the bar with a header in the 73rd minute from a corner. Then 4 minutes later Burnley scored with a goal from an unmarked Andre Grey – the leagues top scorer. It was a poor defensive display that resulted in Grey getting his only clear chance of the game.

I was gutted as we were mugged again. Blues continued to press but things got worse when 'Bluenose' Burnley player Lloyd Dyer dived to the ground when Jon Toral was nowhere near him and resulted in a somewhat unjust red card for Toral in the 94th minute. No way was it a foul or a second yellow card and I left the stadium really disappointed. It was Blues first red card of the season and yet another undeserved home defeat. I am starting to dread the home games at the minute.

On the positive side the Villa relegation part had been brilliant and the result had not put a dampener on the party atmosphere at all. Karma is great. I loved it when Bluenoses sang 'you laughed at us when we went down – who the fuck is laughing now!'

Tuesday night saw the third home match in a row at St. Andrews against Preston and I have to admit that due to recent results I was not really looking forward to it. I was still hopeful though. It still wasn't mathematically impossible for Blues to make the play offs but it wasn't very likely.

Blues did play well and we were 1-0 up at half time so things were going well. Clayton Donaldson scored the second to make it 2-0 in the second half of the game and Blues were cruising. That was till about 15 minutes from time when Blues imploded again and threw away a two goal lead in a 10 minute spell. I could not believe it. To make it worse Blues didn't seem to try very hard after that. It was the worst 5 or 6 minutes of injury time I've seen. Blues didn't go all out for a winner, they looked lifeless.

I left feeling very disappointed as the jubilant Preston fans sang '2-0 and you fucked it up'. Don't I know it. So that was our play off hopes over for another season. Oh well, I can't complain really. It has still been a good season and hopefully Blued will continue to improve under Gary Rowett and perhaps put in a promotion challenge next season.

It was an early start for the trip to Huddersfield as the coaches were leaving St. Andrews at 8.30am. We had a stop at the services on the way and I enjoyed a KFC – lovely. The coaches arrived in Huddersfield in plenty of time so we headed off to find a pub. The first one we came across was 'The Gas House' but they wouldn't let us in, saying it was members only – a likely story. So we headed up the road to the 'Yorkshire Rose' which was a really nice pub with a few Bluenoses already inside. It wasn't packed either.

We were joined by Brendon and co and a bit later my friend Micheal also made an appearance with his friend. We all had a good catch up and then we left them to walk to the stadium. Huddersfield's ground is one of the nicer of the new stadiums with a bit of character to it. The away end was already buzzing when we got inside and there were several singing Bluenoses around the bar area. There were a few 'St. George's' scattered about due to it being St. Georges day. In fact we had see a few of them enjoying a pint in the Yorkshire Rose before the game.

Blues had the majority of the stand behind the goal and we were separated from a section of singing, flag waving Huddersfield fans in the far end of the stand. They were making quite a lot of noise and were impressive for home supporters which seems to be sadly lacking these days. The Bluenoses were in full voice though and were more often than not drowning out the home support. The teams came onto the pitch and 'Keep Right On' rang out loud and proud.

The game got underway but wasn't really much to write home about. The players looked like they were already on holiday. At half time the score was 0-0. The half time entertainment at the bar was more fun than the game as Blues fans sang and danced and a blue flare added colour to the scene.

The second half got underway and we finally had something to cheer as David Cotterill fired Blues ahead in the 73rd minute. We cheered and sang and danced about in the away end. Our fun only lasted 10 minutes though, Huddersfield drew level with only 8 minutes left to play. Huddersfield looked the more lively after their goal but it really was a game Blues should have won. It's the story of Blues season though.

Still, I was happy with a point a we headed back to the coaches and bumped into the 'villa funeral'. It was hilarious. They had a claret and blue villa coffin and a big claret and blue villa wreath which was leading a procession in celebration of villa's relegation to the championship. Really funny. I took a few photos then got on the coach ready for the trip home. Overall, yet another great away day following the Blues of Birmingham.

Blues last home game of the season was on a Friday night because of the Sky TV cameras and the fact that we were playing Middlesbrough. I was looking forward to the match although sad that it was the last home game of the season. I was a bit worried about the atmosphere as Middlesbrough had sold 4,800 tickets and had the whole bottom section of the 'Railway End' due to a combination of them being in contention for automatic promotion and their club putting on free coach travel plus match tickets priced at £15.

My concern was that the Blues attendance would be reduced and subdued due to the fact we had nothing to play for, it was a Friday night and on live TV. I need not have worried though as the Bluenoses were out in force and in fantastic voice. The stadium rocked and was the best atmosphere all season. 'Keep Right On' echoed around the ground. The attendance was 21,380 and it was buzzing.

The match kicked off and it was end to end stuff. Blues were playing really well against high flying Boro and it must have been a really entertaining game for the neutrals watching on TV. Blues stunned the traveling fans when Stephen Gleeson hit a long range rocket that flew into the bottom corner of the net in the 33rd minute. Cue delirious celebrations around 3 sides of the ground.

As seemed to be the norm of late though, the lead didn't last long as Boro snatched a close range equaliser 7 minutes later and the first half ended all square at 1-1. Blues came out all guns firing for the second half and won a corner in the first minute which saw a Ryan Shotton header go just over the bar. A few minutes later Boro hit the post, it was a cracking game.

Just as Blue were starting to dominate Middlesbrough scored with a header from close range from an unmarked Ramirez. Very poor defending in my opinion. Blues never gave up though and were relentless in attacking the Boro goal. It paid dividends in the 68th minute with another spectacular goal, this time from David Davis. He hit a cracking right footed shot from the edge of the box that flew into the bottom corner of the net. Brilliant! 2-2.

The action continued end to end, right into the 95th minute when the referee blew for full time. It had been a fantastic game of football with both teams having had 16 shots on goal each.

So the match finished 2-2 which was a fair result and we headed home happy. For me I had been really impressed with the atmosphere as the Bluesnoses had all united in song. The new group Called 'the Tilton Alliance' had taken up their new position in block 4 and had sang and bounced throughout the game. I really hope this group of singing fans gets bigger and brings the old atmosphere back to St. Andrews. It is a really great idea and I would love it to be like the 70's and 80's again before the all seater stadiums.

Last game of the season and an early kick off in Wales awaited us. As is tradition for the last Blues away game it is usually enjoyed in fancy dress. Myself, June, James and Jack had been planning our outfits for weeks and we were all really looking forward to it. On the way to the coach we stopped for a newspaper and ended up blocking a bus. It was quite funny when June (the driver) was in the shop, so James got out in his green dragon outfit to go round to the drivers side to move the car but June came running over dressed as a nun and got in and we drove off. It must have looked really funny to those on the bus. The driver didn't look amused though.

There were 7 official Blues coaches that were due to depart at 8.30am. As we arrived I spotted Jack arriving as a brown beer bottle – very funny. I was going as a nun with a long blue wig – hence 'Blue Nun' – the retro wine for those of you who don't remember it. The coach stewards were in fancy dress and looked brilliant. Most of them were dressed as Thunderbirds with a 'where' Wally girl' also. The coach drivers had Gary Rowett masks – brilliant! There were several Blues fans also in fancy dress including superheroes which included a family of Batman, Batgirl and a Bat child. I particularly liked Laurel and Hardy who were travelling on our coach. They were fabulous.

As usual we were late getting away and late arriving in Cardiff due to us missing the police escort that the other Blues coaches were on time for and had gone on ahead of us. This meant we had to wait forty minutes at the services which was prolonged due to a couple of idiots not coming back on time. We finally arrived at Cardiff City's stadium just before 12 o'clock for the 12.30 kick off. It was buzzing in the concourse below the stands when we entered through the turnstiles into the away end. It was brilliant – fancy dress everywhere.

I headed to the programme booth whilst Steve headed to the bar and June, James and Jack to the other bar. Good job I went straight for the match programme as they ran out of them just afterwards. The young girl behind the counter said to me (in a welsh accent) "I've never seen anything like this before, what's it about?" She looked overawed as I explained that it is a Birmingham City tradition to wear fancy dress for the last away game of the season.

The fancy dress clad Bluenoses were in full voice as I made my way to the others to claim my nice cold cider. A few Blues fans did the sign of the cross or bowed as I passed them – very funny. There were 5 or 6 green beer bottles who were leading the singing and soon spotted Jack – the lone brown beer bottle and gave him some stick. They broke into a chorus of "shit on the brown" which I thought was quite funny.

Then a loud rendition of 'Dele Adebola' broke out and I turned to,see ex-Blues player Dele Adebola amongst the Blues fans. I think he was heading for his seat but was being sidetracked by lots of Bluenoses wanting photos with him. Yes we also had a snap with him!

There were some great costumes on display. There was a bloke with a dress and a bright pink wig who looked good, and a great postbox. There were a couple of sheep and a few bananas. As we went up into the stand I saw five sheikhs and a belly dancer – really good! Inflatables were bouncing around the Blues end and these included sheep and penis's – yes you heard correct and no I don't know the relevance of the Willy's either. There were also England flags being waved throughout the away end. There were lots of empty seats around the home sections and their fans were silent but the Blues end was sold out and was in full voice. 'We're Birmingham, We're Birmingham' was being belted out.

The game kicked off and the Blues fans continued to sing. Neither team had anything but pride to play for but that wasn't going to stop us Bluenoses enjoying ourselves. Fun was had by singing 'we hate villa more than you' from each half of the away contingent. A reaction was finally gained following a loud rendition of 'God save the Queen' from the Blues end. The Welsh fans didn't seem to like this as all and a few gestures were aimed our way to which we laughed and returned with gusto.

This enticed loud renditions of 'Enger-land! Enger-land!' With St.Georges flags waving madly, and 'Swing low sweet chariot' was sung. Then followed 'we'll see you in France!' Good clean fun! Blues were playing well and when the ball fell to our Welsh wizard David Cotterill he fired home a shot into the bottom corner. This caused scenes of mass celebration and two blue flares and a smoke bomb in the away end. I was, of course, also dancing around in celebration as the blue smoke seemed to engulf us. '1-0 to the Enger-land!' broke out from the Blues fans. It was great fun.

The lead didn't last long though as Jonathan Grounds cocked up about 2 yards in front of goal as he brought the ball down for a tap in for the Cardiff player. 1-1 but it didn't stop us singing. It spurred the Cardiff fans into life though for about a minute but that was drowned out by a loud rendition of 'Keep Right On'. Our manager Gary Rowett was told after the game that the Blues fans were the loudest at Cardiff this season

The Blues fans also sang 'is this a library?' and other songs and generally had a fantastic time. The match ended with a draw and all the Bluenoses stayed behind to applaud out team as they came over to us at the end. We sang 'We're Birmingham, We're Birmingham' and 'Keep Right On' as the players applauded our support. Gary Rowett did the 'worship' gesture to us as he bowed with his arms raised and we all returned the gesture and sang 'there's only one Gary Rowett!' as he and the players left the pitch.

As we were heading towards the exits the Cardiff team were doing their lap of honour and the Blues fans got to ruin their parade by singing 'who the fucking hell are you?' to them – quite loudly I might add too. Gary Rowett was asked after the game if he was interested in Burton, to which he replied '3,000 fans when we have 20,000 at Blues'. He also said he loves when

Blues fans sing 'Keep Right On' and it makes his heart tingle. What a man! In Rowett we trust.

So Blues finished in 10th place, the same as last season with 63 points. It could have been so different though if we had won some of the games that we drew but should have won. Overall though it was a fabulous season and I am already looking forward to next season.

Burnley were crowned champions and Middlesbrough were promoted with them to the premier league. Below them were Brighton, Hull City, Derby County and Sheffield Wednesday in the play off places and it was Hull City who were promoted after winning the play off final.

In the premier league 5000-1 shot Leicester City surprised everyone and won the title. Villa finished bottom of the league and were relegated along with Norwich City and Newcastle United. It will make for another interesting season in the championship next season. Incidentally the league will be renamed for next season and will be the EFL – the English Football League. Manchester City won the League cup beating Liverpool 3-1 on penalties after drawing 1-1. In the FA Cup Manchester United beat Crystal Palace 2-1 to lift the trophy.

Me and Ballie at Wembley with Blues Ladies in the 2017 FA Cup Final

At the Nou Camp Barcelona

June, Stephen, Steve and Me at Charlton away

Cardiff Away last game of the season in traditional fancy dress

Me, June, Steve, Brendan Dele Adebola and Barry Away at Cardiff

Me (blue nun) and June at Cardiff

Me and Paul Hockey setting of from St. Andrews for Cardiff

Me and Steve at Cardiff

At a Tenerife game

Me and my sister Annette with the Carling Cup (while is was at St.

Andrews)

Chapter Twelve - In Rowett We Trust

Following the end of the season and no more matches for my beloved Birmingham City I headed off on holiday to the sunshine island of Tenerife. I visit Los Cristianos each year these days as I love the place and it's lovely and relaxing. On this trip though, me and Steve (brother in law) decided we would love to go and see local team CD Tenerife play in the Spanish second division. As it happens there was a home game scheduled for the Saturday 21st May (yes that's right – FA Cup Final day but who wants to sit in watching Manchester United when you can be out at a live game?). So it was off to 'Soy Del Tate shop' where we obtained match tickets and travel with the supporters club coach – all for a total of 27 euros!

Kick off coincided with the FA Cup Final which did affect the amount of fans traveling to the game at the Estadio Heliodoro Rodriguez Lopez in Santa Cruz in the north of the island. This time there would be one coach rather than the normal two.

On the day of the game my mom and sister made their own plans for the day and evening whilst we went to the pick up point in Los Cristianos to get the coach. There were a few others waiting there too and all the group traveling with us were lovely and friendly and made us welcome from the start. Most of the supporters traveling on the coach were British and were in good voice. We were given a free fanzine on the coach and joined in the first and last goal competition taking place. The total journey time would only be about an hour but we had a stop on the way at a lovely café at the service station with a fabulous view of the sea where we all enjoyed a few beers plus supplies for the rest of the journey.

Before long we were arriving in Santa Cruz and we were dropped off at a lovely little bar just down the road from the stadium where other Tenerife fans were already gathered. A few cars honked their horns and waved as they saw us all embark in Tenerife shirts and scarves. We joined the others sitting outside the bar and I admired all the massive banners and flags whilst Steve got the drinks. I chatted to a lot of the Armarda Sur Club and thoroughly enjoyed the experience. The stadium was in view at the top of the road and we headed there about ten minutes before kick off which was at 5pm. We browsed the memorabilia stalls and I obtained a nice silk scarf before we headed into the stadium.

On entrance to the stadium the match programmes were available for free and you could take as many as you wanted. We couldn't really understand where exactly our seats were but everyone seemed to just sit or stand where they wanted so we headed for the main section where the singing was being led by a man on a microphone. The singing was great and continued throughout the game – in Spanish of course. I joined in where I could. There were loads of flags being waved in this section and there was a large banner at the front. It was a completely different (and better) atmosphere than when I visited the Nou Camp recently as these were real football fans here rather than a load of tourists.

I did look around for any Real Valladolid fans but couldn't see any. The attendance was around 8,500 which was reduced due to the FA Cup Final being shown live in bars and the game was a mid table affair with Tenerife in 15th place with not more than a very slight chance of reaching the play offs.

Tenerife were playing well and local hero Nano scored two goals to put Tenerife 2-0 up at half time. Nano is only 20 years old and looks an exciting prospect. After the interval Real Valladolid came into the game more and pulled a goal back before Tenerife took control again and had a goal disallowed. Unfortunately Nano had to go off with what looked like a hamstring injury but that didn't stop Tenerife as they grabbed a third goal to seal the points and moved up to 12th and only 5 points behind 6th place and a play off place.

So game over and a 3-1 win for Tenerife and we headed back to the bar for a quick drink before boarding the coach back to Los Cristianos. What a great day out and I met some lovely people. Good luck to Tenerife for the remainder of the season, it would be great if they could get promoted – either way I will go and watch them again when I am next visiting.

The summer of 2016 saw the Euro's taking place in France so at least we would still get some football. In England's first group game they took on Russia who had brought thousands of hooligans who had been training for this for some time and all hell broke lose as they attacked innocent England fans before, during and after the game. My nephew Stephen was there and him and his mate were briefly attacked before one of the Russians said 'tourist!' and left them alone. Russia should have been kicked out of the tournament! If it had been English fans attacking others we would certainly have been kicked out. The game finished in a 1-1 draw.

A few days later England played Wales in their second Group game. Wales took the lead when Gareth Bale scored but Jamie Vardy got the equaliser for England and then Sturridge scored a 92nd minute winner for England.

Brilliant! The day before the final group game I was heading off on yet another holiday this time to Sicily.

It was my sister Annette's birthday the day we boarded our flight to Sicily and we were all really excited. We arrived in the evening and a coach took us to our hotel in Taormina and although it seemed to be in the middle of nowhere it looked really quaint. I woke up the next morning to discover the most amazing view from our patio of the bay below and the volcano - Mount Etna - simply stunning! In the evening me and Steve (my sisters boyfriend) headed to an Irish bar called 'Time Out' to watch the England v Slovakia game which ended 0-0. Not much to cheer about to be honest. This meant that England finished second in the group behind Wales and means we will get a more difficult route to the finals.

I was back in England for the next Euro match as England were beaten 2-1 by little Iceland. It was so embarrassing as we exited the competition to a country with part time players and the same population as Leicester! Their manager is a dentist! It was the worst England display I have ever seen as players worth millions couldn't string a simple pass together. They didn't have a clue and showed no passion whatsoever. England manager Roy Hodgson resigned after the game.

It seems ages since the last game of last season against Cardiff in Wales but with the pre season friendlies beginning, the new season was almost upon us. It had been a nice summer with a holiday in Tenerife where I had enjoyed my trip to Santa Cruz to watch CD Tenerife play Real Valladolid in the Spanish second division.

I seemed to be working for most of this seasons friendlies but I was able to go to the first one away at Solihull Moors. I am already a regular at Solihull Moors following Birmingham City Ladies. It seemed strange going there to see Blues play. It was a sell out crowd of over 2,000 mainly Blues fans and it was a nice evening.

Gary Rowett played a different team in each half, as did Solihull Moors. Both Birmingham teams played well although the first half team edged it and scored three goals without reply. A couple of blue flares were set off by the Blues fans which added a bit of colour to the night. The second half team missed a load of chances and then conceded a goal which meant the final score was a 3-1 win for Blues. Overall it was a good pre season training exercise although I couldn't really see any improvement from last season. Early days yet though and I remain hopeful.

Next it was away at Forest Green Rovers and Blues scored 3 again to win the game 3-0. Great stuff. Blues then sent 2 different teams for 2 friendly games at Shrewsbury and Walsall on the same night. The Blues side at Walsall won 1-0 with a goal from Caddis in the 80th minute whilst the other Blues side lost 1-0 at Shrewsbury. Quite a few hardy Bluenoses travelled up to Scotland for the next friendly game against Hibernian which Blues lost 1-0. This was followed by a trip to Port Vale where 2 second half goals gave Blues a 2-0 win.

The only home game of the pre season saw Blues face Dutch first division side Roda at St. Andrews and I was able to get to this game. It was a lovely sunny day and I headed to the Cricketers to meet the others before the game. It was great to see everyone again. We all headed to St. Andrews together and made our way into the KOP. Nowadays pre season friendlies only attract smaller crowds hence only the KOP was open for Blues fans and the away section in the Railway End for the visitors. Credit to Roda as they did bring a few fans.

It was a good game too, with Blues being the better team and spurning several chances. It was pretty much the same team that finished last season, which is quite disappointing to be honest. However, when whiz kid Jack Storer came on as well as Reece Brown it improved the team considerably. Still the chances were spurned though and the match finished 0-0. A draw that Roda would be happier about that Blues though.

Gary Rowett is hoping to bring a striker in for the new season and we do really need one. It is still exciting at the thought of a new season about to start though. There was one last friendly away at Kidderminster which I was unable to attend on the Tuesday night due to work. Blues played a 3-5-2 formation and won 4-0 with two goals from Jack Storer. He could play an important part this season.

I was really looking forward to the new season and I was filled with new hope for the visit of Cardiff City to St. Andrews. The buzz around the stadium as well as inside was fabulous. I even went to the Cricketers for a pre match drink with June, James, Jack and Steve and we met the others there too – Brendan , Marie etc. It was a lovely day with most Bluenoses proudly wearing their new Blues shirts – me included. It's a lovely Addidas shirt this season with three white stripes down the sides. Let's hope it brings us some luck. The away kit this season will be all red with the 3 addidas white stripes on the sleeves and down the sides and looks very nice.

There was nearly 20,000 inside the stadium and the Bluenoses were in good voice. Before kickoff there was a minutes applause for Alex Goven who sadly passed away recently. Alex was the ex Blues player who began our proud anthem 'keep Right On' back in the 1955 season. What legacy! As the whistle sounded for the minutes applause the stadium began the loudest and most poignant rendition of 'Keep Right On' I have ever heard. It sent shivers down my spine and brought tears to the eyes of some.

There were quite a few Cardiff fans that had made the trip but the Blues fans drowned them out. The match got underway but it was the same old story that Blues could not put the ball in the net. With it being pretty much the same team that finished last season so poorly, it wasn't filling me with hope. It did look much better when Jack Storer and Reece Brown came on in the second half but Blues still couldn't score. The two youngsters displayed something the rest of the team didn't - passion. I felt we missed Paul Caddis and his attacking wing play and at least Caddis had passion. The game finished 0-0 and left us all feeling somewhat disappointed. At least we didn't lose though and we have all season to look forward to.

The following Tuesday I was back at St. Andrews on a surprisingly cold night for the visit of newly promoted League One side Oxford United in the League Cup. Once again I was disappointed by manager Gary Rowett's disrespect of the competition as he made nine changes and virtually played the reserves. Admittedly it is still a fairly strong line up though.

There were a fair few supporters who had travelled up from Oxford but overall the stadium was fairly empty with 7,202 present. We were in for a long and painful night as Blues again failed to score. The game went to extra time and in the dying seconds, with penalties looming, Oxford grabbed a surprise goal with a far post header that Blues failed to defend. It was shocking to be honest, the manner of the defeat was pretty disgraceful. A reserve side that looked woeful throughout. Once again where was the pride and passion? I left St. Andrews thoroughly despondent. On a positive note Villa lost to League Two Luton Town with their best team on the pitch.

The first away game of the season was at Leeds but I couldn't go as I was working and no one would swap with me. Trust me to miss a great result! Blues won 2-1 with goals from Maghoma and Morrison and this result really cheered me up. The best news this week though is the signing of two new players, both strikers. Oh how we need them. Che Adams has signed from Sheffield United for £2 million and looks very promising and joining him is Greg Steward from Dundee for £500,000 and he looks promising too. I am filled with hope again

I couldn't make the Wigan away game due to work commitments again which meant that I didn't get to benefit from the free coach travel put on by

Blues new sponsors 888. Apparently it wasn't a great display from Blues as we went 1-0 ahead and then sat back and defended for the rest of the game as we so often do under Gary Rowett. Of course this resulted in a last minute equaliser from Wigan as Blues invited Wigan to come at them and then failed to defend an attacking move at the far post. I suppose we should be happy with a draw but it felt like two points dropped- again. This means that Blues sit 9th in the table. Early days yet though.

Blues first derby game of the season saw us take on Wolves at St. Andrews at 3pm on a Saturday, a welcome change from the enforced early kick offs. However, the match prices remained somewhat high therefore discouraging a high turn out with a relatively low Derby day attendances of 18,569. I wasn't very well and was breathless and struggling. It transpired that I had pleurisy which developed into Pneumonia and I was really poorly for a while.

It was a good atmosphere though and the fans were in good voice. Blues started well and new signing Che Adams looked really good and scored the opener for Blues in the 24th minute. So at half time with the score at 1-0 to Blues all looked well. Then came the second half and Blues imploded by conceding after only two minutes. From there on in we were woeful. It didn't take long for Wolves to take the lead when they scored again on 61 minutes.

Gary Rowett immediately substituted our best player Che Adams to loud boos around St. Andrews (maybe injured?). This is the first time I have ever known Bluenoses boo a decision by Rowett, even though I too was disappointed by his decision. To make things worse Gary Rowett then took of Jonathan Spector (defender) to bring on Jack Storer (striker) and dropped David Cotterill (winger) back to right back. Admittedly Spector is at times woeful but Cotterill is not a defender. Jack Storer- a passionate Bluenose, then put the game beyond Birmingham when he reacted to a challenge by putting his head in the face of the Wolves culprit and was shown a straight red card.

So Blues were down to ten men and it was no surprise when we conceded a third goal in the 89th minute as the Wolves fans revelled in their victory. I left just after the final whistle extremely downhearted at our first defeat of the season. Wolves do seem to be our bogey team but I was more disheartened at the display and the decisions from manager Gary Rowett.

Following the defeat to Wolves the next game was once again at St. Andrews as Blues played host to Norwich City. After last weeks performance I wasn't very hopeful against a strong Norwich side that were relegated from the Premier League only last season. Therefore I didn't foresee the amazing performance the Blues team displayed as they brushed aside Norwich City to win easily 3-0. It could easily have been by more goals too.

David Davis scored the first goal after 22 minutes as Blues went in at half time leading 1-0. The second half saw a brace from Clayton Donaldson with his first coming from the penalty spot and his second a calmly taken goal with a left footed shot into the bottom corner. Despite a crowd of only 16,295 the place was buzzing and we all left the stadium in good spirits, apart from the Norwich contingent of course.

Then it was off to London to see Blues take on an in form Fulham side at Craven Cottage. As was usual with the London trips we made the trip down south by train. We arrived early at Euston station and headed over to Putney Bridge by underground and then crossed over the bridge and into the Rocket pub.

It was only about 11.30 so there were plenty of tables available so we found ourselves a nice booth and all five of us (me, June, James, Steve and Jack) ordered the fabulous Wetherspoon's big breakfast – and big they were! There were already several Bluenoses in the pub and it wasn't long before many more arrived including my nephew Stephen who I had a match ticket for in the away end with us. I love to meet up with him for the London games and it's great for him to see his beloved Birmingham City again.

I love the walk through the park to Fulham and once again it didn't disappoint with hordes of Bluenoses making their way to Craven Cottage. I did struggle a bit walking through the park as I had only recently recovered from pneumonia and I had to keep asking everyone to slow down a bit so I could breath okay. Blues have 4,500 heading into the away end today. Once inside the atmosphere in the away end was fantastic with the Bluenoses in full voice.

The game got underway and Blues were playing well. In the 25th minute Che Adams was fouled in the area and a penalty was given to cheers from the Bluenoses. Up stepped Clayton Donaldson only to see his shot saved by the Fulham goalkeeper. Then just before half time Fulham had Michael Madl sent off for a second yellow card. At half time the score was all square at 0-0.

The second half started brightly with Che Adams again winning a penalty after being fouled in the area. Gary Rowett had already instructed Maghoma to take any penalties following Donaldson's first half miss but Donaldson took the ball from Maghoma and stepped up to take the penalty. This time he coolly converted the spot kick, sending the ball into the bottom left hand corner of the net.

A wall of noise erupted from the 4,500 traveling Bluenoses as we cheered and bounced around. New signing Lucas Jutkiewicz came on for Donaldson late on and looked quite good. Blues had several chances to add to the score line as we sang our hearts out but the game finished Fulham 0 Birmingham City 1 and we were happy with that. Blues are now 4th in the Championship, only 5 points behind surprise leaders Huddersfield Town and only 1 point off 2nd placed Newcastle United.

A few days later, on a Tuesday night, we headed off by coach to the Madejski Stadium to see Blues take on Reading. As usual the official coaches were late leaving and hit the rush hour traffic, thereby only arriving at Reading about twenty minutes before kick off. We still managed a quick walk around the stadium and got some food from one of the several outlets outside the turnstiles.

It wasn't a great game as Reading had most of the possession (70%) but both teams had several attempts on goal and the match finished 0-0. The atmosphere amongst the 1,186 of us that travelled to Reading was really good and we had some good banter with the Reading fans. It's great that our sponsors 888 are putting on free coaches to the away night games up to Christmas. Blues dropped down to 5th place in the table following this result. Only 4 points behind leaders Huddersfield now though although both Newcastle and Barnsley are gaining on them.

Next up it was Sheffield Wednesday who travelled to St. Andrews sitting comfortably in 9th place, only 1 point behind Blues. It was buzzing at St. Andrews with 18,786 in attendance although 2,135 had travelled from Sheffield. I do wonder when all the 'I'm not coming back till Carson Young goes!' Brigade will actually return. Probably for the Villa game!

Anyway, it was a great day and a fantastic result as Blues ran out 2-1 winners despite going behind in the 77th minute. The Sheffield Wednesday fans celebrated and taunted us relentlessly until Clayton Donaldson (man of the match) silenced them with a goal in the 81st minute. It was a tense and exciting game as it headed into injury time and Blues pressed for a winner which, amazingly, came in the 92nd minute with a great goal from Jutkiewicz. St. Andrews erupted with noise as we celebrated wildly and the Sheffield contingent looked stunned. Oh what sweet revenge after they robbed us last season.

Blues remain 5th in the league with 15 points, still only 4 points behind leaders Huddersfield Town who are surprising a few people this season. Norwich City are up to 2nd place and Villa are down in 18th place with one win in 8 games.

Another trip to London as Blues took on QPR which means a nice train journey and a meet up with my nephew Stephen. We met at a pub within walking distance of the ground called 'The Shepherd and Flock'. It wasn't too packed and was mostly Bluenoses including Brendan and co. We got chatting to a cockney who looked just like Peter Andre – although a bit older. He wished us luck as we set off for the ground. This time QPR only gave us the upper tier (after the farce of last season) which was already sold out to 1,616 Bluenoses. This was probably because of the trouble of last year, which was caused by the disorganisation by the police on duty.

Everyone that has been to Loftus Road will agree that there is very little leg room in the away area but at least the entire Blues end were standing, as they do at all the away games, and in good voice as usual. Blues started the livelier and took the lead on 23 minutes when that man Jutkiewicz scored again for the second game in a row. It came from a corner that was headed on by Michael Morrison to Lucas Jutkiewicz who headed home from close range. The away end exploded in celebration.

However, our joy was short lived as we conceded another soft goal from a corner and it was all square again at 1-1. And that was how it stayed, and we all headed back to the tube station and bid goodbye to Stephen till the next London fixture. This meant that Blues drop down to 6th in the league table, Norwich have overtaken Huddersfield to go top and Brighton have moved up to 3rd. Still, it's not looking too bad as Blues are only 4 points behind the leaders and still in the top six.

I had to miss the next game at St. Andrews against Preston North End as I was enjoying a mini break in Weymouth with my family. I got to visit the Nothe Fort and had a Portland crab sandwich. We also visited Portland Bill (the lighthouse) with stunning views and had one of their famous Portland crab sandwiches. I had a lovely time although from what I heard I don't think many of the St. Andrews faithful enjoyed twice going behind to Preston although at least Ryan Shotton and Che Adams scored to maintain Blues unbeaten run and secure a 2-2 draw. A point meant that Blues remain in 6th place but the chasing pack are catching up. Huddersfield regained top spot again.

I was back from Weymouth and able to go to St. Andrews for the game against Blackburn Rovers. Blues played well and Stephen Gleeson scored a great goal in the 64th minute to put Blues 1-0 up. Blues then had a lot of chances including David Cotterill hitting the post in the 83rd minute. There was a long delay when both Jonathan Spector and Blackburn's Sam Gallagher needed treatment following a clash. This resulted in ten minutes of injury time being played and the game finished with a 1-0 win for Blues. This kept Blues in 6th place on 20 points.

A cold Friday night saw us depart St. Andrews on our free coach travel and head to Nottingham for the match against Nottingham Forest which was being shown live on TV. As usual the coaches left late and hit the rush hour traffic and got to the ground not long before kick off. We ended up grabbing burgers outside the stadium before heading inside for the game. There were a lot of Bluenoses who had made the trip – 1,996, excellent! It was great banter. I love when Blues taunt Forest fans with 'you're not famous anymore!' as it always gets a reaction.

Blues played well but went a goal down before half time and then 2-0 down on 63 minutes. Then in the 71st minute Lucas Jutkiewicz pulled a goal back and Blues looked likely to go on to salvage a point. However, Forest hit us with a sucker punch when they made it 3-1 in the 83rd minute. Despite another ten minutes of 'injury time' the game ended with a defeat for Blues and a long cold trip home. Blues remain in 6th place with not much change in the leading places.

A few days later I was off to St. Andrews as Blues were aiming to bounce back against a Rotherham team rooted to the foot of the Championship. We do usually tend to bounce back after a defeat under Gary Rowett so I was hoping that we would do exactly that on this occasion. However, Blues also have a poor record against teams at the bottom.

It was another good atmosphere inside St. Andrews under the floodlights as 16,404 turned up to cheer our team. It turned out to be an entertaining game as Rotherham played well but Michael Morrison put Blues ahead in the 15th minute. Unfortunately Rotherham then equalised on 31 minutes but four minutes later Lucas Jutkiewicz scored to restore Blues lead. Then, two minutes before half time, the lively Jacques Maghoma scored to send Blues in at half time with a 3-1 lead.

I was starting to relax, something I can very rarely do watching Blues but I should have known it was too goo to be true as Rotherham reduced the arrears in the 56th minute and it was now 3-2 and a bit nerve wracking. I had to wait till the 84th minute before I could relax again when David Cotterill scored to restore our two goal advantage and that was how the game finished with Blues winning 4-2. Blues moved up to 5th in the table.

Apart from it being a night match, I was looking forward to the trip to Burton. As Blues have never played Burton Albion before, it would be a new ground for me and it was really exciting. The game was being shown live on TV but was still a sell out for the Blues end and we were all looking forward to standing on the terraces once again.

We travelled on the official coaches which dropped us on the main road next to the Pirelli Stadium. As we arrived a bit later than usual we headed through the turnstiles once I had been to the club shop to get a badge and a programme (the last one!). Once inside I was delighted to discover a lovely little bar and so me, June and James ordered drinks while Steve went in search of chips which he returned with shortly afterwards and we all pinched a chip. Then it was onto the small but modern terrace, in fact three sides of the ground were terrace areas. I loved it.

The atmosphere was fabulous amongst the Blues fans as we sang our hearts out. There were 1,734 Bluenoses here tonight and our noise filled the small stadium. However, it failed to inspire our heroes as Blues were poor and lost 2-0 to a team near the bottom of the table. Of course ex Blues player Lloyd Dyer scored and celebrated in front of the away end who in return showered him in abuse and gestures which he thoroughly deserved. He really is a toe rag. It had been a good trip that ended in disappointment. I quite like Burton's stadium, it has a nice feel about it. Blues are now down to 7th in the league.

We were all really looking forward to the game against Villa and my nephew Stephen was coming out up from London for the game. He was traveling by train for the early kick off and I would be meeting him at St. Andrews. As it happens I met him as he was walking up towards the stadium. There were police everywhere and they were using drones for the first time at a football match and the drones could be seen high up in the sky.

It was a mass of blue and white around the stadium and the villa fans arrived by coaches and were taken straight into the fenced off away coach park. Local derbies are always a little nerve racking with so much local pride at stake. The atmosphere amongst the 26,656 fans inside the stadium was electric. 'Keep Right On' and 'shit on the villa' were resounding around the stadium.

It was a real feisty second City derby as always and Blues were up for it from the start. It has been quite a while since our last derby meeting. Blues threw everything at Villa but the Vile managed to grab and undeserved lead. The Bluenoses got behind our team and when David Davis fired a cracker into the bottom corner from long range the place exploded in celebration. A blue smoke bomb was thrown in front of the away end and the Villa fans were engulfed in blue smoke - I had to laugh. We were all on our feet punching the air and jumping around madly. I felt we would now go on and win the game but it was not to be and we left the ground happy with the 1-1 draw. This meant Blues remained in 7th place in the league table and looking good.

The following Saturday it was bonfire night as 1,671 Bluenoses travelled to Yorkshire as Blues took on Huddersfield. It was a pleasant trip up to Huddersfield on the official coaches and we were soon headed to the pub 'the Yorkshire Rose' for a pre match drink and chat. The pub was already getting full with the arriving Bluenoses which then meant that the local Huddersfield fans then had to wait in a queue outside for people to leave before they could gain access. We then headed back to the ground and the traveling Blue army were in great voice as always.

Blues were poor in the first half and fell a goal behind but happily we recovered in the second half with Lucas Jutkiewicz scoring with a great header and the away end erupted in celebration. The game ended in a 1-1 draw and we headed back to Birmingham fairly happy with the result as Blues remained in 7th place just outside the play offs. On our way out of the stadium they were selling the pies off for a pound so I purchased a balti pie which I really enjoyed.

Chapter Thirteen - Rowett Out - Zola In

A few days after the Huddersfield game we headed off on holiday and it was back to my old home of Abu Dhabi and we were staying at the Sheraton again in the club class rooms. It was lovely to be back and a nice sunshine break. We went to the Fairmont on the Friday for a champagne brunch and had a lovely time and to cap it off England beat Scotland 3-0 at Wembley in a World Cup qualifier. Unfortunately I came down with a cold and felt unwell for a few days but it didn't spoil my holiday. We dined in Flavours and also visited the Souk at the Shangri-La and watched the beautiful sunset.

We visited my friends Trish and Tracy at their luxury apartment and it was great to see them again and we enjoyed a nice takeaway before enjoying a drink on their massive balcony overlooking the city. I did start to feel a bit unwell again so we left early armed with beers, wine and coke that Tracey gave to us. The next day I met up with my friend Liz and we all enjoyed a brunch in Flavours and had a lovely time.

I was still in Abu Dhabi on the Saturday as Blues entertained Bristol City at St. Andrews and I was quite hopeful that we could get back to winning ways as 18,586 made their way into the stadium. Blues played well but it took a late goal by Che Adams to give Blues a 1-0 win and the stadium was in raptures as we dared to dream because Blues were now 5th in the table and sitting pretty in a play off place.

The next day we had a horrendous trip home due to weather conditions in Europe. Our plane was unable to land at Amsterdam and after 2 aborted landings during which most of the passengers were sick, we were diverted to Brussels where we sat on the plane for 3 hours. A doctor came onto the plane to see a couple of passengers while we refuelled and then headed back to Amsterdam for another attempt at landing! I just wanted to get off and lie on the ground! This time we did manage to land safely but missed our connecting flight to Birmingham. This meant a later flight on a small plane with propellers! We arrived home freezing and minus our luggage. What a day. I was still feeling sick the next day.

We dared to dream as we headed to London to meet Stephen and get the train to Brentford via a couple of pubs on the way. It took us ages to get to Brentford though as Steve got us on the wrong train so we then had to get off at Clapham and wait for the next train which then broke down. You couldn't make it up! I really like going to Brentford as I love the terraces and the character of their small ground. Blues took 1,659 of us and we all really enjoyed the trip as a penalty converted by Clayton Donaldson and a great back heeled goal from a Ryan Shotton ensured a great 2-1 away win and Blues were now 4th in the table.

What a fantastic day! I was beginning to think that this could be our season! It took us a while to get out of Brentford as the trains were delayed due to trespassers on the tracks. We made our connection to Birmingham with minutes to spare. What a day.

As Barnsley came to town for our first match in December I was still hoping for great things this season as I headed for St. Andrews on a cold Saturday as winter descended. Me, mom and Annette had been to see Rod Stewart on the Friday night and stayed at the Hyatt hotel as part of moms Christmas present so Steve picked us up and dropped us home before coming back to give me a lift to the game. Perhaps the cold affected the attendance or perhaps it was the proximity to Christmas as only 17,072 made their way into St. Andrews. It was an awful day all round really as David Davis got sent off for two yellow cards and accompanied by a poor performance from Blues, I was sent crashing back to earth as Blues lost the game 3-0. This meant that Blues dropped to 5th in the table but still in a play off spot. I can still dream.

Even though it was getting closer to Christmas over 3,000 Bluenoses headed to Newcastle for the long trip up north on another cold day. We traveled by coach (10 official coaches) and we were impressed by the sheer number of Bluenoses as we arrived at St. James Park. After our very long climb up the stairs to the away end up in the gods (stunning views though) we made our way into the bar area which was quickly filling with Bluenoses in good voice already and we purchased our pre match drinks.

We made our way into the stands and the singing in the away end was incredible. Our anthem was loud and proud and we never stopped singing throughout the game. Unfortunately Blues were awful and Newcastle easily dominated. Bluenoses spent most of the time singing 'we've got the ball' swiftly followed by 'we've lost the ball' and when we did have a shot 3000 Blues sang 'we've had a shot'. It was a very poor performance by Blues as we lost the game 4-0 but the fans were supportive of the team throughout and never stopped singing. As atmospheres go amongst the Bluenoses this was up there with one of the bests despite the result.

Rowett said he was disappointed with the performance saying that "we didn't play enough balls or play with enough quality when we did win the balls. We were too passive at times". After the game the Newcastle fans were full of praise for the Blues fans on social media saying that we were the best group of fans to travel to St. James Park in years and that we were way better than the traveling fans of the Vile. The Newcastle fans loved us. Unfortunately this result meant that Blues dropped out of the play off places and down to 7th.

The following Tuesday saw Blues lowest home crowd of the season as only 15,202 were in attendance at St. Andrews as Blues took on Ipswich Town. I was surprised by the low attendance and wondered if it was due to our recent performances as some Blues fans are not that happy with the football we are playing at the moment but you can't argue with our current position which is really promising. Blues played much better against Ipswich and took the lead from the penalty spot as Clayton Donaldson converted to put Blues 1-0 ahead but he was later carried off on a stretcher. Michael Morrison scored Blues second before Ipswich pulled a goal back and also had a goal disallowed as Blues held out to win 2-1. Although Blues remain in 7th place we are only outside the play off places on goal difference and only 3 points behind 3rd place.

This is why I was stunned the following morning at the news of manager Gary Rowett's sacking. Everyone was surprised and disappointed. It was only two days after two new directors had joined the board and Gary's backroom staff were also sacked. It was obviously a premeditated sacking as later that day as we tried to digest the shock news it was announced that former West Ham and Watford manager Gianfranco Zola would be Blues new manager with a two and a half year contact. Zola confirmed that he had been approached about the job some time ago. Blues chief executive Panos Pavlakis said "his pedigree, philosophy and ambition fits with what we want to achieve as we move in a new direction. Gianfranco has a wealth of experience top level experience as both a manager and a player and we are extremely excited with his appointment".

It was reported that Blues players were fuming when Rowett told them he had been sacked. Zola met with some of the senior players and outlined his plans to make it attacking, adventurous football although he said it would be foolish to try to implement too much too soon. I felt sorry for Gary Rowett as I felt he had done a brilliant job at Blues and had steadied the ship and was moving us forward. It all sounded exciting with Zola's plans but I felt the owners were taking an unnecessary risk and should be careful what they wish for. I felt Rowett had been treated disgracefully. Of course there were rumours that he had been talking to other clubs (Fulham and Wolves being examples) at times and had then approached the Blues for improved contacts but it was all rumours.

There was a strange atmosphere for Zola's first game against top of the table Brighton at St. Andrews as a lot of the fans were really angry at Gary Rowett's shock sacking although everyone was also going to get behind the new manager as we felt he was in no way to blame. Over 17,000 turned up for the game and Blues started well with Kieftenbeld hitting the post in the first minute.

Blues were not to be denied though and Lucas Jutkiewicz scored with a header. Despite Blues being the better side Brighton grabbed an equaliser and then a winner in the 94th minute which in no way reflected the game and Zola's first game ended in defeat. At least the fans had got behind him and sang his name (after a loud rendition of 'one Gary Rowett') at the beginning of the game as a message to the owners. Blues were now down to 8th in the league.

There were over 3,000 Bluenoses who travelled to Derby only to see Blues lose again, this time to a very soft penalty which meant we dropped even further down the table to 11th. I could see what Zola was trying to do with the team as he was trying to get Blues to play attractive attacking football and I really hoped it would come together.

The last game of 2016 saw us travel up to Barnsley and we popped into the nearby leisure centre for a pre match drink when we arrived. Inside the ground the traveling Bluenoses were in good voice and I was hopeful of getting a good result. It started really badly as Blues went 2-0 down but they fought back as Lucas Jutkiewicz scored from the penalty spot before Maghoma grabbed the second to ensure that the points were shared in a 2-2 draw. Blues were still in 11th place as Zola searched for his first win.

It was back to St. Andrews after our New Year celebrations and a home game against Brentford which we really should be looking to win. We headed into the Cricketers before the game to have a catch up and pre match drink. Lucas Jutkiewicz scored to put Blues 1-0 ahead and we all celebrated and though that our luck might be about change. How wrong we were as Blues made mistakes that lead to Brentford scoring 3 second half goals and missed a penalty as they beat us 3-1. This meant Blues dropped down to 13th and it was getting worrisome.

On Saturday it was a break from League action as Blues took on high flying Newcastle United at St. Andrews in the FA Cup 3rd round. I love the FA Cup and was as optimistic as ever of progressing, hopefully, to a Wembley final. It's a shame all the other Bluenoses, who used to turn up in their numbers in years gone by, don't feel the same as only 13,171 bothered to turn up and 4,671 of them were from Newcastle. So very sad. I'm sure there would be about 50,000 (I go to all the games) fans who would want tickets for the final though, should we make it!

Hence the atmosphere inside St. Andrews was mainly created by the traveling Toon army. I much prefer away ties in the FA Cup to be honest because at least then the Blues fans create more atmosphere. The Newcastle fans were selling half/half FACup scarves outside the ground with the date as well as the two teams on it. Blues played really well in this game but despite Lucas Jutkiewicz scoring again, the game ended in a 1-1 draw which meant a long distance replay next week in midweek. Not what I had hoped for but at least Blues were in the draw for the next round.

It was back to St. Andrews and on a positive point Craig Gardener had returned to Blues on loan from West Brom and it would be good to see him don the Blues shirt again and hopefully add some class to our midfield. It was a poor game to be honest and ended in a 0-0 draw but at least it brought our 5 match losing streak to and end and Blues moved up a place to 12th in the league.

The trip to Newcastle for the FA Cup replay would be a long journey and not one that appealed to many especially midweek. My mate June couldn't go as she was working so it was just me but I sat with Baz on coach one so it was ok. There were 818 hardy souls that made the trip and I was proud to be one of them as we sang our hearts out from the start on a cold January night. As always our coaches were late to leave St. Andrews and we arrived with only 30 minutes to spare. Blues did play better than our last trip and I thought we were really unlucky to lose 3-1 with their third goal coming on the break as Blues looked likely to equalise. But it was not to be and we were out of the FA Cup for another year so I was heartened by our display but disappointed in our cup exit. It was a long journey back and we arrived in the early hours of the morning to find our cars had been locked on the car park! Typical Blues. It took ages to get a number for the night watchman to came and unlock the gates. I was knackered when I got home.

The highlight of January was the return of Craig Gardener on loan which I was quite happy about and hoped he would help turn things around for us. It was then off the play Blackburn as Blues took on a team in 23rd place in the league. It was a cold day but I like the trip to Blackburn and we headed into the nearby social club where we saw other Bluenoses that we knew and had a good catch up. Then it was back to the stadium and Blues were soon 1-0 up when Lucas Jutkiewicz scored from the penalty spot after David Cotterill had been fouled. Blackburn then equalised just before half time and that was how the game finished in a 1-1 draw. It was a good atmosphere in the away end but the rest of the stadium was nearly empty. It was frustrating to have scored after 3 minutes and then throwing it away with poor defending.

The next Saturday we were off on our travels again, this time to Norwich and I was meeting my nephew Stephen who was traveling from London. It was a nice sunny day and we met Stephen at a pub on the river and he was already with the Bluenoses from the party bus. We all had a drink then walked up the the stadium for the game. Blues had two new signings who would be in the team today, Kerim Frei and Emilio Nsue (from Middlesbrough) and we were quite excited about the prospect. Today there was a good away following of 1,026.

In all fairness Blues did play some exciting and entertaining football and hit the woodwork twice but didn't defend well and lost the game 2-0. I said goodbye to Stephen as he headed to the train station and got the coach back feeling disappointed again. It's a long time to the end of the season though and I can see what Zola is trying to achieve and it will be nice if we can play exciting football again. Blues remain in 12th place in the league table.

There were only 16,672 at St. Andrews to watch the Tuesday night game against Reading and I was amongst them. Blues would be without the Welsh wizard 'David Cotterill' who had made a transfer deadline day move to Bristol City on loan after being told he had 24 hours to find another club as he did not fit in with Zola's plans. Blues played well and deserved at least a point but Reading scored in the 71st minute to condemn Blues to a disappointing defeat again and we are now winless for 8 games under Zola. I am beginning to wonder if he is capable of keeping his promise of entertaining football at Blues.

The night before the Fulham game I had a fantastic time at the Donny Osmond concert that was part of my birthday presents with on overnight stay at the Crown Plaza with my mom and sister. I had a fantastic night with a bottle of champagne in the hotel before heading to the concert. Brilliant! It was back to St. Andrews the day after as Fulham came to town and Blues finally got their first win under Zola as Lucas Jutkiewicz scored the only goal of the game after Fulham had a player sent off for a foul on Craig Gardener. Lucas had earlier hit the crossbar and today's goal was his 10th of the season. His partner today had been new signing Jerome Sinclair. Blues remain in 12th spot.

The Sheffield Wednesday away game had been moved to the Friday night for live TV viewing which of course made it more difficult for fans to travel and therefore only 953 made the trip to Hillsborough. That's not too bad really though. Once again Blues tried to play attractive football and hit the woodwork 3 times but our defence was poor and we managed to lose the game 3-0 and I'm beginning to feel a bit despondent. It doesn't feel good at the moment and there is rumours of unrest in the dressing room. I Really hope we turn the corner soon.

Blues next game was another midweek away game and I was one of 614 Bluenoses amongst a low crowd of 10,233 who spent valentines night in Preston. David Davis was suspended for this game, Che Adams was recalled and Craig Gardener was give the captaincy. It just didn't go for us yet again as we lost 2-1 and Craig Gardener was sent off for a foul. Blues are now down to 14th in the table. Zola said he was fed up of talking about luck, he said "the reason we keep losing games like this is not because we are unlucky, at the moment we are very poor, simple as that". It was another depressing trip home on the coach wondering where the next win would come from. When we arrived back at St. Andrews our cars had once again been locked in the car park!

There were 20,265 inside St. Andrews as we finally played on a Saturday again but the majority left extremely disappointed. Lucas Jutkiewicz was out injured and so Adams and Sinclair played up front in a 3-5-2 formation. Nsue managed to miss a sitter and then QPR scored. Keita went off with concussion and Jack Storer mad an appearance but it was a poor performance as QPR were 4 goals up before Nsue got a consolation in injury time but most of the Bluenoses had left by that point. I was disgusted by the defeat to a poor QPR team who were languishing down the bottom of the league. We remain in 14th but I am really worried that we could slip down near the relegation places if Zola doesn't get it sorted soon.

It was back to Friday night football for the trip to Wolves as once again we were being shown on live TV. At least it was only a short trip to Wolves and we went in a hotel bar by the train station for a pre match pint, then walked up with the arriving Bluenoses to the stadium. It was buzzing inside the away end and it was a carnival atmosphere as 2,151 made the short trip. Blues started well and were playing some good football even though we were playing with only Adams up front and when the Wolves keeper dropped the ball at the feet of Kieftenbeld he fired home and the away end exploded in celebration. A couple of bottles were thrown down at us from the Wolves fans above up but they were returned ten fold in response. 'Always shit on the old gold and black' rang out as the Wolves fans looked despondent.

It got even worse for the Wolves fans when ex-Wolves David Davis curled home a shot to make it 2-0 to Blues and he ran to the Blues fans in celebration and the blue end erupted. It was brilliant and I jumped around in celebration. I prayed we could hold out, especially when Paul Robinson got a straight red for allegedly punching a Wolves player (later rescinded). Wolves did manage to pull a goal back once Blues were reduced to 10 men but we held on for a 2-1 win and the celebrations began. It was a happy journey back to the car and Blues moved up to 13th. It makes a change to win in front of the cameras as we usually lose and to win in a Derby game was even better. I was very happy.

Blues had yet another Friday night game for live TV again when 4th placed Leeds came to town bringing over 3,000 fans with them which bolstered the crowd to over 20,000 inside St. Andrews and the atmosphere was great. Blues played really well and Leeds manager Garry Monk said he didn't enjoy the first half hour of his team's visit to St. Andrews. However, our luck in front of the TV cameras remained the same as ex Blues Chris Wood scored twice as Leeds beats us 3-1 despite Blues having 27 shots. It was our best display of the season but we were mugged. I was very downhearted. Zola said that despite the mistakes it was his team's best performance of the season. The result sees Blues slip back down to 14th place.

The next day I was off on my holidays again. This time it was a girls holiday with just me, mom and Annette for a week in Tenerife and I was really looking forward to the break. It was a lovely sunshine break at a time when I was knackered and I had a fabulous time.

On the Tuesday night Wigan came to St. Andrews and I was worried as I know that Blues traditionally lose to low placed teams and they don't come much lower that Wigan in 23rd place. It was a really awful performance from Blues as another ex Blues player Dan Burn scored the only goal of the game to give Wigan the 3 points with only 340 of their fans present to see it amongst the 15,596 as Blues tumbled to 17th place. I really fear a relegation battle is now certain.

Despite Blues current form 1,500 Bluenoses made the trip to Cardiff in the hope of cheering our team on to a win. It was a great atmosphere even when Blues fell a goal behind. We never gave up hope though and when Lucas Jutkiewicz scored in the 89th minute to make it 1-1 the away end exploded in celebration as blue smoke filled the air. It still means that Blues are in 17th place and only 6 points off the relegation places. Once again we are getting nervous.

Back to St. Andrews for the game against top of the table Newcastle and Clayton Donaldson would be back from injury so I was hopeful that the turnaround would begin. I can see what Zola is trying to achieve but many Bluenoses just want him out before it is too late as Blues have only achieved 1 win in the 18 he has been in charge and have lost 11 including the cup defeat. Newcastle brought 3,229 fans amongst the 19,796 inside the stadium and the atmosphere was great. Blues played well and the 0-0 result was probably a good one although it dropped Blues down to 18th, and closer to relegation and took Newcastle to the top of the table. Blues are only 5 points off the bottom 3.

Despite our current predicament there was still a good following away to Ipswich as 952 Bluenoses made the trip. We nearly missed our coach as our the Blues website said the coaches were leaving at 10am when it was in fact 9am. It was a mad rush but we made it in time.   It was a nice journey and once in Ipswich we had chips by the ground then headed into a pub called 'Punch and Judy'. Then it was into the away end for the game. Just after halftime Defender Jonathan Grounds scored to put Blues 1-0 up and we all celebrated and sang our hearts out. Unfortunately Ipswich scored 'a wonder goal' or more likely a fluke as a cross into the box flew into the net. What a disappointment. I'm beginning to think that the gods are against us and we looked doomed to League One football next season if this continues. Blues remain 18th.

Due to work I was unable to make the long trip to Brighton on a Tuesday night but 675 hardy souls made the trip. Despite Brighton taking the lead after only 2 minutes Blues had the better of the first half but just couldn't score. Brighton then extended their lead to 3-0 before Adams scored a consolation goal in yet another defeat. The natives are getting very restless and calling for Zola to be sacked. Blues still in 18th place.

Next up at St. Andrews was Derby and they were now managed by Gary Rowett who Blues had sacked back in December and once the Blues fans had given him a warm reception they then got behind current manager Zola by singing his name. Blues played really well too but as our luck seems to be out at the moment Derby scored a lucky goal as a shot rebounded of the post, hit goalkeeper Tomasz Kuszczak and went into the net. My heart dropped. Why is it always this way?

Lucas Jutkiewicz then scored but his goal was disallowed and afterwards both managers said they couldn't see a reason. But on 69 minutes Blues did equalise as Adams scored to deservedly put Blues level. We were playing really well and it looked likely that Blues could get the win but in injury time Derby hit Blues on the break to score a very unlikely and unjust winner and our hearts were broken. Blues had been the better team and did not deserve the defeat. Despite the defeat Blues are still 18th in the table.

It was Good Friday and 2,600 of us headed to Rotherham in the hope of a good day out and getting a good result against a team who had just had their relegation confirmed after losing their last 10 matches. Surely Blues could win this one? Zola said it was a must win game but Blues didn't look like they were fighting for our lives whereas Rotherham did and it didn't help that Clayton Donaldson was out with a knee injury.

We had travelled up on the coaches and walked into town to find a pub. As usual Steve had a certain pub he was looking for but after walking round in circles me, June and James got fed up and headed into the Wetherspoons to join other Bluenoses and had a great time while Steve went off to find his pub. On our way back to the ground we passed armed police which is reassuring but a sign of the times at the moment with the recent terrorist attacks.

Into the ground and on 73 minutes Blues were awarded a free kick just outside the area and as Gardener looked like he wanted to take it Kerim Frei pushed him aside, placed the ball and showed him how it should be done as he fired a cracker high into the net and the away end exploded. Blue smoke bombs were let off and as the blue smoke filled the air many Bluenoses spilled over the barrier to celebrate. Stewards were running everywhere to try to contain us and many Bluenoses were arrested and taken away - a shame really as they were only celebrating and had just become a bit over excited.

With just 5 minutes to go the win was snatched from our grasp as Rotherham equalised and they could have won it in stoppage time when a Rotherham player blasted over from close range. That was all too much for the traveling Bluenoses as they chanted 'Zola out!' and some Bluenoses fought amongst themselves, a very sad sight indeed. Zola responded afterwards that he had no intention of leaving and as long as the fans turned on him and not the players there was not a problem. However. During the post match warm down Emilio Nsue had to be restrained by his teammates as arguments broke out amongst the players. Blues drop to 19th.

Easter Monday brought a big decision for me as I had to decide between Blues v Burton or the Ladies FA Cup semi final with Chelsea at Solihull Moors for a place a Wembley. I have to say I made the wrong choice opting to watch the men's team lose 2-0 at home to a poor Burton side languishing at the bottom. My mate June made the best decision as she went to the Moors and saw Blues ladies book their place at Wembley for the Ladies FA Cup Final as they beat Chelsea on penalties.

The games against Burton was one of the worst performances I have seen by a Blues team. We were shocking and allowed that tosser Dyer to score against us yet again - everyone knows he always scores against us so why not just mark him out of the game! Not rocket science is it! It was a disgraceful performance and saw Blues drop to 20th just 2 places from relegation.

Zola resigned after the match. He said " I sacked myself. I gave my resignation. I am sorry because I came to Birmingham with hugh expectations. Unfortunately the results have not been good and I take full responsibility. It is not that I like quitting but Birmingham deserves better. If I feel I cannot help the players why stay? If I cannot help the team it is better I leave and let someone else do that."

During Zola's time Blues won only twice in 24 games and fell from 3 points off the playoffs to 3 points off the relegation places with only 3 games remaining. It had been a very poor Easter period too with 2 very poor performances and the prospect of relegation is looking very real indeeed. It is very anxious times as a Bluenose. Things did look a whole lot better just 16 hours later when Harry Redknapp was announced as Blues new manager till the end of the season. He would work unpaid till the end of the season and receive a bonus if he kept us up. Harry brought in Steve Cotteril to assist him and I was really hopeful again. Harry contacted Gary Rowett prior to his first match to get more insight into his players.

Chapter Fourteen - We've Got Redknapp - Harry Redknapp!

Today would be new manager Harry Redknapp's first game in charge of Birmingham City and what a first game to start with – a big derby game against Villa at Vile Park. After all the despondency of late under Zola I felt more optimism now that Harry is at the helm. Can he steer Blues away from relegation in what seems like an impossible task at present with only two wins in twenty five games during Zola's reign?

Because the match was an early kick off and on a Sunday some friends had persuaded a local club to open early for around 15 – 20 Bluenoses to get a pre match drink in our local area. We got there about 9am, enjoying a McDonalds sausage and egg McMuffin on the walk there, and already the pre match preparations were in full swing. We were all looking forward to the game and we took a 'team photo' whilst singing 'shit on the villa'. Spirits were high. My nerves were jangling when local taxi company Elite massively let us down (again I must add) as our pre booked taxis were nearly an hour late, meaning a mad dash to the 'dark side' to make it in time for kick off.

It wasn't helped by traffic around the ground. We had to get out and walk, and the local police made us walk even further out of our way to get to the away turnstiles. That part was chaotic but at least we made it into the ground in time for kick off. The atmosphere was buzzing with over 40,000 inside and the Blues fans were in great voice. The banter was great and 'Keep Right On' was belted out.

The match kicked off and Blues were playing really well. Bluenoses sang 'Harry Redknapp's blue and white army' and 'Harry give us a wave' to which he responded with a wave to the Blues supporters. The players certainly rose to the occasion and were playing their counterparts off the pitch. I did feel it may not be our day when Che Adams missed a sitter in the first half. Despite Villa not posing any threat to us they managed to nick a goal in a goalmouth scramble in the second half. We were gutted but never stopped singing. 'We're Birmingham City we'll fight to the end!'

And fight we did, the players gave their all but just couldn't find the killer touch and get a goal that would have at least given us what we deserved. After the game Harry Redknapp looked stunned as he gave his TV interview saying "our keeper never even got his gloves dirty, I don't know how we lost that" he said "Steve Bruce has got a big job on his hands there". I love this man! There's only one Harry Redknapp. So we headed home disappointed but with heavy hearts because Blues had outplayed Villa and been unlucky to lose and with Harry now at the helm we have hope in our hearts again.

The result means that Blues are 21st in the table only two points ahead of Blackburn who occupy the last relegation place. Our goal difference is much worse than Blackburn so we have to win our last two matches to avoid relegation. How on earth did we get into this situation? Brighton are top of the table with Newcastle United in second spot.

Today I was finally really looking forward to going to St. Andrews again for Harry Redknapp's first home game as Birmingham City manager. I still can't believe I'm saying that – 'Harry Redknapp – Birmingham City manager!' I am both excited and nervous as the game is of such importance to us with Blues needing a win to give us any chance of staying up and keeping it in our own hands.

I was also looking forward to seeing a sold out St. Andrews – even the Olympic Gallery had been opened in order to meet the demand for tickets. Outside the stadium there was a buzz in the air. It was great to see Dave surrounded by fans buying his 'Made In Brum' fanzine and match day badges. He has some fantastic Women's FA Cup Final – Birmingham City Ladies v Manchester City Women badges ready for the Wembley Final in two weeks time. As we were early we headed round to Bar 8 at the back of the Main Stand. It was so busy that there was a queue to get in and with many of them taking their drinks to the outside area it didn't take us long to get in and get a drink to calm the nerves.

At 2.30pm I headed back round the other side and into my seat on the KOP. The stadium was already buzzing with an air of excitement. When the players came out onto the pitch for kick off, the loudest version of 'Keep Right On' that I have heard for a long time was belted out from all four sides of the stadium. It was absolutely fantastic. Harry must have been impressed by the 28,000 Bluenoses in full voice! In his programme notes Harry said "Birmingham City is a big club, a proper club, and my sole ambition at present is to help keep us in the Sky Bet Championship. That's all there is to it - we know the situation and what's ahead of us and that's all everyone has to concentrate on at present."

The match got underway and Che Adams was brought down in the box in the 7th minute and Blues were awarded a penalty much to the delight of the Bluenoses. Lucas Jutkiewicz stepped up to take the penalty and to our horror saw his spot kick saved by the Huddersfield goalkeeper. To make matters worse Che Adams then received a straight red card (unfairly so and the club appealed afterwards and it was rescinded) in the 23rd minute and Blues were reduced to ten men against a team currently 3rd in the Championship – even though Huddersfield had made ten changes.

Now I was worried as it was obviously not going to be our day. How wrong I was. The ten men of Blues fought like warriors with the partisan crowd cheering them on like a 12th man (or in this case the 11th man!). Just before half time Craig Gardener crossed the ball into the box, Morrison headed it back across goal and the unlikely Jonathan Grounds was on hand to head it home from two yards out. Goal!!! The stadium exploded with noise and I was jumping all over the place.

Having reached half time with a 1-0 lead I could only pray that we could hold on with only ten men in the second half. Amazingly Blues came out for the second half and continued to play like their lives depended on it. Then in the 76th minute Maghoma jinxed into the penalty area and was tripped by a Huddersfield defender and the referee pointed to the spot – penalty! Harry shouted over for Craig Gardener to take it and he stepped up to smash the ball past the goalkeeper and into the net. 2-0!

Once again St. Andrews exploded with noise and celebrations. Gardener ran towards the KOP/Tilton corner in celebration and several Bluenoses were over the wall and celebrating with the players. Unbelievable scenes! I was busy hugging those around me. 2-0 with only ten men! The match resumed and the tannoy announced "please do not go onto the pitch at any time during the game or afterwards" to which 28,000 jubilant Bluenoses sang 'we're Birmingham City we'll do what we want!'

What an amazing match, Blues always do it the hard way. I was also immensely proud of our support as we all sang our hearts out throughout the 95 minutes as we got our vital win. I also loved singing 'Harry Redknapp's blue and white army' – something I never dreamed we would get to sing. And I loved it when we sang 'Harry give us a wave' and he turned and waved at us. Fantastic!

I was absolutely buzzing as I left a jubilant St. Andrews. I had witnessed one of the rare special days this season has given us. However, as expected, Villa put in a poor performance at third from bottom Blackburn which of course delighted the sad 'Blackburn shirt wearing Vilers'. How sad. So it remains in our own hands that we now have to win at Bristol City next week to avoid relegation to League One. At least Blues moved above Nottingham Forest who lost at fellow strugglers QPR.

I woke really early on the morning of the Bristol City game with the excitement/ nervousness of what lay ahead. This was Blues most important game since the last great escape at Bolton three years ago and today would be just as nerve wracking due to a dramatic turnaround in form of the two teams below us. Blues have to win – no doubt about it. If Blues draw or lose then we would need Nottingham Forest or Blackburn to draw or lose and to be honest I think they will both win because that's the sort of luck Blues have. No pressure then!

Because of the early kick off time of 12 o'clock the coaches would be leaving St. Andrews at 8.30am from the Main Stand car park because the KOP car park is being used by those going to church. Yes us fans come second once again. To top it off the coaches were late leaving again, wether this was down to poor organisation by the stewards again, or the fact that we had to wait ages to get the gates to the car park open due to the wrong key being sent, I don't know.

The coaches did finally get away though at 8.37am and we were on our way. It was me, June and James on coach one heading to Bristol. There were loads of Blues coaches (around 15 – 20) and we were all told to meet at the Bristol services to meet the police escort who were planning to escort all the coaches to the ground. This was mainly because there was a 10K Run through Bristol happening today and many of the roads were closed. We met the police escort and were soon on our way through the back roads with the police motorbikes stopping traffic and taking us straight through. The coaches parked at the usual place on the industrial park and we had quite a walk over the railway lines and on to the away end of the stadium.

I was impressed to see that an outdoor bar had been set up near the away turnstiles which was selling beer and cider. Fabulous! I had a nice cold Thatchers cider (when in Somerset eh) as we watched the Bluenoses arrive, many in fancy dress. I had on a long blue wig, face paint and a pair of massive blue sunglasses. I said Hi to Batman and we headed into the stadium.

Inside the stadium the away end was buzzing with over 2,600 Bluenoses on their feet and in full voice. There was a mixture of nerves and excitement in the air, though it was probably mostly nerves to be honest. The game got underway and Blues looked up for the fight. However, news soon reached us that Blackburn were leading 1-0 at Brentford – not what we wanted to hear as this meant that only a win would prevent Blues from being relegated to League One. Then it was 2-0 to Blackburn and I became even more nervous. This was not good.

Blues fans sang continuously and got behind the team and in the 16th minute Che Adams turned his man and fired the ball past the Bristol City goalkeeper – 1-0! The away end erupted as we all celebrated and some of the tension lifted. A new song was born and was belted out with passion 'we've got Redknapp, Harry Redknapp, I just don't think you understand, he saved us from the drop, he'll take us to the top, we've got Harry Redknapp'

As the match went on and we sang our hearts out, more news kept coming in. Nottingham Forest were leading Ipswich 1-0. Then in was 2-0 and Blackburn were 3-0 ahead. As ninety minutes approached, Forest were winning 3-0 and Blackburn 3-1. This meant that Blues had to win and as the fourth official held up his board showing six minutes of injury time we all knew that a Bristol City goal would send us down to League One.

Bristol City were now relentless in their attacks on the Blues goal in their attempt to send us down (and we will never forget this Bristol City!) and those six minutes were probably amongst the most stressful six minutes of my life! I could hardly bear to watch. It was awful and my nerves were wrecked. Even their goalkeeper came up for their corners! Then the sound of the final whistle rang out and the roar of celebration and relief in the Blues end was deafening.

Strangers hugged each other, barriers were climbed and many surged towards the pitch and some of the barriers collapsed under the strain as police and stewards tried in vain to keep the celebrating Blues fans off the pitch. The players had sprinted the length of the pitch, jumped over the barriers and dived into the mass of celebrating Blues fans!

Harry Redknapp came over and punched the air in celebration before appealing for calm as the barriers collapsed. Calm? No chance! He then went around the players hugging them and someone got a Blues scarf to him which he proudly put around his neck. The players were now in a group and bouncing around singing 'we are staying up!' Craig Gardener, who had been celebrating with the fans, noticed this and ran and dived on top of them. Fantastic celebrations and I was privileged to be part of it all.

So the season was over and Blues moved above Burton Albion to finish in 19th place. Nottingham Forest just avoided relegation, finishing fourth from bottom. So the relegated teams were Blackburn Rovers, Wigan Athletic and Rotherham United who will all play in League One next season.

Newcastle United clinched the championship title as Brighton were held to a draw at Villa Park and were promoted in second place. Surprise package Huddersfield Town were also promoted following play off victory at

Wembley. Hull City, Middlesbrough and Sunderland will join us in the championship after being relegated from the Premier League and from League One comes Sheffield United as champions, Bolton Wanderers in second place and Millwall via the play offs.

Blues had 3 managers during the season - Gary Rowett, Gianfranco Zola and Harry Redknapp. Our top goalscorer was Lucas Jutkiewicz with 11 and our average home attendance was 18,717. The highest was 29,656 against Villa and the lowest was 7,202 in the League Cup against Oxford United.

It was a nice hot summer which I enjoyed immensely, making the most of my garden and enjoying my days off. England Under 20's won the World Cup in June which was a fantastic achievement. I went back to Tenerife for my summer holiday with my family and had a lovely time by the sea.

Chapter Fifteen - Harry Spent The Lot

There has been a lot of excitement since Harry Redknapp has agreed to stay on as Birmingham City manager for the forthcoming season. Season ticket sales have rocketed and most Bluenoses are filled with optimism and hope again. Harry is known for his entertaining brand of football and his success. Hopefully he will be able to attract some big names and talented players to the club.

Goalkeeper David Stockdale was the first to arrive, a move that took us all by surprise as he had been Brighton's number one goalkeeper in their promotion to the Premier League last season, and on a free transfer as well. Then came defender Marc Roberts from Barnsley, their player of the season last season, for 3.4 million pounds.

Highly rated midfielder Cheikh N'Doye came in from French Ligue One club SCO Angers on a free transfer and looks really exciting. Ahead of all this Harry had already secured the signing of Craig Gardener who had already been at the club on loan from West Brom. A great start so far.

It was amazing to see Harry Redknapp up on stage at an event singing 'Keep Right On' and he knew every word. Oh but we do love him. Harry was chosen as the manager of an all-stars line up against Sir Alex Ferguson's Manchester United 08 side for Michael Carrick's testimonial in June (2-2) at Old Trafford and it was fantastic to see Harry on the sidelines wearing his Birmingham City badge with pride!

Blues kit for the 2017-18 season was blue shirts with white strips down the sides, white shorts with blue strips down the sides and blue socks. The away shirts were lovely - white with blue strips down the sides and the third kit was all red with the 3 white Adidas strips on the shoulders. Of course I had to have all three!

Pre season started with a tour of Austria and then the first proper friendly back in England was away at Oxford United on 22nd July. I really wanted to go as it would have been a new ground for me as I have been to the old 'Manor Ground' but not to their new ground. Unfortunately I was working so I couldn't go but the team did well without me with Blues winning the match 2-0 with goals from David Davis and Che Adams and over 1,500 Bluenoses outnumbering the home contingent. I was also unable to go to the next friendly away at Kidderminster as Blues came away with a 1-1 draw having scored at both ends with Blues Paul Robinson netting an own goal after ten minutes.

I was able to go to the final friendly on Saturday 29th July as Premier League Swansea City were the visitors to St. Andrews. It was great to see everyone again especially June and James. June picked me up and we were soon heading into 'My Happy Abode' for a drink only to be told they had nothing on draft. As I didn't want a bottle we headed round to Bar 8 following assurances from staff that it was open. So we walked all the way around the ground to discover that Bar 8 was in fact closed so we headed to the Cricketers and it was great to see lots of Bluenoses that I knew.

Only the KOP was open today and as we arrived at the turnstiles there were massive queues. I bumped into Harry and Terry and as there were already people in our seats the stewards found us a row of seats together.

Harry Redknapp played a good team but we just couldn't score. Blues had loads of possession but seemed a little goal shy. "Shoot!" Everyone kept shouting, but they just kept passing it about. Swansea scored against the run of play and added a lucky second with a deflection in the second half. Che Adams had a good game and was unlucky not to score at least two goals. The game finished with a 2-0 defeat but at the end of the day it was against Premier League opponents and I did feel Blues were the better side, we just lacked firepower. We really need a prolific goal scorer.

My mobile beeped with the sound of a text message which said simply "happy opening match of the season" accompanied by a photo of a pint of beer. This summed the day up nicely as all over the country football fans were keenly anticipating the first day of a new season as the Championship and Football Leage got underway.

Blues were away at Ipswich Town who had lost their last friendly game 6-1 against League One Charlton and despite the long distance and early start I was quite excited about the trip. The seven coaches left St. Andrews late as usual at 09.26 (should have been 09.15) and it was me, June, James and Barry on the back seat – reunited after the summer break.

It was a long trip broken by a stop at the motorway services where we enjoyed a KFC feast before re commencing our journey – late again due to poor organisation from the stewards. We arrived in Ipswich about 1.30 pm and me, June and James headed off in the rain to a pub called the Punch and Judy. It wasn't too packed and had both Blues and Ipswich fans drinking in there.

We found a table and got talking to some Blues fans from Redditch on the next table. They were telling us how the four of them (4 lads) had come in a taxi from Redditch all the way to Ipswich which cost them £40 each return. By the time we left the pub and headed to the ground the heavens had opened and it was pouring with rain. We pulled our hoods up and sprinted across the car park as we prepared to get very wet.

Once inside the ground I took my coat off to dry as it was still quite warm and so my new White away shirt got its first outing. The away end was buzzing and the atmosphere was fantastic amongst the 2000+ Birmingham fans who had made the trip and the singing was brilliant. 'Keep Right On' – the first of the new season – was loud and proud.

The home fans were silent whilst the away contingent sang our hearts out. The match kicked off and Blues, in our new White with blue shorts away kit, were the better team. It looked like it would only be a matter of time before we scored. 'We've got Redknapp, Harry Redknapp' was belted out and the sun was now shining. All looked well.

One of the Ipswich players went down with what looked to be a serious injury and a small buggy thing with a stretcher drove onto the pitch. The bemused Blues fans sang 'what the fucking hell is that?' and I had to laugh. The player was then put onto the stretcher which was then strapped to the buggy and it drove off and the match resumed.

It was 0-0 at half time and Blues took up where they left off and had a good chance to score which was wasted. We never looked like losing the game but then 10 seconds later the ball was in our net from an Ipswich breakaway and Blues were 1-0 down. We were stunned. 'Keep Right On' echoed round the ground in defiance and a bit of banter was exchanged between both sets of fans with the odd bottle or two flying through the air. One Ipswich fan in particular was taunting the Blues fans until several stewards went to speak to him amid chants of 'wanker! Wanker!' and 'does your mother know you're here?'.

From then on Blues lacked the firepower to get a goal from a "very weak team" as Harry said after the game. He looked across the bench and we had no one he could bring on to make a difference. If he doesn't bring in new players we will struggle and he said this himself. Let's hope we can get some more players soon. We desperately need a striker. Somewhat disappointingly Blues lost 1-0 to a very poor Ipswich team. It's only one game though so it's still early days yet. So it was off back to the coaches and the long trip back home.

Once again it was pouring with rain as we headed up the Coventry Road to St. Andrews. It is August and we should be sitting in our gardens sipping Cocktails! Anyway, despite the weather we made our way into the KOP – the only stand open due to the poor support the League Cup gets these days. No doubt there will be about 80,000 die hard Blues fans wanting tickets if we get to the final again.

Well the real 'die hard' fans were braving the weather tonight and the KOP was pretty full. There were a handful of Crawley fans in the away end – bless them. We were treated to a really entertaining game and a brilliant result. It began when Che Adams fired Blues ahead with a shot from the edge of the penalty area which flew into the bottom corner of the net in the 27th minute. Blues were on fire and David Davis made it 2-0 with another great goal in the 38th minute and then three minutes before half time Che Adams got his second goal to send us into the break 3-0 ahead.

Blues played just as well in the second half and I for one was pleased to see David Cotterill back in the team as he fired in some pin point corners and crosses. It was one of these corners that found the head of Robert Tesche who powered it into the net to make it 4-0. The rout was completed in the 66th minute as the man of the match – Che Adams completed his hat trick to make it 5-0. Blues did get a bit sloppy in the last fifteen minutes and allowed Crawley a consolation goal four minutes from time. So a fantastic 5-1 win and progression to the next round of the Cup. Shame there was only 7,814 there to see such an entertaining game.

Two days later following the Bury v Sunderland tie the draw was made for the next round and Blues were drawn at home to Bournemouth – the team that knocked us out of the FA Cup (somewhat luckily) last season. Not the best tie we could have hoped for but a chance for revenge and a home advantage.

Blues first home game of the new season against Bristol City with Harry at the helm and there was a sense of excitement in the air. Unfortunately my season ticket has still not arrived – shame on you in the ticket office! To say I am a bit pissed off is an understatement. I paid in full on the 2nd June, I am a gold member and they only posted it this last Monday - disgraceful.

Once they had given me my match day ticket I got my match day badge and headed into St. Andrews with June and James.

It was fantastic inside St. Andrews and it looked pretty packed as over 21,000 buzzed with excitement. It was great seeing Harry Redknapp with his team and he was given a fabulous reception from the Blues fans as he came out. I was a bit nervous as I think Bristol City have a really strong team this season and could be the dark horses. The stadium was still settling in their seats when Bristol City took the lead on 57 seconds after hitting the bar twice in their first attack. I was worried. The fans responded with a loud rendition of 'Keep Right On' as red flares went off in the Bristol end.

Blues then started to play well although Bristol City looked dangerous and it was a really exciting game with chances at both ends. Then in the 30th minute the ball dropped to Craig Gardener on the edge of the penalty area and he fired a low shot into the bottom corner of the net. Goal! 1-1 and St. Andrews exploded. What a noise! 'Craigy Gardener is a Blue – he hates villa' rang out around the stadium. When the half time whistle blew the place was buzzing again.

The second half got underway and Harry was forced to make three substitutions during the half due to injuries. Blues were playing really well now and the atmosphere was unbelievable. If this is the 'Harry factor' it is brilliant. In the 74th minute Jacques Maghoma shrugged past three Bristol players before hitting a unstoppable shot from distance that flew into the bottom corner of the net and the roof was lifted off the stadium. It was an incredible explosion of noise as everyone were on their feet and celebrating like crazy. What an incredible comeback.

The only dark cloud on the horizon was the referee who, having already been widely booed and been the object of 'you don't know what your doing', then proceeded to send off Blues Michael Kieftenbeld to a crescendo of boos. Three quarters of the stadium then sang the loudest version of 'you don't know what your doing' that I have heard. And yes, I did join in.

So with ten minutes to go Blues were down to ten men and hanging on valiantly. Intent on proving to everyone that he was a complete dick the referee then proceeded to show a yellow card to Blues Stephen Gleeson who was sitting on the bench at the time. No idea what for. Then, despite no injuries, the board was held up for 5 extra minutes! I don't think any of us were really surprised though. Every time he gave Blues a free kick cries of 'off! Off! Off!' Rang out around the ground.

The final whistle went and St. Andrews erupted in cheers. What an amazing game and a fantastic 2-1 win for Blues . We all headed home very happy indeed. It is only early yet but Blues are in 10th spot.

It was great to be back at St. Andrews again a few days later and following a pre match drink in the Cricketers we were amazed by the massive queues at the turnstiles. This hasn't been seen for a long time for a night match and just endorses the 'Harry effect'. It's really quite exciting these days. To add to the excitement just a few days earlier Birmingham had signed a bright new prospect from Luton Town – striker Isaac Vassell and he had been named in tonight's squad.

There were 20,215 inside St. Andrews which was great to see and the atmosphere was great. Newly promoted Bolton were not the best of teams and I thought Blues really should see them off. However, it turned out to be a poor game really, the highlight being the introduction of our new striker Issac Vassell. He looked fast and very promising for the future. I still think Harry has a lot of work to do though after this uninspiring 0-0 draw against what I thought was a poor Bolton side. Hence I left St. Andrews disappointed with the draw but excited about the addition of Isaac Vassell.

The 1,715 away tickets for Burton sold out by the time they reached bronze members and never even made it to the season ticket holders or general sale. I was lucky enough to get one though as I am a gold member, as did my friends June, James and Steve. So I was really looking forward to the trip. I like Burton due to the good old fashioned 'terraces' and I relish the opportunity of standing on them amongst a partisan Blues following in full voice.

We travelled on the official Blues coaches and for once (despite leaving late again) we arrived in plenty of time so headed up the road to the away pub 'The Beeches Hotel'. There was also a bar in the pub car park and there were already loads of Bluenoses drinking there. It was a bit cold to be honest so once we had our drinks me, June and James headed inside with Steve following us not long afterwards. There was a bit of singing going on and the cricket was on live from Edgbaston.

It was soon time to head to the Pirelli Stadium for kickoff and we joined the queue at the turnstiles. Once inside we got chips and headed for the already packed terraces. There were loads of Blues fans trying to get on the terraces which seemed full and I just pushed and squeezed my way through as I was used to from the 80's. It was a bit tricky with a tray of chips in my hand but the pre match Thatchers probably helped my quest. We found a spot near the corner just as the teams were out.

The game kicked off with Lucas Jutkiewicz back after injury and Blues started brightly. The Blues fans were in great voice with loud renditions of 'Keep Right On' and 'we've got Redknapp, Harry Redknapp'. They also taunted the home fans with 'your grounds too small for us'. Then in the 29th minute Jacques Maghoma fired the ball home and the away end erupted in celebration. Blues were in control and went in at half time 1-0 ahead (just as I had predicted on FanScore).

I have no idea what went wrong in the second half but we were awful. We let Burton back into the game and it was soon 1-1. Blues just let Burton have the ball, didn't close them down or tackle them and gave the ball away easily. They didn't run or chase the ball and that tosser Lloyd Dyer, who always taunts the Blues fans, managed to score the winner against us yet again! Burton seem to be our bogey team as we have lost every one of the three competitive games we have played against them.

The Blues fans were not impressed with the way some of the players performed in the second half and rightly so. Once again the only bright spot was the introduction of Isaac Vassell who looked fast and dangerous. Blues fans sang 'we've got Vassell, Isaac Vassell I just don't think you understand, he came from Luton Town to send the villa down, we've got Isaac Vassell!'

The game finished in a 2-1 defeat and Harry Redknapp didn't pull any punches afterwards. He said that four or five players went missing in the second half and the team needs surgery and he will bring in more players and these players need not come crying to him when they don't get in the team because they have had their chance and he doesn't care. Harry said the Blues fans are fantastic and deserve better and if it's the last thing he does in management he will give them a good team, he said this team ruined Zola last year. Harry still maintains Blues will finish in the top six. I love this man! Birmingham are now 15th in the table.

Harry is working very hard in the transfer market and it finally seems to be paying dividends with the loan signing of Carl Jenkinson and Cohen Brammall from Arsenal and Sam Gallagher from Southampton. For tonight's game against Bournemouth only Cohen Brammall will be available to be in the squad.

As is the case these days for the Cup games only the Kop and the away section were open. The Kop was full though and it extended around the Kop/Tilton corner up to the border of the Tilton as over 8,000 were in attendance. The good news was that Isaac Vassell and Cohen Brammall were in the starting line up, hence Blues started the game lively.

Isaac Vassell was outstanding and has frightening pace which was almost matched by the lightning fast Cohen Brammall attacking from full back. Blues looked threatening and deservedly took the lead when Michael Kieftenbeld scored following a Gleeson corner. The Bluenoses on the Kop were on their feet. 'We're gonna win 8-0' rang out as the Bournemouth fans looked on. It was a brilliant first half and the improvement the new players have brought was clear for all the see.

Unfortunately it remains a tale of two halves and without our two best players Vassell and Brammall, who were withdrawn with injuries, we defended poorly and conceded two second half goals to lose 2-1 and exit the cup. Very disappointing but many positives to be seen in the first half performances of Isaac Vassell and Cohen Brammall. Another positive was the outstanding performance of youngster Wes Harding who came on as a substitute at right back.

Blues have been hit by the injury jinx again and it seems to be the curse of the strikers as four of our five strikers are now injured. In particular the promising new signing of Isaac Vassell and also the lively Che Adams. On the positive though, new signing Sam Gallagher and Carl Jenkinson are able to play. I do admit to being a bit concerned when I saw the line up as Harry seems to have opted for a very poor midfield with Gleeson starting. It was a lovely warm sunny day at St. Andrews as 20,000 came to enjoy the game. I even popped into the Bar 8 before the game for a cold drink to cool me down.

Unfortunately it turned into a day to forget as Blues lost 2-0 to the most boring side I have seen and the only word I can use to describe it was crap! Well that's the polite version anyway. I would love to know how much time the ball was actually in play as Reading spent the majority of the game time wasting, in particular their goalkeeper, and the very poor (crap) referee did nothing about it. I read recently that fans were being short changed as a recent Premier League game was shown to have had the ball in play for a total of 47 of the 90 minutes. It was probably the same today.

The fans were frustrated as Blues couldn't defend and our midfield was nonexistent. Our new player Sam Gallagher looked good but had no service. When the second Reading goal went in five minutes from time there was a mass exodus. Although I understand how they feel it breaks my heart to witness it. So Blues down to 20th but still a long way to go yet and if Harry can get another five or six players in before transfer deadline then there is still hope. If not then another relegation battle looks on the cards. It would be lovely to see nice entertaining football again as the last couple of years have been hard to watch and very disappointing.

Transfer Deadline Day

What an exciting transfer deadline day on 31st August 2017! Harry Redknapp made it brilliant for all us Blues fans as one player after another was linked with Birmingham City. Some were seen heading into our training ground at Wast Hills. I have never before been glued to Sky Sports deadline centre before or checked facebook for signings and fans updates. At one point Harry was linked with an audacious bid to get Arsenal's Jack Wilshere to Birmingham. But that never came off. The really exciting coup was Alex Song (former Arsenal and Barcelona midfielder) which looked certain as Harry told reporters he was joining on loan but at the very last minute it seems that the two clubs couldn't agree on the details and the deal was lost, much to our disappointment.

Blues did make some fantastic signings though and broke our transfer record to sign Brentford's highly rated Spanish midfielder Jota for a reported eight million. So by the end of the transfer window Harry has brought in a total of 14 players, all of them look exciting. They include David Stockdale (Brighton), Craig Gardener (WBA), Marc Roberts (Barnsley), Maxime Colin (Brentford), Isaac Vassell (Luton Town), Harlee Dean (Brentford), Cohen Brammall (Arsenal), Cheikh Ndoye, Sam Gallagher (Southampton- Loan), Jeremie Boga (Chelsea – Loan), Jason Lowe (Blackburn), and Liam Walsh (Everton – Loan).

Outgoing players included Clayton Donaldson (Sheffield United), Maikel Kieftenbeld (Derby), Robert Tesche on loan to VFL Bochum and Cheick Keith on loan to an Italian club. So it looks like we will have a completely new and exciting team to hopefully take the Championship by storm.

The following weekend after the transfer window closed was international weekend and with England already top of their group they headed to Malta to take on the team at the bottom of the group on a Friday night. Surely this would be a chance to add to our goal difference. I watched the game on live TV but have to admit being somewhat bored. I find the current England team boring as they just pass the ball around slowly all game and it seems to take ages to create a chance on goal. What happened to speed and urgency and, yes the passion of the England teams gone by!

Malta were quite a physical team putting in some pretty tough tackles and at half time the score was 0-0. It remained a dull game and it was with some relief that we cheered Harry Kane's opener in the 53rd minute. As the game drew towards it conclusion it looked as though it would remain 1-0 until the game came to life in the last seven minutes. The goals came from Bertrand on 85 minutes, Welbeck on 90+1 and Harry Kane's second goal in the 92nd minute which somewhat flattered England with a 4-0 score line.

The following Monday night saw second placed Slovakia come to Wembley to take on England. I wasn't looking forward to this game, which is unusual for me, but I think it is a really poor England side that we have at the moment. My worst fears were confirmed when poor defending contributed to Slovakia taking a shock lead in the 3rd minute. It was a shock to the system and the England players looked stunned. Slovakia continued to look threatening as England continued the slow passing approach in search of an equaliser. England looked nervous as several chances were either hit wide or over from the England players.

England won a corner in the 37th minute which Marcus Rashford hit low to the near post and Eric Dyer smashed the ball home for the equaliser. Wembley were on their feet, maybe more out of relief that anything else and England went in 1-1 at half time. We did play a bit better in the second half and Marcus Rashford scored a cracker to make up for his first half mistake that led to Slovakia's goal. So England got their result with a 2-1 win which keeps us top of the group and also helps Scotland's cause but it was still a boring game. I was happy with the win though.

It was a bit of an early start for the trip to Norwich as the coaches were due to leave at 9.30 am although they actually departed at 9.36 late as always. There was also a stop at the services at Cambridge which we were told would be 30 minutes but was in fact 45 minutes, again, as always! Hence we didn't arrive in Norwich till 1.45pm.

This was really disappointing for me as I was hoping to spend some time with my nephew Stephen who was traveling across from London for the game and his train arrived at 1pm. Luckily Steve, Brendan and Co were already in Norwich as they had travelled on the 'party bus' which left Birmingham at 8.30am and went directly to Norwich so that they were there early. They were all in the Nelson having lunch, drinks etc, so Stephen went to join them when he arrived and it was right opposite the train station.

When our coaches did finally arrive (we passed the Nelson and I could see them all outside enjoying their drinks) me and June headed straight to the Nelson to join them. It was lovely and sunny and everyone was outside by the river as the boats sailed past. I really liked it there as did June and Stephen. We had a great catch up discussing the new team and the comings and goings. It turns out that Maikel Kieftenbeld has had to return to Blues as some of the transfer paperwork wasn't completed correctly.

As we walked up to the stadium the sun was shining and we could hear the Blues fans singing in the away end. The Blues section was sold out again with over 1,500 making the trip. The game got underway and Blues did not start well and conceded a sloppy goal in the first 5 minutes. The Blues fans were unusually subdued after this apart from the occasional banter with the Norwich fans in the nearby stand.

Blues had the majority of the possession but had only one chance on goal and didn't defend too well and could easily have conceded a couple more goals. New signing Liam Walsh looked really good before he was substituted and Jota also looked exciting and he was the fans man of the match at the end of the game. Overall it was not a great performance, quite poor to be honest but I tried not to be too disappointed as it will take time for the team to gel. Harry had played six new signings from the onset and they need time to get used to playing together so I remain hopeful. The pouring rain that began just before half time and soaked us didn't help the mood.

Stephen walked back to the coaches with us and then headed to the train station to get his train and we set out on the long journey home. Blues are now down to 21st but with 40 games still to go we are not too concerned.

Two days later and I was off for a short break in Looe in Cornwall with my family. I had never been to Looe before and I was driving down in my new mini. We were staying in a lovely apartment at Black Rock holiday camp which was a short drive from Looe. It was lovely. It meant that I would miss the away match at Leeds on the Tuesday night. At least I wouldn't have to fork out the £37 for a match ticket! Once we had unpacked in our hillside apartment with a side on view of the sea me, mom Annette and Steve took the coastal path into Looe (big mistake as it was really far, up and down hills and through the undergrowth!) and had a lovely pub lunch in Ye Olde Salutation Inn. Then we got a taxi (£10) back to our apartment and a storm swept in.

It was torrential rain and high winds which meant that there was no way we could head into Looe (even in the car) and as there was no onsite food/shop we had to make do with beans on toast. On the bright side though, it meant I could watch the Leeds game on a live stream till the last ten minutes when it went off air.

Although Blues lost 2-0 to an in form Leeds (who then went top of the table) I thought we were the better team and did not deserve to lose. The team played really well together and were caught on the break and couldn't score ourselves. I was heartened by our performance though. Unfortunately we picked up injuries again which is rather worrying. Our star player Jota looks like he has an hamstring injury as does Che Adams who had just returned from injuring his other hamstring. We are having a lot of bad luck with injuries. Blues are now third from bottom in 23rd place.

The next day I drove into St. Austil and then on to Charlestown which was a lovely little bay where they filmed Poldark as well as lots of other films. There were lots of old ships in the bay and a lovely pub called the Pier House, where we stopped off for a drink before heading back. In the evening I drove into Looe and we had a lovely steak in the Ship Inn.

The following day I drove into Polperro, another historic little bay. It was a bit bigger the Charlestown with little cottages and shops and a few traditional pubs, one in particular called the Blue Peter Inn (known as the Blue House) was the last pub before France. We visited the model village and had lovely fish and chips from the 'Chip Ahoy' which I promptly dropped when I fell backwards over a cobblestone and onto my backside! Oh well, at least I had eaten the fish. In the evening we went into Looe to the Golden Guinea for dinner and the following day we were off home to Birmingham feeling relaxed.

It was great to be heading back to St. Andrews to see Harry's new look Blues take on a Preston team doing very well for themselves so far this season. It was a good crowd of 21,268 with several having travelled from Preston too. The game got underway and although Jota is out as well as 3 of our 4 forwards, Blues played really well with some good football on display. In the 35th minute Blues deservedly took the lead with a brilliant goal from Maxime Colin who scored from a tight angle after losing his player in the box.

The team were playing well with Jeremie Boga terrorising the Preston defence and Liam Walsh, who came on for the injured Jason Lowe in the first minute, running the midfield. Maghoma was also having a good game and Blues went into the break 1-0 to the good.

Blues looked a different team in the second half though and conceded on 56 minutes when they allowed Preston's Johnson to pass everyone for at least 40 yards before firing home. Goalkeeper Stockdale rightly went ballistic at his defenders and from then on Blues players heads seemed to drop and we conceded another two sloppy goals. So in a 12 minute period Blues lost the plot and conceded three goals. Despite attempts to get back into the game Blues lost 3-1 and we went away feeling downhearted. When will our luck change? I can see this will be an exciting team (once they gel and our injuries are sorted) given time though.

However, time is something we don't have as I was to discover whilst out in the evening at the lovely Marco Pierre White restaurant an the 25th floor of the Cube for Steve's birthday meal with Annette, mom and Steve. The beautiful views of the city were ruined for me by the news that our owners had sacked Harry Redknapp. To say I am gutted is an understatement. I have waited 40 odd years to see a manager like Harry at St. Andrews, a proper football manager and he was our best ever hope of seeing exciting, proper football back at Birmingham City. I cannot believe that these clueless owners from China could be so foolish.

Once again the owners have made a massive mistake which will no doubt cost us again. First they sacked Gary Rowett when Blues were 6th in the League, then they gave Zola 20+ games despite winning only 2 (and he had to resign!) yet they give Harry Redknapp only THREE games with HIS team, a total of ONE WEEK! They have no idea at all about football and it doesn't help that they don't even speak English.

Chapter Sixteen - Harry's Gone

I am heartbroken to see Harry go as are the vast majority of Bluenoses. When interviewed on the radio he remained a gentleman saying these things happen but he should have had longer. The team he inherited were a disgrace but he has given us the nucleus for a very good team. I wonder if he has been 'used' as most of these new players came in because of Harry Redknapp (and most people bought season tickets because of Harry Redknapp). What now?

Blues have announced that Lee Carsley will be caretaker manager until a replacement is found. Lee Carsley is a brummie and was in charge of Blues U23's and England U23's

For the first time in ages I wasn't really looking forward to a match. I was looking forward to the trip to Derby but I am still really downhearted about the loss of Harry Redknapp and the lack of confidence in our owners. Of course I will get behind Lee Carsley and the team and hope and pray that we can turn this around soon.

There were lots of coaches heading to Derby today and the short trip passed quickly. Great to be traveling with Terry and Nigel again (as well as June & James of course) and we had a real laugh on the way. Once there me, June and James headed off in search for a KFC which we found nearby and had a lovely lunch before heading back to the stadium. There was about 3,500 Bluenoses in the away end and the atmosphere was electric. 'Keep Right On' was being sang and everyone seemed jovial.

The game got underway and the team resembled Harry's team as Lee Carsley had not made many changes. Goalkeeper David Stockdale was out with a broken arm (yes another injury!) and Bluenose Craig Gardener was back in the team. Blues were playing well and I thought we were the better team. I didn't think much of Gary Rowett's Derby to be honest and thought Blues would go on to win the game. That said we don't seem to create many chances or look clinical in front of goal. Chelsea loanee Jeremie Boga was terrorising the Derby defence and would easily go passed three or four of their players each time he ran at them. Half time came with the score 0-0.

In the second half Blues took up where they left off. Boga and Gallagher had to come off in the second period to be replaced by 'the Juke' Lucas Jutkiewicz and Isaac Vassell. The effect was immediate as 'the Juke' scored with his first touch of the ball in the 44th minute, a stooping header into the bottom corner of the net from a Craig Gardener free kick – 1-0!

The Blues end erupted with wild celebrations that seemed to go on for ages and a flare sent blue smoke into the air. It was pure elation and relief and was the first time this season that Blues have taken the lead in a game and boy did we enjoy the moment. And a 'moment' is what it was as Derby were level two minutes later.

I couldn't believe it – well I could as we can still be really poor at defending balls into the six yard box. The Derby fans were delighted and they were taunting us from our right side which resulted in hundreds of Bluenoses attempting to confront them across the dividing barrier. The police and stewards were suddenly called into action to keep the two sets of fans apart and a few arrests were made. It have to say though that it was only Blues fans who were arrested despite the Derby fans doing exactly the same things and inciting the Blues fans.

Despite Blues having several corners and looking the better team we couldn't get the winner and the game finished 1-1. Still a good away point at Derby that I would have gladly accepted before this game but I felt a little disappointed that we hadn't won the game. Blues remain second from bottom as bottom club Bolton lost again.

With Lee Carsley still caretaker manager and no news of who Blues new manager would be, Blues were up against Sheffield Wednesday at St. Andrews. There were 20,365 inside St. Andrews which is really good for a midweek match especially with our current form and all the uncertainty and it was pouring with rain.

As always though the fans got behind the team and were rewarded when Isaac Vassell fired Blues in front in the 76th minute as he latched onto a through ball from Jacques Maghoma. The stadium exploded with noise as the Bluenoses celebrated. I jumped around wildly. We haven't had many goals to celebrate this season so it was really great, especially as it turned out to be the winner as Blues secured victory with a 1-0 score line. Are we about to turn the corner? I really hope so. Blues are in 22nd position.

Blues have finally decided on the new manager and Steve Cotterill was appointed in the post. I am not really sure this is the right decision but I will get behind him and hope that he can bring the team together and take us forward. It was announced that he will take over after the Hull game which would now be Lee Carsley's last game in charge. So it was with some optimism that we headed off to Hull with Blues once again selling out the away allocation with 1,500 making the trip.

As usual we headed into the Walton Social Club which already contained quite a lot of Bluenoses so it was nice to catch up with a few of those we knew. Then we headed off through the fair and after purchasing a Hull City fanzine we headed into the away end where the Blues fans were in great voice as always. I had been talking to a Hull fan outside who had said that Hull have been awful so far this season so what was to follow was truly shocking. It was Blues who put on an awful performance, going behind after only 7 minutes and we were so bad that we were 3-0 down with only 26 minutes played.

The Blues fans never stopped singing though. Even though Blues were playing so shockingly bad we still did our club proud with our support. It remained 3-0 until the 72nd minute when Blues again caved in and conceded another 3 goals in 15 minutes and an embarrassing score line of 6-0. The Hull fans were taunting us and throwing bottles and missiles at us and yet it seemed to be only Blues fans being evicted or arrested.

In the 91st minute Sam Gallagher scored his first goal for the club as he added a consolation to make the final score 6-1. Blues fans sang 'how shit must you be – we scored a goal' and chants of "easy!" It did look like it took a deflection though and Hull fans responded with 'how shit must you be, we scored for you'.

The Hull fans were now taunting the Blues fans whilst safely behind the police line separating the two sets of fans but some Blues fans left the ground and went round into their section appearing behind them and taking the Hull fans and the police by surprise. Hence it was kicking off for sometime outside as the police tried to keep them apart which then led to a bit of a delay in the coaches leaving. So it was a long trip home after such a heavy defeat and Blues remain in 22nd place. I don't know when this nightmare will ever end. I will be glad to be going away on holiday next week.

The following weekend was the international break and England beat Slovenia 1-0 at Wembley on the Thursday to qualify for the 2018 World Cup in Russia. On the Sunday England won 1-0 in Lithuania which I watched in the Smugglers Inn in Cap Salou as we enjoyed a Sunday roast.

I was going to miss the Cardiff game due to my holiday and should have been heading off to Tenerife but due to Monarch going bust a week before we were due to fly it meant we lost our Tenerife holiday. However, just days before we had been due to travel we managed to book a holiday in Spain. The original holiday would have meant that I also missed the Millwall game but the new holiday meant flying back on the Friday so I would now be able to make the trip to Millwall.

So we watched the Cardiff game in Salou in a British pub called The Red Lion which had loads of TV's showing the Blues match and two very large screens, one of which we pulled up our chairs in front of along with some other Bluenoses. We were also joined by a Wolves fan who was hoping that Blues would do them a favour by beating top of the table Cardiff which would then mean they could go top if Wolves beat Villa tomorrow – which he tells us he is flying home for. He had also been left without a holiday and had booked last minute like us when Monarch went bust.

Just before kickoff I thought I could hear loads of Bluenoses coming up the road singing 'Keep Right On' but it turned out to be the Bluenoses inside St. Andrews as they had just put the sound on. The atmosphere sounded great and I was as excited as usual, although after last weeks game against Hull I was just hoping to avoid a thrashing from the current table toppers Cardiff.

The game got underway and I was pleasantly surprised as Blues played really well and had the best of the play. I was on my feet when Che Adams scored in the 19th minute to put Blues ahead. It was fantastic and we outplayed Cardiff for the entire game. Despite over 6 minutes of injury time (which always seems to happen if Blues are winning) Blues held on to achieve a great victory and move us up to 19th in the league table. I had also predicted the first goal time on the Blues FanScore so I was well pleased. I happily headed off to get the bus back to our hotel in Cap Salou.

So I was back in England and looking forward to the trip to Millwall. I thought Blues may be able to win this game. Unfortunately it was a 5.30 kick off due to the game being shown live on Sky again. Our coaches arrived about an hour before kickoff and we were taken directly to the away turnstiles. Once again it was a sell out away allocation of 2000 and the Blues fans were in great voice.

I don't think the players responded to our support though as they didn't play at all well. We did have probably the best of the first half though but halftime came with a score of 0-0. Millwall came out for the second half with more hunger than Blues and they went ahead in the 48th minute much to our disappointment. Blues fans responded to the Millwall fans with 'nobody likes you – because your shit'. 'Keep Right On' also rang out in an effort to lift our team but it didn't work and Blues conceded another soft goal on 76 minutes and never looked like getting back into the game. Despite having 16 shots we never seemed to look like scoring.

So a really disappointing 2-0 defeat with the highlight being a text from my nephew Stephen at half time with a photo of me, June and James being shown live on Sky as we pondered the first half. Very funny!

The police kept us locked in the outside away area with the gates closed which led to a bit of a crush and it did kick off a bit. We had to wait over an hour before the coaches were allowed to leave and then we were taken by police escort through central London. It was quite nice really with all the bridges illuminated. We didn't get home till late though and we were knackered.

Even though it was an early kick off on a Sunday I was really looking forward to the derby game against Villa. Blues are overdue a win against them and although our current form is poor, form goes out of the window in these games.

We arrived at St. Andrews in plenty of time and awaited Stephen's arrival as he had travelled up from London for the game. As usual it was great to see him again and we headed into the stadium. A few drinks were purchased as we soaked up the atmosphere in the concourse as the usual songs rang out, 'shit on the villa' being today's favourite.

Then we made our way to our seats and St. Andrews was buzzing with 24,408 inside the stadium. Blues started well and were by far the better team. Cheikh Ndoye should have scored with a header in the 39th minute but it was saved by the keeper. All the Blues fans had been given clappers on their seats to add to the atmosphere (as if it needs to be added to!) and these were soon used as missiles to pelt any villa player that came into range. If villa had a corner they were pelted, if they had a throw in they were pelted and if they feigned injury (which they did often) they were pelted. It was quite amusing really and did seem to intimidate the villa players.

It was goalless at half time and in the second half Blues continued to dominate and had the better chances. Jota was put through for a one on one with the villa goalkeeper but the occasion got the better of him as he blasted high and over. Villa hit the woodwork twice in the last few minutes but it would have been a travesty if Blues had lost. So the game finished all square at 0-0 but I was filled with optimism as Blues had been by far the better team and really should have won. I was happy as I headed home and Stephen headed off to get his train back to London. Perhaps Steve Cotterill will change our fortunes after all.

I thought Blues stood a good chance against Brentford despite manager Steve Cotterill saying they are light years ahead of us in the football they play at Brentford. This is why Steve Cotterill does not inspire me and makes me doubt that he is the man to lead Birmingham City to better things.

He proved to be right though as Blues succumbed to two goals in the last 15 minutes on a cold Wednesday night at St. Andrews. Blues did manage 15 shots though, Brentford had 16, and only 2 of Blues shots were on target. It was a pretty depressing night overall and another game in which Blues failed to take their chances and conceded too easily.

Despite the cold 19,045 hardy souls turned up to get behind the team. Many left before the end though, after Brentford scored their second, I'm sad to say. These days when Blues go behind you know that it is very unlikely that they will get back in the game – unlike years gone by when our team fought till the end and often rescued a draw or snatched a win. In recent times there is just no urgency or passion.

Next up was an away trip to Barnsley and with our current away record I wasn't overly excited. We had a pleasant trip on the coach with Terry, Nigel and Charlie on good form and a few laughs were had. On arrival we headed into the local leisure centre bar for pre match refreshments and as usual the bar was already full of Blues fans. Once our glasses were empty we headed back down the hill and into the away end of Barnsley's Oakwell ground.

It wasn't long before we were wishing we hadn't bothered. Once again our allocation was sold out and we were singing 'Keep Right On' as Marc Roberts should have put us ahead in the first minute with a header. It would prove to be a costly miss as seconds later Barnsley took the lead with what was a poor goal to concede. It was disheartening conceding in only the second minute.

The Barnsley fans celebrated but the Blues fans sang 'your nothing special – we lose every week!' As it neared half time with the score still 1-0 Bluenoses sang 'how shit must you be – it's one 1-0'. I think everyone was fed up by now with months, years even, of Blues playing without passion, but our singing continued throughout, all be it gallows humour.

In the second half Blues were really poor again and Barnsley grabbed a second goal in the 68th minute. The Bluenoses had finally had enough and sang 'we're fucking shit'. Blues never looked like getting back into the game with passes going astray and showed no passion whatsoever. Some of the Blues fans sang 'your not fit to wear the shirt' and this continued loudly as the final whistle sounded and the players had to pass the away fans to get to the dressing room. I personally was embarrassed by this and many of the Blues fans also took offence and fought amongst themselves and blue flares were set off. It was horrible to witness and to realise how low we have sunk. Hearing them sing this was probably the lowest point of all my years following Blues.

All in all it was an awful afternoon and if we continue like this I can see Blues playing in League One next season. Something needs to happen and now! The dressing room needs to be sorted out immediately and any bad apples removed. On that note we boarded the coaches and headed home somewhat despondent.

The following Saturday Blues were entertaining Nottingham Forest, who were on the back of a 4-0 win while Blues were losing at Barnsley. For the first time ever I really wasn't looking forward to my afternoon at St. Andrews. I feel despondent at the recent form Blues have been showing, at times they can't even pass a ball to each other. I will never give up on my beloved Blues though.

A crowd of 21,071 were in attendance and amazingly Blues played well, with the lively Che Adams scoring a cracker to put Blues 1-0 ahead. Also amazingly, Blues played well for the full ninety minutes to secure a valuable win which takes us out of the bottom three and gives us some breathing space. It's a shame we just can't play consistently well at the moment. I still don't have much faith in Steve Cotterill though but hopefully that will come.

On Wednesday Blues travelled up to Middlesbrough and I was working and so I couldn't make the long trip. The same must have been said for many others too as, for once, Blues didn't sell out our allocation and only around 400 hardy souls made the trip. I did watch most of the game on a live stream before it was taken down and I wasn't really impressed with a 2-0 defeat and another Jekyll and Hyde performance. It is somewhat embarrassing that Blues still have the worst away record in the entire football league. At least we have managed to stay out of the bottom three for now.

Following the defeat at Middlesbrough we headed to Sheffield to see Blues take on high flying Sheffield United having once again sold our allocation and we noisily filled the bottom tier behind the goal at Brammall Lane. Blues fans were in excellent voice and filled the aisles as well as the seats.

The game got underway and although Blues are still poor and sending passes astray they did look a bit better than of late and surprised everyone when Jeremie Boga scored, what must be goal of the season, from outside the penalty area and curled perfectly into the top corner of the net just before half time. The away end went mental at the rare sight of an away goal and the home contingent were silent.

So at half time Blues went in with a 1-0 lead and smoke from a blue flare rose into the air from a celebratory flare set off in the Blues concourse. The question was – could Blues hold onto that lead for the whole of the second half? Unfortunately the answer was no, despite bravely defending, Blues conceded in the 71st minute and we had to settle for a point. We would have been happy with this prior to kick off but having led 1-0 and had a glorious chance to make it 2-0 when Jutkiewicz wasted an opportunity just before half time, we were somewhat disappointed as we headed home.

The next match was a big derby game as Blues took on table toppers Wolves at St. Andrews. Wolves currently have an really good team and are already 4 points clear at the top with a game in hand, whereas Blues have slipped into the relegation zone, although a win or draw tonight would haul us out of it. To be honest I don't think any of us can see us winning. Just before kickoff the draw was made for the 3rd round of the FA Cup and I was really disappointed as Blues drew Burton Albion at home. I fancied a nice trip to a ground I have never been to before.

There was a massive (somewhat over the top) police presence around St. Andrews and they had erected massive metal barriers making it a long trip back to the car after the game. There were 19,641 inside the stadium with around 2000 coming from Wolverhampton and despite the cold weather the Blues contingent were in good voice.

The match kicked off and it wasn't long – eight minutes to be exact – when Blues gifted Wolves a goal as Jonathan Grounds passed the ball directly to a Wolves player on the edge of the penalty area. Stockdale made two great saves but he didn't have much defence around him and each rebound fell to a Wolves player and despite the third attempt being cleared on the line a goal was awarded by the goal line technology system and Blues were 1-0 down and chasing the game.

Blues were awful in the first period with around eight out of ten passes going astray. Wolves should then have been reduced to ten men when one of their players slapped Stephen Gleeson in the face and only received a yellow card! The Bluenoses really got behind their team in the second half which did seem to inspire more fight and passion but we rarely looked like scoring. To add insult to injury Harlee Dean tried to separate some players in a scuffle and promptly got sent off in the 83rd minute. Disgraceful refereeing! The referee was a total idiot and I am convinced he had gold and black underwear on!

So the game finished with a 1-0 defeat and the big headed dingles were gloating. Blues remained in the bottom three, just one point adrift but with a goal difference of -18. This time last year Blues were 6th. What have our Chinese owners done to destroy our club? It's heartbreaking to watch.

I was a bit worried about getting to Fulham as there had been quite a lot of snow fall on the Friday in Birmingham, although none in London. It did indeed prove a bit difficult to get a taxi to New Street station but we did manage to make it for our 9.10 am train to London Euston. We arrived in London at about 10.35 and got on the tube to Putney Bridge and headed into the Rocket pub, which was already full of Bluenoses. We managed to find a table and had ordered a big breakfast by the time my nephew Stephen arrived. The breakfast was lovely and we were treated to a few renditions of the national anthem by nearby Bluenoses which was great.

Just after 2.15pm we drank up and headed out into the cold and through the park to join the 4,100 Bluenoses in the away end at Craven Cottage. It was a brilliant atmosphere as always and the entire Blues contingent were in great voice as 'Keep Right On' filled the air. The match got underway and Blues seemed to start brightly but then conceded another sloppy goal on 13 minutes and it was the same old story as heads seemed to drop. Blues had several corners but didn't look like scoring, despite the vocal support from the 4,100 Bluenoses. A chorus of boos rang out as the players trudged off at half time.

The second half wasn't any better and the players looked like they really don't care. Blues had one shot on target all game apart from when David Davis put the ball in the net after the whistle had blown for offside and the away end exploded in celebration. It was really funny as it was like a real goal celebration and went on for ages and a blue flare was lobbed into the goalmouth, sending blue smoke into the air. Brilliant!

Blues won a penalty 15 minutes from time and up stepped Jeremie Boga to blast it high and over the bar. It just typifies how we are playing these days. Sad to say some Blues fans fought amongst themselves as feelings were running high between the younger fans (snowflakes) who sang songs such as 'your not fit to wear the shirt' and 'Stevie Cotterill – he ain't got a clue' (they were a minority) and older Bluenoses who took exception to this, knowing how it would effect the players in the middle of a game. It didn't help though and Blues lost once again, that's 9 defeats in 11 away games. When will it end?

We then headed off to Parsons Green for a drink before heading back to Euston where we had the misfortune of bumping into the Millwall yobs returning from their trip to Villa. A few missiles were thrown as they met Blues and a couple of skirmishes but it was mostly handbags as the heavy police presence moved in to move them on. To add insult to injury our train was cancelled thanks to Virgin staff not turning in for work (no snow in London remember) as was the train prior to ours. This meant three trainloads now packed onto one train and resulted in me, June and James traveling in the first class luggage rack from London to Birmingham – oh what fun.

I saw Steve Cotterill's post match interview which depressed me even more as he is just clueless and I wondered if I was at the same game. If he cannot inspire us the fans, how on earth can he inspire the players? This is the worst team I have seen at Blues in nearly 40 years. I will Keep Right On as always though.

Some post match comments from the Fulham fans were interesting which included – "unbelievable support from Brum to be fair. Another case of today's generation of footballers not showing simple levels of humaneness. Those little things matter to fans!". Another Fulham fan said "of the teams I've seen this year BCFC were the worst. No fight, they were neither physical nor skillfull. Shame as they had the best fans at the Cottage this year. Loud + good gallows humour".

Comments from the Blues fans – "Blues fans must be some of the best in the country. Haven't won an away match all season, currently 22nd in the league yet we bring over 4,000 to Fulham". Another reported "the humour of the Blues fans yesterday was incredible, the fake celebrations, even Fulham fans were clapping us!"

I was actually quite poorly today with a chest infection but I dragged myself from my sickbed and headed down to St. Andrews. I wrapped up well and enjoyed a festive turkey and stuffing roll inside the stadium with June, which was lovely. Despite the weather, the proximity to Christmas and Blues current form, over 20,000 were once again inside St. Andrews.

The game got underway and Blues looked poor and nervous from the start and conceded another soft goal from a set piece which was headed home by QPR's Robinson – the first goal of his career. Blues went in at half time 1-0 down to a chorus of boos around the stadium. In the second half, with the crowd behind them, Blues started to play a bit better and got a lifeline when Sam Gallagher was quick to react when the QPR keeper failed to hold Kieftenbeld's long range shot. Gallagher got a foot to the rebound and the ball was in the back of the net to an almighty roar that nearly took the roof of St. Andrews. Oh how we have been starved of goals!

It was game on again and with Blues growing in confidence it looked like they would go on to win. But of course we can't defend can we and conceded again, another goal from QPR's Robinson who has never scored before today and now has two! With the goal coming seven minutes from time the Blues fans, somewhat disappointingly, streamed from the stadium. It proved to be the winner as QPR got their first away win of the season. Typical! With Sunderland and Burton Albion winning, Blues have now dropped to bottom of the league and our lowest point of the season. I headed home feeling even worse than I had this morning.

It's been a year since our owners sacked Gary Rowett and began our spectacular decline. It was summed up in an article in the Football League Paper the next day: 'it's a year since Gary Rowett was handed his P45 by Birmingham, a decision that looks more ludicrous with every passing week. His replacement Gianfranco Zola, oversaw a catastrophic nosedive down the Championship table. Harry 'Houdini' Redknapp came in and performed a rescue act in the final three games. Harry departed in September after signing 14 players for more than £15m, which, with the players Zola signed in January, means it has cost Birmingham in excess of £20m to blunder from the edge of the play offs a year ago to the relegation places. As Steve Cotterill tries in vain to galvanise this disparate group, silence abounds from the boardroom, where there appears to be not the merest semblance of strategy. And Rowett? Doing what he does best. Crafting an industrious, professional, united team at Derby, who look certainties for the play offs – at least'.

The following Tuesday Blues announced that our Welsh wizard David Cotterill was leaving after his contract was terminated as he is not in Steve Cotterill's plans. I cannot believe it! Blues have got rid of the wrong Cotterill! David Cotterill said he is gutted to be leaving Blues as he loves playing for the club. I am gutted too, as he is one of the most skilful players Blues have. Someone at Blues is destroying our club. Why else is all this happening since Trillion Trophy Asia took over?

Two days before Christmas and June and I were heading off on the long journey to Sunderland. We must be mad! We were joined on the coach by Terry, Nigel and Charlie and enjoyed an entertaining trip up north broken briefly by a stop at the services where June and I had a Chinese. It was windy and cold when we arrived but once inside the Stadium of Light, where we were sheltered from the wind, it was okay.

I've not been to Sunderland for a while, since Mikel Forrsell scored for Blues in the Cup a few years ago, so I was quite surprised and impressed by the new upper tier where the away fans are now situated. It is really high up like at Newcastle with a cracking view. Over 1200 had made the trip including quite a few Santa's and a banana. Me, June, Nigel and Charlie had blue Santa hats on and Terry had a Christmas pudding hat on! June and I had wrapped thick blue tinsel around our neck as a throwback to the 1980's. It looked great.

We weren't very optimistic about the match but Blues surprised us and played well. Mind you, Sunderland were the worst team I have seen this season so far. The players seemed to have more space and time on the ball and their passing improved and we played well. Sam Gallagher ran his legs off as usual and when he turned and scored from a good through ball, the away end erupted. 'We've scored a goal!' rang out and the Bluenoses were in good voice as always.

However, 5 minutes later Sunderland were level as Blues conceded a soft goal. It is so disheartening that this keeps happening, especially as Blues scoring a goal this season is as rare as rocking horse shit! Blues continued to play well though and created lots of chances, which in itself is unusual. Colin and Jota on the right were tearing Sunderland apart and Jota thoroughly earned his man of the match award and I was really disappointed when Cotterill took him off near the end. By then though, Sam Gallagher had very unfairly received his marching orders following a second yellow card (since rescinded) and Blues were down to ten men. Even with ten men we should have won but had to settle for a point and we remain rooted to the bottom of the table. It was a long trip home but we didn't let it get us down and we sang a few songs on our way back to Birmingham.

The Norwich game would be my first Boxing Day game since I moved back to England as I am usually working it. This year though I had worked Christmas Day (with my blue Santa hat on) and could now go to St. Andrews to watch Blues take on Norwich City. I wasn't looking forward to it to be honest and most Bluenoses seemed really despondent at the moment with talk of relegation to League One. Stephen was home for Christmas so he came to the match too.

What a disappointment it turned out to be. Blues started brightly but conceded another awful goal where our defenders didn't concentrate at a free kick and we were 1-0 down to a poor looking Norwich team. Shoulders dropped again and with only one striker 'Juke' available Blues never looked like scoring. I don't think anyone was surprised when Norwich scored another soft goal on 70 minutes and many left St. Andrews in despair. Those that stayed did try to rally their team with 'Keep Right On' and other songs but Blues lost the game 2-0 and boos rang out at the final whistle.

Chapter Seventeen - Cotterill's Lost The Plot

The situation is just awful at the moment and the football is poor. Manager Steve Cotterill seems clueless in his interviews and all hope is fading fast. Our club is being destroyed and I am not the only one finding this extremely hard to deal with.

A good crowd of over 21,000 packed into St. Andrews for the last game of 2017 as Leeds Utd were our visitors. Leeds currently sit in the play off places and have won their last 4 games in stark contrast to Blues recent results and rock bottom position. Leeds also brought a good away following but they were drowned out by our passionate home support.

I was beginning to feel that it is becoming a chore visiting St. Andrews lately but to my surprise (and everyone else's) Blues started brightly and played really well. It was the best I have seen Blues play since Leeds away at the beginning of the season. The crowd responded by getting behind the team and 'Keep Right On' and 'We're Birmingham' echoed around the stadium. Despite our dominance Blues went in at half time with the score at 0-0.

At half time there was a memorial for all the Blues fans who sadly passed away in 2017 and their names were read out and displayed on the big screen to applause from both the Band Leeds fans. The reading of their names was followed by a chorus of 'Keep Right On' for those we had lost.

The second half got underway and Blues continued to play really well. Every Blues player showed fight and put in a great shift. Blues has loads of chances but no luck and I was beginning to wonder if we would ever score. Then in the 83rd minute Jota hit a cracking shot from the edge of the area which their keeper couldn't hold and the rebound fell to Maghoma who smashed the ball into the net – 1-0 and the stadium exploded in celebration. Some players ran to the Tilton and some to the Dugout in celebration. I was so excited.

What a performance and the final whistle sounded for a well deserved Blues victory. The fans had played their part too and hearing the great escape tune being sang loudly was brilliant. I also enjoyed 'Jimmy Saville – he's one of your own!' which got an immediate reaction from the Leeds fans. So a great result but as is always the case the other teams at the bottom – Bolton and Sunderland both won and Burton drew which means Blues stay rooted to the foot of the table but only 3 points from safety.

The first away trip of 2018 was at Reading and I was praying that our fortunes would change. I was not particularly confident but hopeful as I know Blues well. It was me, June, Terry, Charlie and Nigel on the coach heading to Reading and as usual it was late to leave and took the long route which meant that we arrived at the Madejski Stadium at 7.20pm for the 8pm kick off. It was pouring with rain as I met up with Stephen who had travelled from London and we headed into the away turnstiles. Over 1100 Bluenoses had made the trip and were in good voice as usual.

I enjoyed a nice pre match cider and then the game got underway. Blues were in last season's red away kit and started well. Just like the Leeds game everyone was putting in a shift and playing well although Jonathan Grounds did seem to be letting the Reading players fly pass him at times – again. In the 24th minute the deadlock was broken when Jacques Maghoma smashed the ball in the net to put Blues 1-0 ahead and the away end erupted in noise. I looked around for Nigel, who had been telling us how shit Maghoma is, on the way down on the coach, and I shouted 'he's shit isn't he!' and we all laughed.

Blues were now singing 'how shit must you be – we're winning away!' to a lot a of applause from the Reading fans. They replied 'how shit must we be – you're winning away!' which I thought was quite funny. Blues were playing well but it didn't stop me being nervous. We continued to play well and Jeremie Boga, who was having a great game, sent a lovely ball to Sam Gallagher who shot past the Reading keeper to score. He and the rest of the team ran to the away fans as we celebrated wildly. To be 2-0 up was brilliant, although no more than we deserved. Bluenoses sang 'how shit must you be – we've scored more than one!' as the Reading fans looked despondent.

Even at 2-0 I couldn't relax. Blues fans sang 'we want three' to which I joined in. The final whistle went to a roar from the away end and boos from the remaining Reading fans. As we celebrated and sang 'Keep Right On' the players came over to applaud us. Once again though, I was disappointed that our manager Steve Cotterill did not come over to us. We had travelled a long way on an awful rainy night and got behind our team (as always) and it would have been nice for him to acknowledge that. Maybe he was just letting his players take the plaudits.

We celebrated all the way home, singing several songs including the ten German bombers and we all dream of a team of Kieftenbeld's. We also sang 'if I had the wings of a sparrow' as we drove past Villa Park. What a great night despite the weather and our first away win of the season. This takes Blues off the bottom of the table as we move above Sunderland and are one point from safety as both Bolton and Burton won yesterday.

Birmingham City v Burton Albion is not the most attractive Cup tie but the FA Cup is special – well to me anyway – obviously not to everyone these days as only just over 7,000 turned up at St. Andrews on this winters day. Only the Kop was open, which only succeeded in killing the atmosphere as all the 'singers' were either separated on the Kop or at home. Sad times indeed.

Despite the atmosphere being like a 'behind closed doors' game Blues did manage to win the match with another goal from Sam Gallagher. That's 4 in 5 games now. Burton proved a difficult game and they probably had the better chances but Blues came away with a good 1-0 win and into the hat for the 4th round draw. While the game had been in the final minutes news had filtered through that Villa had lost 3-1 at home to League One side Peterborough. The Blues fans sang 'we're the only team in Birmingham that's going to Wembley, Wembley! Wembley!'.

So a great result and that is now 3 wins in a row. On Monday the draw for the 4th round was made and Blues were drawn away at Premier League club Huddersfield Town. Bring it on.

I was feeling a bit more confident when I headed to St. Andrews for the game against Derby, there was a good crowd of over 22,000 although Derby brought 3,488 fans. Derby were unbeaten in 9 games but I felt we could do well against them. Blues played really well and should have been at least 2 goals up after 6 minutes as Jonathan Grounds hit the post in the first few minutes and the outcome may well have been very different if that had gone in. Instead Blues were well and truly mugged and the 3-0 final score to Derby did not reflect the game at all.

Derby's first goal was deflected for an own goal from their first chance. The second, in the second half was a clearance that fell extremely luckily to them and the third was a result of Blues pushing up with Blues Jonathan Grounds having hit the post for a second time. Derby should have been reduced to ten men when Keftenbeld was deliberately elbowed in the face but it went unpunished as did other fouls committed by the Derby players. I was quite surprised that a Gary Rowett team was playing like this. Somewhat reassuring was the fact that Sunderland, Bolton and Burton all lost which means no change in the bottom four.

I was feeling a bit more optimistic following Blues performances of late. I know we lost to Derby but I didn't think the score was a true reflection of the game and I was heartened by our performance. Hence I, as well as the others – June, Terry, Nigel and Charlie were in good form on the journey to Preston. My sisters boyfriend Steve was traveling on the 'party bus' which left at 8am and was going via a stop in Blackpool. Good luck with that!

Once we reached Preston the coaches were met by the police who escorted us to the stadium and we arrived around 1pm. I wanted to see the new Dick Kerr Ladies monument so we headed there, had a look and then went into the nearby Tom Finney's Bar which Terry, Nigel and Charlie were refused entry into. So me and June had a quick drink as it was a 'home bar' and then headed to the 'away pub' called 'The Sumners' which, in contrast, was full of singing Blues fans.

I had hoped to meet up with my old mate Ballie (who I played football with at Blues Ladies) but she was in a pub by the railway (she had travelled from Liverpool where she now lives) and that was also packed full of singing Blues fans. Ballie said she would try to get to us but didn't manage to, so me and June walked up the road to the ground and got in ten minutes before kick off. The massive concourse was full of singing Bluenoses and there was blue smoke from flares that had been set off below the stands. Even in the toilets you could smell the smoke from the flares. It was brilliant.

We had to fight our way up to the stands, it was that packed. Over 2,200 Bluenoses had made the journey and the away end was buzzing. Blues were playing in red again and started brightly, creating several chances. As is always the case though, we conceded a sloppy goal from Preston's only attack when Blues Marc Roberts headed across his own goal to gift the Preston player a goal at the far post. Blues went in 1-0 down at half time but I wasn't too worried as we were playing that well that I thought Blues could get back into the game.

At half time I popped down to the toilets and found Ballie in the concourse so we had that catch up after all, which was great. Blues came out for the second half and played really well. Even Maghoma (man of the match) was working hard and getting stuck into the tackles. Every Blues player was playing their hearts out and Blues completely dominated Preston.

The goal did come too as Maghoma dispossessed a Preston player on the edge of the area and passed to Sam Gallagher who side footed it into the empty net from just inside the area. The away end exploded with noise and celebration which seemed to go on forever. It was no more than Blues deserved and, despite pushing for the winner, had to settle for a point from the 1-1 draw. After the game Preston's manager said that they (Preston) didn't even deserve a point. It's given us all hope though and despite Sunderland winning Blues remain second from bottom as Burton lost 6-0 at Fulham and they drop to the bottom. Blues are only one point off safety.

The transfer window is not going too well at the moment though with no new signings and Blues letting David Cotterill, Stephen Gleeson and Emile Nsue, all very good players, go. On a positive note Maikel Keftenbeld has signed till 2021 and Jonathan Grounds has had a new contract too (not sure about that one – if it's good or not). There is also interest in Cheikh N'Doye but I don't think that Steve Cotterill will let him go as he is an important part of the Blues squad.

I was really excited for the Huddersfield game as it's the FA Cup and Blues are still in the competition at the 4th round against a Premier League team. I'm glad it's away from home as our support is better away in the FA Cup as it has been 'dead' at St. Andrews in the last round with over half the ground shut. For today's game Blues are taking 18 coaches, a double decker, a minibus, loads of cars and those traveling by train. There should be around 3000 as Blues have sold our full allocation of 2300 so Huddersfield are opening the rest of the stand for pay on the day to away fans.

When we arrived at Huddersfield there were Blues fans everywhere as we headed into the away end. The atmosphere was brilliant as the partisan away following sang throughout the game. Blues were playing in red again, which really seems to be bringing us some luck at last. Me, June, Nigel and Terry decided that we will wear our red away shirts next week to travel to Sheffield Wednesday.

Blues started the game on the attack with the crowd behind them. Manager Steve Cotterill had made seven changes but all the players coming into the team were good players and played their hearts out for their place. Carl Jenkinson was back after injury and played really well and Cheikh N'Doye was brilliant – man of the match for me. Jason Lowe got a rare start and also played brilliantly. Of course Huddersfield then scored with their first chance of the game against the run of play and Blues were 1-0 down.

The Blues fans had some fun when a policeman went over to speak to a Huddersfield fan not far from the away end and he looked chastised as Blues fans sang 'sit down and behave yourself' and then 'he's gonna cry in a minute'. Very funny. There were loads of loud renditions of 'Keep Right On' and 'We're Birmingham, we're Birmingham'. It really was fun in the away end despite the score line and Blues were playing really well and I felt we could get back into it.

In the second half Blues played really well and Jutkiewicz fired in a shot in the 54th minute to bring us level at 1-1 and the Blues end went mental. A blue flare found its way onto the pitch and the away stand bounced in celebration. We can win this, I thought, and when Jutkiewicz headed over the keeper and into the net, I thought we had but the linesman's flag was up (wrongly) and the goal didn't stand. Therefore the game finished 1-1 and Blues will go into the draw for the 5th round on Monday. We headed home where I then went to my cousin Lynn's 65th Birthday party at Weoley Castle WMC. It had been a great day.

The replay will be in a couple of weeks and I hope we get the 'magic' of the FA Cup as I don't think our support or the atmosphere will be as good at home in this competition – I'm sad to say. If Blues open the Tilton it may be better though. Fingers crossed.

There was plenty of impressive feedback from the Huddersfield fans on You Tube and Twitter regarding Blues away support. One wrote that it was 'the best and loudest support at Huddersfield all season – which is why away fans should never be given the whole of the South Stand again!' The Huddersfield fan who had been the subject of the good natured micky taking posted that the Birmingham fans were 'quality support'. He commented that he 'had been spoken to 3 times by the police and the piss taking was relentless – quality support!'. He had loved it.

The next Tuesday Blues were at home in a 'six pointer' relegation battle against Sunderland who were just 1 place above us. Although it was a nerve wracking situation I was feeling a bit more optimistic of late, with Blues recent upturn in form and I felt we had a good chance of getting something from the game. There were 19,601 people inside St. Andrews on a cold night under the floodlights and the Bluenoses were in surprisingly good voice and there was a buzz around the place again.

Blues were back to a full strength team and unbelievably turned into Barcelona for 70 minutes of the game. David Davis scored a cracker in the 28th minute and St. Andrews erupted. Then Jeremie Boga, the smallest player on the pitch, headed in a Maghoma cross in the 44th minute to make it 2-0 and more wild celebrations took place along with 'Keep Right On'. Blues started the second half as they ended the first with Sam Gallagher side footing home another lovely ball from the rampant Jacques Maghoma to make it 3-0 on 54 minutes. Cue a massive exodus of the Sunderland fans to chants of 'is there a fire drill?' from the home support.

After 70 minutes Blues took their foot off the accelerator and allowed a poor Sunderland side to come at them and in the 83rd minute Sunderland pulled a goal back to make it 3-1. Fortunately they didn't score any more and it was a mere consolation but it was still disappointing to concede and took the shine off what was a very good result. Blues leapfrog Sunderland and moved out of the relegation zone and up to 19th in the table .

I was starting to look forward to going to the games again and for the away trip to Sheffield the five of us, me, June, Terry, Nigel and Charlie all wore our red away shirts as they seem to be lucky. We haven't lost in red this season. I even bought along my flag for the back window of the coach. It was a nice little trip but it was pouring with rain when we arrived at Hillsborough, home of Sheffield Wednesday. We didn't let it put us off though as we all headed to the chip shop up the road. The chips were lovely and we ate them in a sheltered area next to the chippie overlooking the stadium.

We headed into the away end and as usual there was a large contingent of Bluenoses in good voice. Blues played in red again and started off positively. It only took Blues 8 minutes to take the lead when David Davis broke through to put Blues 1-0 ahead. The away end exploded and we celebrated wildly. On 21 minutes it got even better when Jota hit a long range shot that went through the legs of the goalkeeper to put us 2-0 up. More wild celebrations followed in the jubilant away end.

Sheffield Wednesday's Marco Mathias was then shown a red card for an off the ball incident as he put his head into Brammall's face. We all cheered and sang 'time to go, time to go' and waved happily as he made for the changing rooms. We were even happier when Jota got his second of the game in 45+5 minutes and send Blues into the half time break with a 3-0 lead. I really couldn't believe it and I was incredibly happy.

Could it last? Well yes and no as ten men Sheffield Wednesday pulled a goal back after the break to make it 3-1 but then had another player sent off on 68 minutes and their fans streamed out of the stadium in disgust. Unfortunately Blues then went down quite a few gears against only 9 men and just passed the ball around for the last 20 minutes. It was incredibly boring to be honest and we never attacked them at all. It was like we were resting and feeling sorry for our opponents, which was exactly what Steve Cotterill admitted to afterward. We really should have gone out to improve our goal difference as it could cost us at the end of the season. Hull City didn't feel sorry for us when they put 6 past us and neither did Bournemouth as few years ago when they scored 8. I really don't know where Steve Cotterill comes from at times. Mind you. I was really happy with what was a very good away win and keeps Blues out of the relegation places and we all headed home happy.

It was back to Cup action on the Tuesday as Huddersfield came to St. Andrews in the FA Cup 4th round replay with the prize of a home tie against Manchester United in the 5th round. Too much to hope for? Unlike the previous meeting, Huddersfield fielded a full premier league team whilst Blues manager Steve Cotterill put out a second string. Disappointing, I know.

To be fair Blues did give it a good go and took a surprise lead on 52 minutes when Che Adams scored a cracker. St. Andrews came to life and thoughts of Manchester United came to mind only to be shattered 8 minutes later when Huddersfield equalised. It was a really cold night and the prospect of extra time was not appealing but the game finished 1-1 and it did go to extra time. It was an awful extra period too as a tired Blues team caved in and conceded 3 goals to lose the tie 4-1 and so our dreams were ended for another season. I headed home chilled to the bone and downhearted. It's been an awful season so far despite all the hope and optimism at the start.

With our unbeaten run at an end and Villa flying at the moment, I was a bit nervous about the trip to Villa but, to be honest, I thought that we were well overdue a win against them. Stephen had travelled up from London for the game and me, Stephen and Steve got a taxi over to Hennessy's bar for 9am to get the party started. The pub was already full of Bluenoses and you had to show your match ticket on the door to get in. It was about ten deep at the bar but there were lots of staff on duty, although it still took the lads about 10-15 minutes to get served. Hence they had a good stock of beers/cider when they joined me.

Despite the cold we headed into the beer garden where Brendan and company were already congregated. The staff were making breakfast rolls and I had a lovely sausage and tomato roll washed down with a lovely cold strongbow. Then we made our way to New Street Station to get the football special, which we were packed onto, taken the long way to Witton and made to tolerate a long stop in the middle of nowhere to ensure that we would only just make the kick off. Typical!

We arrived at Witton and headed to villa park in our numbers and arrived about ten minutes prior to kick off as I joined June and James in the away end. Bluenoses were in good voice as always. There proved to be two turning points in the game, firstly Blues Sam Gallagher hit the post and it rebounded back out for him to miss the follow up at the the point where Blues were on top. The Villa hit the post and it goes in. Our bad luck continues. A tale of two chances and once 1-0 behind Blues players confidence visibly drained and several players looked overawed by the big 'derby' occasion and were not up for it. I was disappointed to be honest. It was a horrible afternoon in a toxic environment as Blues lost the game 2-0 and we headed back to town somewhat downhearted. Our time will come.

Next up was a home game against Millwall and Blues really needed to get back to winning ways so that we don't slip back into the relegation zone. There was a good crowd at St.Andrews on a cold afternoon but we didn't get anything to cheer about as Blues lost 1-0 to a Millwall goal in the 77th minute. Yet more disappointment and many fans calling for manager Steve Cotterill to be sacked. I don't like to see our fans turning on our manager and it made me sad.

A few days later and me and June were off to Brentford on a cold Tuesday night. Despite not having much confidence in Blues at the moment, I do like the trip to Brentford and enjoy standing on the terraces again. We actually arrived early at 6pm despite it taking over 3 hours to get there on the coach. Hence we headed to the Griffin pub on the corner of the ground and I arranged to meet my nephew Stephen in the Griffin. I called him and he was already on his way over from work and joined us at about 6.40pm. Brendan and his mates were already in the pub and it was full of Bluenoses.

The pre match drink proved to be the highlight of the night, as well as the chicken balti pies we enjoyed on the terraces, as the game itself turned into a nightmare. Blues went into the halftime break trailing 2-0 having made two errors to concede the goals. Not long after the break Blues missed a glorious opportunity to score which would have changed the whole game had the score been 2-1. Instead Blues fell apart and were overwhelmed by a rampant Brentford who added another 3 to their tally and beat us 5-0 sending Blues home despondent.

Over 1,200 Bluenoses had made the trip and they vented their anger on manager Steve Cotterill who looked a lost figure as he trudged past the away end. I really don't like to see this happening and times are not good as a Bluenose at the moment. It was a long trip home I can tell you.

The next game at St. Andrews against Barnsley was a must win game. Barnsley were just below Blues in the last relegation place and had not won for the last 18games and defeat was unthinkable. 19,822 turned up in the hope of ending our recent poor run of results. From the opening ten minutes it looked as though we would do just that as both Jeremie Boga and Che Adams had shots saved.

Then it all went wrong as Barnsley took the lead on 12 minutes then won a penalty on 17 minutes. David Stockdale made a great save from the penalty to keep the score at 1-0 and keep Blues in with a chance. Until Blues conceded another poor goal on 38 minutes and it was 2-0. Steve Cotterill came in for a lot of abuse from those sitting behind the dugout, one fan got on the touch line and threw his season ticket at the manager before being escorted out, and another threw a bottle. Disgusting behaviour which meant Steve Cotterill had to be escorted off down the tunnel at halftime. No matter how the team is doing Steve Cotterill is a human being and these fans just bring shame on Birmingham City.

The second half was poor as Blues confidence was low and we are the lowest scoring team in the football league. No surprise then that the score remained 2-0 and Barnsley jumped above Blues sending us crashing back into the relegation places as the boos rang out around St. Andrews with chants of 'we want Cotterill out!'.

None of us expected the Forest game to go ahead due to the 'beast from the east' or 'storm Emma' which had left us more or less snowed in. Only 4 games were still on and the Forest v Birmingham game was one of them. Even the Villa game was called off. This meant clearing my car of its 3 inch deep covering of snow and getting my shovel out to clear a path off the driveway and onto the road before heading slowly to pick up June and then it was off to St. Andrews to get the coach to Nottingham.

The car park was too dangerous for the coaches (okay for our cars though) so we had to walk round to Tilton road where the coaches were now parked up. Unfortunately Terry and Charlie couldn't make it – Terry due to the conditions and Charlie who couldn't get his car off his driveway. Nigel made it though and we all enjoyed a pleasant trip to Nottingham, even arriving early for a change. This meant that June and I could get chips and gravy and I was able to get a matchday badge. It was really cold walking around the stadium though.

Inside the stadium the away end was full and the Bluenoses were in good voice. The news all over facebook was that Steve Cotterill would be sacked after the game and that the owners were already lining up Garry Monk as his replacement. I took this with a pinch of salt because if it was true then this would be disgraceful behaviour by our owners. I also don't think that Garry Monk would be the right man for the job and it would just be more upheaval for the players at a time when they need some stability.

The game kicked off and Blues did start brightly but then we conceded a goal in the 6th minute from a long range shot which Stockdale really should have saved. So at half time it was 1-0 and although Blues were the better team Forest scored again in the 79th minute when Blues left their player in acres of space to run into and shoot past Stockdale – poor defending again. At 2-0 down we all knew it was game over but we were playing really well and as ever I was a little hopeful.

Our hopes were raised when Michael Morrison powered home a header from a Craig Gardener free kick and it was 2-1 in the 87th minute. Blues fans celebrated and sang 'how shit must you be? We've scored a goal!' Forest were now hanging on for dear life and how we didn't get at least a draw I will never know. The game finished in another defeat but at least we had played much better and it was clear that the players were giving their all for the manager. Even Forests manager said it should have been at least 2-2.

We got back on the coach and listened to Steve Cotterill's interview on the way home. He sounded choked as he said his players had given everything for him today as he was cruelly questioned about keeping his job. I felt really sorry for him. When we got home later in the evening we discovered that the worst kept secret in football was true as the owners sacked yet another of our managers and Steve Cotterill was discarded.

Chapter Eighteen - We've Got The Monk! Super Garry Monk!

The following day came the announcement that Garry Monk was Birmingham City's new manager as we already knew would happen. This proved that once again Blues owners have gone behind the back of the current manager, it was left to Steve Cotterill to show some dignity in his departure. I felt immensely sorry for Steve as he had given his best and been treated disgracefully.

So onwards and upwards, what is done is done and although Garry Monk would not have been my choice as replacement I listened to his interview and I was very impressed by what he had to say. It renewed my confidence that perhaps we might get out of this awful mess with our new manager leading the way. Only time will tell though. This is Blues 5th manager in 14 months!

So with one and a half days to prepare his new side, Garry Monk led his Blues team out in front of a partisan crowd of nearly 19,000 inside St. Andrews. I didn't expect much difference to be honest as he hasn't had much time and Middlesbrough are a top side battling for promotion. The Bluenoses were a passionate as usual and a loud rendition of 'Keep Right On' echoed around the stadium to welcome Garry Monk.

Middlesbrough made us change ends, which I didn't like, but I was pleasantly surprised by how well Blues played and it was easy to spot the positive changes Gary had made. Blues created a lot of chances in an attacking 4-4-2 formation with Che Adams and Lucas Jutkiewicz up front. Jota was having a fantastic game and it was much better seeing him take our corners instead of Craig Gardener for a change. Overall Blues were much improved and playing well, so it was really disappointing to concede a goal and go 1-0 down.

In the second half Blues completely dominated and Middlesbrough time wasted whenever they got the ball. It was obvious that they were hanging on for a 1-0 win as a dominant Blues threw everything at them. However, Blues still cannot put the ball in the net and conceded our 7th consecutive defeat. Luckily all the teams around us at the bottom lost, although Blues remain in the bottom three.

So I left the St. Andrews feeling somewhat unusually despondent despite the vast improvement Garry Monk has created. I just cannot see Blues scoring the goals needed or getting the luck we have been denied all season. I bumped into Barry on the way out and he tried to get me to not to be despondent but it wouldn't go away. Please don't let it be impending doom!

A few days later and we were off to Cardiff to take on a team that are currently second in the Championship. Gary Monk is having a difficult start to his Blues career from the fixture list. He hasn't had much time with the team yet and with Cardiff flying high we are not really expecting anything. Lots of Bluenoses had made the trip though and we sang our hearts out throughout. 'There'll be no sheep shaggers in Moscow!' (Referring to the 2018 World Cup in Moscow) was the song of choice as well as 'Eng er Land!'

The team selection was almost the same as the last game except Sam Gallagher started instead of Che Adams who was on the bench. I really like Che Adams but he just hasn't been the same since he came back from injury and I'm not alone in thinking that. He doesn't look interested anymore. The first half got underway and despite having 58% possession our defence let us down again and Blues went in 3-0 down at half time and were booed off by some of the away supporters. No way back from this, obviously. Goal difference is becoming a concern also.

In the second half Blues upped their game and completely dominated the half with 68% possession. Craig Gardener pulled a goal back with a penalty in the 54th minute. 'We're gonna win 4-3' rang out and we enjoyed celebrating a rare goal. Ten minutes later a Michael Morrison close range shot was cleared off the line when it really should have been a goal. Blues continued to attack a Cardiff defence that were clinging on at this point and in the 95th minute Maxime Colin fired a shot into the top of the net to make it 3-2. The away end exploded in celebration. 'We're Birmingham City we'll fight to the end' was belted out.

Blues really should have got at least a point but the match finished in a 3-2 defeat. We were all really heartened by the fighting spirit in the second half and we all applauded our team loudly. The players came over to applaud the fans and then we headed back to the coaches with a bit more hope that Garry Monk can lead us out of danger. Blues remain 3rd from bottom, 3 points adrift of Barnsley just above us. Next up is a crunch match against Hull City and I was off to Tenerife on holiday.

On the day of the Hull game I was off to Birmingham airport to embark on my 'winter break' holiday to Tenerife and I was concerned about the forecast of snow and our chances of getting away before it hit. Luckily we did and when the match kicked off in front of a partisan St. Andrews crowd of over 22,500 I was in the air. I admit to having a case of the butterflies at the thought of such an important game and me not knowing how things were going.

As soon as I got in our apartment in Tenerife I checked the scores and was ecstatic to discover Blues had won 3-0 with 2 goals from Jota and one from Che Adams. Apparently the bad weather had hit just after we took off and the game had gone ahead during blizzard conditions. Some of the photos I saw of the conditions were truly amazing with fans covered in snow and unable to see the other end of the pitch. I saw a great video of the Tilton singing 'can't fucking see!' Brilliant. What a fantastic win though!

I had a wonderful holiday, a real relaxing break, and my first game back was at St. Andrews as Blues entertained Ipswich Town. It was another good crowd of 20,555 and as usual we were in good voice and from kick off we got behind the team. It wasn't as good a performance as against Hull and was a bit scrappy but Blues stuck at it.

On 21 minutes, from an Ipswich attack, our keeper David Stockdale made a long throw to Jacques Maghoma which he collected and ran with the ball all the way into the Ipswich penalty area where he was brought down by an Ipswich defender – penalty! We all cheered. Up stepped Jota to smash the ball home and St. Andrews erupted. 'Keep Right On' echoed around the stadium. The rest of the game was a bit of a slog although Blues could have made it 2-0 early in the second half. The final whistle confirmed Blues as 1-0 winners and the celebrations began as Blues are now out of the bottom three.

So far it had been a good Easter and I was looking forward to the trip to Bolton on the Tuesday night for the crucial game against a Bolton team just 3 points ahead of us. I had expected about 800 – 1000 Bluenoses to make the trip on a Tuesday night but Blues had already sold their allocation and 5000 of us were heading to Bolton. I was so excited. I was traveling with June on one of the 17 official coaches making the trip. As usual the Blues stewards struggled to organise the boarding of the coaches and as usual we left more than 10 minutes late, which meant we hit the rush hour traffic on the Aston Expressway and it took an hour to get as far as Walsall's stadium on the M6. We arrived at Bolton 3 hours after setting out.

It was buzzing in the away end of the Macron Stadium and June and I were in the upper tier. Once we had downed a quick drink and caught up with various people we knew we headed to our seats. Blues were already singing 'there's more of us than you' to the Bolton contingent. The top tier and the lower tier were singing 'we hate Villa more than you' to each other as they were getting no joy from the Bolton fans. When 'Keep Right On' rang out it was truly epic and echoed around the stadium.

The players came out to cheers and the game got underway. It was a hard fought scrappy game but Blues were up for the fight. 'Garry Monk's blue and white army' rang out. On 40 minutes Blues won a free kick which was floated into the box for the 'Juke' Jutkiewicz to fire into the net to send 5000 Bluenoses into raptures. It was completely mental as blue flares were set off and we bounced around with the blue smoke and the smell of the flares in the air around us. The loudest 'Keep Right On' of the night filled the stadium and Garry Monk punched the air in delight and Blues went in 1-0 up at half time.

The second half got underway and Bolton were throwing everything at us in an attempt to get back into the game. Blues were holding on but on 63 minutes Che Adams received a straight red card for a tackle and Blues were down to ten men. This meant Gary Monk having to make several changes but Blues held firm despite the added 3 minutes somehow turning into 7 minutes as the referee seemed to forget to look at his watch!

When the final whistle sounded the away end erupted in celebration. As 'Keep Right On' rang out the players and staff came over the join in with us and they applauded our fantastic support. It was brilliant to watch Maghoma and Ndoye enthusiastically joining in with us as we sang 'Birmingham, Birmingham, Birmingham! Brilliant! Garry Monk applauded us and we sang 'Garry Monk's blue and white army'. It was well worth making the trip with the fantastic night that we had just experienced.

On checking facebook on the way back it was great to see that 'football away days' had put on a photo of the away end at Bolton and had praised Blues fantastic away following on a Tuesday night. Amongst the comments was one from someone from Bolton who said that he lived a mile from the stadium and heard the Birmingham fans singing in his living room. Brilliant. It was also fantastic to see Blues Harlee Dean, in his post match interview say that Blues support was fantastic and he has never seen anything like it ever, coming from Brentford.

One Bolton fan Theo said 'Birmingham City fans loudest that have come this season for sure. Very good support and louder than any club I've ever heard come to the Macron'. Another Bolton fan Sam 'embarrassed to be a Bolton fan today we were shown up in front of the Birmingham fans, could still hear them chanting when we had all left the stadium and were outside-embarrassing'.

What an amazing night, one of those rare occasions that stays long in the memory. Bolton seems to be a favourite place to visit for us Bluenoses. It also means that Birmingham are now level on points with Bolton, Reading and Hull who are all just above Blues on goal difference and most importantly Blues are 5 points clear of the relegation zone.

Although I was excited about the next game at St. Andrews I was also dreading it a bit as Burton Albion are our bogey team. Blues have only ever played them 3 times in the league and have lost all 3 with Lloyd Dyer scoring in every game for them. Mind you it has been over a period when

Blues have not been doing very well. It didn't put people off going to the game though as over 22,000 were packed into St. Andrews.

Blues were forced into making a change due to Che Adams 3 match suspension with Jeremie Boga coming in to replace him, only this time Boga would be up front with Lucas Jutkiewicz as Garry Monk stuck to his 4-4-2 formation. I love this formation as it is more exciting and finally has Blues scoring goals and proves that previous manager Steve Cotterill's "Blues can't play with two up top" to be wrong. With 3 wins on the trot Blues would be going into today's game against bottom club Burton full of confidence.

Blues started well and had the ball in the net on 6 minutes only for it to be disallowed and the ball pulled back for a free kick on the edge of the box – wrongly I must say! It was a terrible decision as was the Burton hand ball in the area that should have been a penalty for Blues but was missed by the referee. 'You don't know what you're doing' rang out. Blues totally dominated the first half but went in at half time 0-0.

The second half saw Blues continue to dominate but totally against the run of play and with their first shot, that man Dyer scored and somewhat surprisingly gave Burton the lead. I couldn't believe it. The Blues fans got behind the team and they hammered at Burton as we laid siege on their goal. Nigel Clough the Burton manager took off Darren Bent and replaced him with a defender as they sat back and 'parked the bus' in an attempt to keep us out. It looked like it would work too as Blues hit the post (Jota), the crossbar (Davis) and had an effort cleared off the line. Blues had 25 attempts on goal 13 of which were on target but their keeper played out of his skin pulling off a string of saves to keep Burton in the lead.

The crowd roared the Blues on and in the 87th minute the 'Juke' headed the ball into the Burton net via the crossbar and St. Andrews exploded. The roar was deafening as we all went completely mental. There was then 5 minutes of injury time as Blues went in search of a winner and how we didn't win the game I will never know. So the game finished in a 1-1 draw and the point could prove vitally important at the end of the season, especially with some of the teams around us winning. Bolton lost at Derby though which moves Blues up to 19th place.

The games were coming thick and fast now and before I knew it, it was time for the trip to Bristol on a Tuesday night. We arrived at Bristol City's Ashton Gate around 6.30pm and headed straight for the outdoor bar at the back of thr away stand. I love this area to be honest as it's easy to get a drink and chat to other Bluenoses and music is playing too. I like the way Bristol City put this on.

Inside the stadium there were 1,500 Bluenoses who had made the trip and as always were loud and proud. We were treated to another good attacking performance from Blues but we fell behind on 12 minutes when Bristol scored from a free kick which was straight at our keeper Stockdale and I felt extremely disappointed that he didn't save it. Fifteen minutes later Blues were 2-0 down and really didn't deserve to be.

Lucas Jutkiewicz pulled a goal back on 34 minutes and we went in at half time trailing 2-1. In the second half Blues continued to dominate but failed to take any of the many chances we were creating. To make matters worse the referee was awful, allowing Blues players to be pulled, pushed and fouled and he was giving every decision to Bristol. Blues had 51% possession, 13 shots and 7 shots on target compared to Bristol City's 4 shots. To make matters even worse Bristol then grabbed a third goal on the counter attack to make the final score 3-1, a really unfair reflection of the game. Blues fans sang 'we're Birmingham City, we'll fight to the end' and that is just what our players do now under Garry Monk.

A really disappointing result but another inspiring performance from Blues. It gives us hope although our run in is the most difficult of all the bottom placed teams and it's off to table toppers Wolves on Sunday. At least tonight all the other teams at the bottom lost so we stay out of the relegation places.

By the time we headed to the Molyneux for the midday kick off, Wolves had already had their promotion to the Premier League confirmed by Fulham's failure to win their midweek fixture. Not that Wolves intended to ease up as they want to secure the Championship too. Fair play to them.

Me, James and Steve were going by train and June was traveling by coach. Therefore the three of us got a taxi into town and following breakfast in the Trocadeer (they weren't serving alcohol till 11am) we then headed to the Shakespeare for a pre match drink as they were serving from 10am. We saw loads of Bluenoses we knew in there and had a good chat before heading off to New Street Station to catch a train to Wolverhampton.

The train was packed with Bluenoses and we were soon arriving at Wolverhampton and heading to the stadium only to find that the programmes had allegedly sold out. There were 2000 in the away end and we were in good voice. Wolves put on a display of flames around the pitch which made a hot day even hotter and probably singed a few eyebrows. For once the dingles were actually quite noisy as they were in celebratory mood.

The game was one to forget for us Bluenoses as the team was changed completely – positional wise, with Jota playing in defence and Colin further forward and we looked completely disorganised. It just wasn't working. Mind you, Blues could and should have opened the scoring in the first half as the Wolves keeper made 2 great saves. But that was as good as it got as Wolves Jota put them ahead on 22 minutes. Wolves do have a very good team but what let them down was their foreign players who kept diving whenever a Blues player came anywhere near them – it was blatant cheating at times and I quickly lost respect for them.

Things got even worse in the second half when Morrison gave the ball away which then resulted in Harlee Dean receiving a red card for his tackle on the Wolves player charging through. Somewhat unfair I thought but we were now down to ten men with only 52 minutes played. Surprisingly Blues played better with ten men but were caught out on 87 minutes when Wolves made it 2-0 and game over. I felt we set out all wrong for this game and we should have stuck to 4-4-2 and gone for it. That just my opinion although ex Blues player Robert Hopkins had agreed with me during our half time chat as he was sitting near me.

The tannoy announced that the Wolves fans should remain in their seats at the end of the match for the celebrations. Their fans sang 'we're Wolverhampton, we'll do what we want'. The Blues fans responded with 'you're Wolverhampton, you'll do what you're told!' That was the only part of the day that raised a smile from me. It had also been nice to catch up with ex-Blues player Robert Hopkins too. I headed back to get the train with a heavy heart as I was again wondering if Blues would stay up. Blues are now 4th from bottom just 2 points clear of Barnsley in 21st place and they have a game in hand. Every game is now a Cup Final for Blues with only 3 games left to save ourselves.

It was a lovely sunny day and there seemed to be a buzz around St. Andrews. I was excited although nervous as each game is so important at the moment. Sheffield United have a good team that are currently pushing for a promotion spot and they have brought 2,700 fans with them today. It was a big crowd inside and St. Andrews was rocking. 'Keep Right On' was so loud.

The game kicked off and Blues were up for it from the start. Unfortunately Sheffield United caught us on the break and an ex-Blues player (typical!) scored a soft deflected shot that Stockdale really should have saved easily.

Mark Duffy, being the tosser that he is, ran to the Blues fans and taunted them so much that he received a booking for his trouble and he's lucky that's all he got! This only succeeded in spurring on the the Bluenoses as 'wanker! Wanker!'rang out followed by a deafening rendition of 'Keep Right On'. Duffy was booed every time he touched the ball from then on and Blues and the Bluenoses moved it up a gear or two.

Revenge was sweet just after the half hour mark as Marc Roberts fired home a well worked corner from Jacques Maghoma who was having a great game. Jota was running the show and the Juke was running his heart out. St. Andrews erupted with noise as we celebrated for ages. The feel around the place was incredible. So at half time it was 1-1.

Blues continued to dominate in the second half and with around 20 minutes remaining Che Adams sent Jacques Maghoma clear and in a one on one with the keeper he calmly fired home. St. Andrews exploded with the loudest cheer for a long time. I hugged my neighbour and everyone (except the away end) went proper mental. 'Keep Right On' rang out and the stadium was rocking. Not long afterwards Mark Duffy was substituted to loud boos and as he took his place on the bench all you could hear was 'Duffy what's the score?' Brilliant. Garry Monk said after the game that it had been the best atmosphere so far at St. Andrews.

So the game finished in a brilliant 2-1 win for Blues and for once thousands of fans stayed in the stadium applauding our team and singing 'we're Birmingham City we'll fight to the end' and 'Garry Monk's blue and white army' as the players walked around the pitch applauding the Blues fans. To make the day even better Bolton and Barnsley both lost which means that Blues are 19th and 5 points clear of the relegation places although Barnsley do have a game in hand. Burton beat Sunderland away which means that Sunderland are relegated.

Elsewhere Manchester City are champions in the Premier League, Wigan are promoted to the championship and Accrington Stanley and Luton Town are promoted to League One. Wolves have clinched the Championship after winning 4-0 at Bolton. Next up its an away trip to QPR and I'm already looking forward to it.

Up early and into the Briar Rose in town by 9.40am along with several other Bluenoses prior to the trip to QPR. We even had a cheeky visit from Derby fans in town early before their game with Villa but the bouncers wouldn't let them in. Then it was off to New Street Station to catch the 10.30 virgin train to Euston which had us in London by 12.00. We immediately jumped the tube to Shepherd's Bush Market and walked to the Crown and Spectre pub not too far from the away end of the ground.

Today it was me, June, James and Steve and my nephew Stephen was on his way to join us. It was a nice old pub with a Thai/English menu and already there were mostly QPR fans inside. We found a table with a couple of Bluenoses already on and ordered food just as Stephen made an appearance closely followed by Natalie and her boyfriend. It was great to have a drink and a laugh. I had seen a lot of fancy dress on the way with many dressed as blue or white monks (no prizes for guessing why with a manager named Garry Monk).

Following a 'team photo' outside the pub I put on my long blue wig and massive blue sunglasses and we headed to the ground singing 'Keep Right On' on the way. We entered the away concourse just as a blue flare had been set off and the corridor (as that is all their concourse is really) was filled with blue smoke and some of it went up into the stand. None of us really minded the blue smoke though as we went about chatting, singing and laughing at all the fancy dress. The stewards were in a bit of a panic though and I have to say their stewards are the most horrible, difficult and unhelpful stewards any of us have ever come across. It was quite funny when Natalie was shown first a yellow and then a red card from a referee with a white stick. Brilliant!

We found our way to our seats despite being sent the longest way possible by the steward – sent to the furthest end of the row that we were at the start of. The view was the worse I have ever had (and that includes the packed terraces of the 70's and 80's) – restricted view doesn't even come close. We could not see the goal or the goal line/ corners at our end. Loftus Road really is a shit hole. I could not believe it. The whole of the upper stand apart from the front row must have been restricted view. The entire stand needs to be demolished.

If Blues win today it will ensure our safety for another season, perhaps even a point and we are all hoping that Blues can achieve this as no one wants to go to the last game of the season – again! The match got underway and Blues looked a little shaky to be honest – almost like nerves had taken hold again. Amazingly Blues took the lead on 27 minutes when Che Adams fired home and the away end went mental. Everyone was jumping on each other and I had to keep hold of my blue wig to stop it flying off as me and Stephen jumped around together.

Just what Blues needed! Could we hold the lead? No! Just 60 seconds later and QPR were level. Due to the restricted view I didn't see their goal but I did see the QPR player that ran to celebrate in front of the away end and I also saw him spit at the Blues fans and I saw the bottles and coins that headed towards him in response. What a tosser. So half time and it was all square at 1-1.

The second half got underway and I thought Blues were the better team and had the better chances but QPR were more clinical and took their chances in the 70th and 92nd minutes thereby inflicting a 3-1 defeat on us. We were devastated and I just can't bear the thought that it will go to the last game of the season as both Burton and Barnsley won. It couldn't be a more difficult game either, with high flying Fulham coming to St. Andrews needing to win for a chance of automatic promotion. Blues would only need a draw but I'm sure we will not get anything to be honest.

The day of reckoning arrived on a lovely sunny day and I admit to being really nervous. So much so that I couldn't even eat before the game. It was a full house at St. Andrews with the Olympic Gallery open for the first time this season and the atmosphere was the best and loudest that I have known for a good few years. My nephew Stephen had travelled down from London and was bringing his girlfriend Alice to her first live football match – he couldn't have made a better choice for her. It was lovely to meet up with them and I think Stephen was as nervous as me.

It really was in our own hands today and Fulham had come in the hope of winning and leapfrogging Cardiff, if they failed to win, into the automatic promotion place. Fulham also arrived unbeaten in the last 23 games. Surprisingly though, Blues started on the front foot and completely surprised Fulham as they attacked them from the start. Blues were fast and wanted it more than Fulham and completely outfought them. On 15 minutes the outstanding Wes Harding made a fantastic run up the wing and crossed for the 'Juke' Lucas Jutkiewicz to fire home to a crescendo of noise inside St. Andrews and Blues had a deserved 1-0 lead. Blue smoke poured from the Tilton stand.

My nerves began to settle a bit and the singing from the blues fans was loud, passionate and continuous. The stadium was buzzing and the 3,300 Fulham fans were now silent. Then 2 minutes before half time Jota collected the ball from a Blues corner and crossed for Harlee Dean to head home and claim his first goal for Blues and made the score 2-0. St. Andrews exploded as Harlee Dean sprinted to the KOP, gesturing to the away fans on his way passed them and he was mobbed by his teammates. I was in heaven and hugging my friends as everyone celebrated. It was no more than Blues deserved and we went into the halftime break with a 2-0 lead. Amazingly all the other scores were going our way, in sharp contrast to last year, not that we needed them.

I was worried that Blues wouldn't play as well in the second half but my fears were soon gone as Blues took up where they left off and continued to trouble Fulham. The stadium was rocking and 'Keep Right On' was so loud. Blues seemed to be cruising towards 3 points until Fulham's Tom Cairney pulled a goal back for them in the 84th minute. This rallied Fulham and within a couple of minutes Stockdale pulled off a fantastic save to deny them an equaliser.

Why is it always this way? I thought as the the nerves returned with a vengeance. However a point would have still been enough as all the other scores were still in our favour. Then in the 89th minute Jota sent Che Adams through and he outpaced their defender to fire past the Fulham keeper, 3-1 and St. Andrews exploded again. Parity was restored and the party began in earnest. 'We are staying up! Say we are staying up!' Was belted out followed by 'we're Birmingham City, we'll fight to the end'. This meant that Paul Robinson could come on in place of Jacques Maghoma and he received a standing ovation (Robinson that is) for his last appearance in a Birmingham City shirt as he is hanging up his boots at the end of the season. Chants of 'Robbo, Robbo' rang out around the stadium as he played out the last 7 minutes.

The referee had added 6 minutes but when the final whistle sounded the joyous scenes were incredible. Despite the tannoy pleading "please stay off the pitch or the players will not come back out for their lap off appreciation", loads of Bluenoses poured onto the pitch singing 'we're Birmingham City, we'll do what we want'

The rest of the Blues fans booed those on the pitch and chanted 'off! Off!' as everyone wanted to see the players do a lap of appreciation. The Blues fans on the pitch then headed towards the Fulham fans and the barrier of stewards and police in front of them, but happily the Blues fans just wanted to applaud them and the Fulham fans applauded the Blues fans in return and the Bluenoses then peacefully left the pitch and returned to the stands for the players to return.

The players returned and proceedings began with an award presented to Paul Robinson who then made an emotional speech to the fans and ended it with 'let's sing our song' and he paused for a moment as I think he had forgotten the words to 'Keep Right On' so he went with 'we are staying up' instead and everyone happily joined in. Then the players did their lap of appreciation with their families and everyone had stayed behind to see this. It was lovely, a real bonding between players and fans.

So that's it for another season as Blues maintain our place in the Championship. There was so much great feedback from the Fulham fans after the match as they credited the Bluenoses for our efforts throughout the afternoon and some claimed it was the best home atmosphere they had heard in the Championship.

There were lots of positive postings on social media from the Londoners: "must say Birmingham City's fans were incredible. Incredible atmosphere". The Grizzler said "I know Birmingham fans get a bad reputation, and the fans running on the pitch trying to goad the Fulham fans...but...walking to coach a Birmingham fan wished us the best of luck in the playoffs, and shook hands...class"

Tom FFC "a great atmosphere today though, Birmingham fans were class, deserved the win". ElliotVan B "honestly want to be angry at Birmingham but I can't. Sound club, sound fans and great noise for their goals". Michael Cox "not too sure why our fans mocked Birmingham today. Comfortably the best support I've ever seen in the Championship". Sam Lockheart "Birmingham fans were unreal today. When that first goal went in the noise was something else'. Jamie "Birmingham fans have been class with us today".

This result meant that Blues finished in 19th place and live to fight another day. The other results of the day saw Bolton escape relegation thereby sending Barnsley, Burton Albion and Sunderland into League One. Exiting from the top of the table to the Premier League are Wolves and Cardiff. The play off final saw Fulham and Villa contest the last place after beating Derby and Middlesbrough in the semifinals and it was Fulham who were victorious at Wembley. Joining the Championship from the Premier League will be Swansea City, Stoke City and West Brom who all suffered relegation. Blues incredibly came 8th in the average away support in the EFL with 1,922 – the highest for a club in a relegation battle.

Blues average attendance was 21,041 with the highest being 27,608 against Fulham and the lowest was 7,623 against Burton in the FA Cup 3rd Round. Blues top goalscorer in the League was Sam Gallagher with 6 and over all competitions was Che Adams with 9.

Manchester City won the Premier League, Chelsea beat Manchester United 1-0 to win the FA Cup and Manchester City won the League Cup as they defeated Arsenal 3-0. As usual the same teams getting the silverware - boring!

Chapter Nineteen - World Cup Fever

I was really looking forward to the World Cup even though it was in Russia. For the first time in years England have a good young team who seem to be full of confidence and have said they are going to Russia to win the World Cup. The competition was due to kick off on Thursday 14th June with Russia v Saudi Arabia and this was my last day at work for a couple of weeks as I was then off on holiday on the Saturday. This meant that I would watch England's first group match in Fuerteventura. I did record the opening ceremony though and watched Englishman Robbie Williams singing to open the World Cup Finals. Hopefully an Englishman will be closing the World Cup with his hands on the trophy.

My start to the holiday was a nightmare which began with a Norwegian airplane en route to Madrid declaring a midair emergency and then crash landing on the one and only runway at Birmingham airport which resulted in Birmingham airport closing just as we sat in Wetherspoon's in the airport departure lounge waiting for our gate to be announced. Happily everyone got off the plane safely but it took a while to clear the runway of the airplane and all the foam. To cut a very long story short whereby we waited hours with no information, no TUI representative and no water or refreshments forthcoming we were shipped off to a hotel in Coventry over 8 hours later after being told out flight was cancelled and would depart from Manchester in the morning. The whole thing was a nightmare and we were finally collected by taxi at 8am to race us to Manchester airport for our rearranged 10am flight to Fuerteventura which had to wait for us and finally departed just before 12.00 midday. We had already lost a day of our holiday.

We arrived at our hotel in Corralejo to find that it was a bit of a way out, it was cloudy and very windy. However, as the days went by and we found our way around we got to love the place and the sun came out and the winds dropped. Our apartment had a beautiful sea view and I could see nearby island Lanzarote across the sea – it's only 10 kilometres away. The sea itself was only feet away – wonderful and relaxing. I could watch the ferries come and go to lanzarote and back. My brother Neil and his wife Sue were holidaying in Lanzarote for the second week.

The first England game was on the Monday night 18th June against Tunisia for a 7pm kick off. We had been told of a TUI event in a pub called Flicks and given a buy one get one free drink ticket. Hence we headed off to Flicks in our England gear to watch the match and got seats not far from the big screen. It was full of England fans in Flicks and a great atmosphere and the pub exploded when England scored after 11 minutes. Despite lots of missed chances England couldn't get that killer second goal and Tunisia were awarded a penalty to bring them back into the game. I couldn't believe it – well I could really to be honest! At half time I was given raffle tickets and won a lovely England towel. The second half was much the same as England had several chances but could not score.

It looked to be heading for a draw but in the 90th minute Harry Kane headed in a late winner and the pub erupted. 'England, England, England!' Rang out and we celebrated our win. Apparently the fans inside the stadium were plagued by midges with the 2,100 England fans being attacked by clouds of flies that got everywhere. Back home one England fan fell through the roof of a bus shelter during celebrations. This leaves England in second spot behind Belgium who beat Panama 3-0.

England's second group game was a 1pm kick off on Thursday 24th July against Panama. By now we had found a really nice English pub called the Seven Pints and decided to watch the match there. As it was a lunch time kick off mom and Annette wanted to go off and get lunch somewhere else so I went with Steve to the Seven Pints to watch the game. We got there early and it was already packed with England fans and it was twice the size of Flicks where we had watched the previous game. We got a seat though and I had a nice full English breakfast before kick off with a nice cold pint of Strongbow.

The match kicked off and England looked really good despite Panama being really dirty and constantly fouling our players. Jessie Linguard was deliberately elbowed in the face in the area and left polaxed and requiring treatment but the referee missed the obvious penalty and sending off that should have been awarded. The Redditch Birmingham City flag could clearly be seen behind the goal. Despite the fouls England took the lead on 11 minutes when John Stones headed home from a corner and the pub erupted and beer shampoos commenced near the bar area. I was in the air, jumping around my table when a spontaneous chorus of 'it's coming home!' broke out.

On 22 minutes the lively Jessie Linguard was brought down in the area and a penalty was awarded. We all cheered! Up stepped Harry Kane and hit the perfect penalty into the top corner giving the keeper no chance, 2-0 and cue more wild celebrations! Once again 'it's coming home!' broke out. On arrival we had all been give a card to get signed with each pint purchased and if you could drink Seven Pints (name of the pub) a free Seven Pints, Fuerteventura, Russia 2018 t-shirt would be given. Steve was currently trying to drink his way through the Seven Pints to get the t-shirt and doing quite well. England were totally dominant and Jessie Linguard curled a fantastic shot from outside the area into the top corner of the net to make it 3-0 and the pub exploded. More beer shampoos at the back and this time the pub played 'it's coming home' and everyone joined in. It was brilliant! Four minutes later John Stones headed his second of the game to make it 4-0! The loudest cheer of the night met this goal as we all celebrated again amongst the flying beer.

I couldn't believe the score line and it got even better when the referee again spotted the Panama players wrestling Harry Kane to the floor and awarded another penalty to England just before half time. We all cheered again. Up stepped Harry Kane to fire the ball home and make it an unbelievable score line of 5-0 at Half time! The Seven Pints went absolutely crazy. I didn't want half time to come as I thought it might interrupt our momentum. I had began to think of goal difference as earlier Belgium had beaten Tunisia 5-2 which meant they had a goal difference of +6 and had gone top but England had now equaled that and I think that makes us top.

The second half began much the same as the first and Harry Kane claimed his hat trick in the 62nd minute to make it 6-0! Cue unbelievable scenes in the pub. 'It's coming home' rang out again. Apparently a group on England fans at the bar had brought along their German friend and decked him out in England gear and flag and had promised to soak him in beer each time England scored. He was very wet at this point! Steve had managed to drink his seven pints and proudly clutched his t-shirt and all was good.

That was until Gareth Southgate started with his substitutions with Harry Kane being the first to come off just after scoring his 3rd goal. Panama then scored their first ever goal of the World Cup to make it 6-1. Their fans in Russia were delirious and celebrated for the rest of the game as if they had won the World Cup. So both sets of fans were happy with the 6-1 result. I felt we could have scored a lot more had it not been for the 3 substitutions in the second half but perhaps the manager was resting them for the last 16 as England now topped the group and qualified for the next round. The next game against Belgium would determine who finishes top. Gary Lineker tweeted 'This is getting silly. Last time England scored 4 or more goals in a World Cup was the 1966 WC Final'.

Wednesday 27th June saw holders Germany getting eliminated after losing to South Korea 2-0 and finishing bottom of their group (they also lost 1-0 to Mexico). This was probably due to the fact that I had Germany in the sweep at work! Overall it was all looking pretty hopeful. The question was did we want to finish top of the table or take the easier route by finishing second? I think Garage Southgate was opting for second place with his team selection against Belgium although they rested a few players too. Back home fans in Wiltshire had placed two giant red ribbons across the historic White Horse to create a massive St. George's Cross flag until the English heritage removed it.

The last group game against Belgium was an evening kick off on the 28th June so mom and Annette went off on their own again and I headed to meet

Steve at the Seven Pints where he was keeping a table. It was already quite full when I arrived and ordered a chicken curry and a Strongbow. This time I was trying to fill the card to get a free Seven Pints - Russia 2018 t-shirt! The pub was buzzing as World Cup fever has well and truly gripped the nation. The game got underway but it was a poor performance from the England 'reserve' team which had eight changes. Belgium also fielded a 'reserve' side but looked sharper.

Several England players looked average although goalkeeper Jordan Pickford made a couple of good saves. In fact he got his fingertips to the Belgium goal which won them the game. The best part of the goal was when a Belgium player picked the ball out of the net and went to fire it back into the net but only succeeded in blasting it against the post and it rebounded straight into his face and knocked him flying. I laughed at that for the rest of the game and it definitely received the biggest cheer of the day!

The game finished with England defeated 1-0 and second in the group - quite handy really although I never like to lose. This means England will face Colombia- winners of group H, in the next round and I will be back in England for this match. The rest of the holiday went fantastically and I was sad to be heading away from the rest and relaxation. Before I headed back I saw more big nations get knocked out as Argentina were despatched by France and Portugal were sent home by Uruguay. Another big shock was hosts Russia beating Spain 4-3 on penalties as yet another big side head home. It is getting even better for England. Can it be our time?

I was back at work on the day of the last 16 game against Colombia but as it was an evening kick off I worked an early duty and was home in time to watch the game on TV. Everyone is excited at the prospect of England reaching the quarterfinals and I was no exception as I rushed home to watch the match. Unfortunately I had no one to go out to see the match with as my mate June was away in Scotland watching the golf so I had to watch it in the house. Mom and Annette called in for a while though. What a game it turned out to be, with loads of excitement as England played the dirtiest team in the tournament who would stoop to anything to put England off their game.

It was a really tough game as the Colombian players tried every dirty trick in the book to defeat England. One of the Colombian players head butted Jordan Henderson in the penalty area as we were preparing to take a free kick but all he received was a yellow card! Unbelievable! When the Colombian players weren't busy fouling the England players they were rolling around on the floor faking injuries. Despite all of this England played really well and did not react to the constant cheating. During the game Colombia received a total of six yellow cards. In the 57th minute England were awarded a penalty for yet another foul on Harry Kane and while the Colombian players surrounded the referee another of their players was busy scuffing the penalty spot with his boot. Shocking behaviour. It didn't put Harry off though, he stepped up and fired home to make it 1-0 to England and I was running around the room in celebration.

Despite dominating the game England then conceded in the last minute from a rare Colombian corner to send the game into extra time. I couldn't believe it. Colombia did not deserve the draw and they sat in and defended throughout extra time and the game went to the dreaded penalty shootout. England have never won a penalty shootout in the World Cup so not looking too good. I was so nervous as was the rest of the country. Colombia took the first kick and scored 1-0. Then it was the turn of Harry Kane who confidently despatched his kick into the net 1-1. Colombia then made it 2-1 before England's Marcus Rashford fired home to make it 2-2. Again Colombia went in front as they scored to make it 3-2. Jordan Henderson stepped up to hit a good shot but the Colombian keeper made an outstanding save to keep the score 3-2. I was devastated as I have seen England lose so many of these penalty shootouts. Mateus Uribe for Colombia then hit the crossbar with his penalty and I was jumping up and down! Up stepped Kieran Trippier who very calmly converted his penalty and it was now 3-3. It was getting tense and Colombia's Carlos Barca stepped up to be denied by a great save from Jordan Pickford. This meant that if England scored the last penalty we would be in the World Cup quarterfinals.

Up stepped Eric Dier and he fired the ball home to set off unbelievable scenes of celebration as England won 4-3 and made World Cup history as we won our first ever World Cup penalty shootout. I was running around in ecstasy and couldn't believe that we are in the quarterfinals, something that none if us expected from this young England side. This now means that England will face Sweden on Saturday 7th July and I would be off work and able to go out and watch it. The news channels were showing unbelievable scenes of celebrations all around the country as World Cup Fever well and truly took over. 'It's Coming Home' was being played everywhere and video clips were being adapted to incorporate the song, some of them really funny. It was brilliant and totally united the country. Around the country 36 million Pints were consumed in pubs everywhere as fans celebrated in bars, streets and on the roofs of buses!

I managed to get the day off for the Quarterfinal match against Sweden and decided to watch it at the Harborne Village Social Club. Not the best place really but at least I would be watching with friends and there were loads of England fans to cheer the lads on. There were 5,000 England fans inside the stadium in Russia to watch the game. It was a much more comfortable game to watch after the stress of the last game as England took the lead on 30 minutes with a great header from Maguire and we went mental as we celebrated madly. England had total control and scored a second from Dele Ali on 59 minutes and we began to dream, Sweden tried to come back but keeper Jordan Pickford made a couple of outstanding saves to ensure that England booked our place in the World Cup Semifinals for only the third time in our history. I couldn't believe it and I was so excited! It's coming home!

Kensington palace tweeted 'you wanted to make history @England and you are dong just that... Football's Coming Home! W.'. Around the country 32 million watched in pubs, clubs and homes and the RAC declared this the quietest Saturday afternoon of the year as many held World Cup barbecues in the 30 degree heat. However, 999 calls rocketed as the London ambulance service appealed to fans to calm down. England fans celebrated around the country as World Cup fever hit a new high. In other quarterfinals Belgium knocked out five time World Cup winners Brazil, Uruguay were beaten by France and hosts Russia were eliminated on penalties by Croatia. The semi finals would see France take on Belgium and Croatia against England. I was still a bit too scared to dream as it looked like England's best chance since 1966 of reaching the World Cup Final.

Somewhat reluctantly I decided to head back to the Harborne Village Social Club for the semifinal against Croatia and as was usual I was decked out in England gear and flags. I was nervous! The match began well with Kieren Trippier scoring a fantastic goal from a free kick with only 5 minutes played. The place went barmy as we jumped about and dreamt of a World Cup Final. Surely we could beat Croatia as we were playing so well and the Croatians didn't look a threat. England should have been further ahead before half time but went in only 1-0 ahead. In the second half Croatia changed their tactics and England did not adapt to these but started to look tired. We stopped passing as much and started hitting hopeful long balls which was very disappointing. Croatia got their equaliser on 68 minutes and the game went to extra time. I was finding it all unbearable as was many others around me.

England looked better in extra time but looked tired. Trippier had a header cleared off the line by a Croatian player. On 109 minutes Croatia scored as an injured Trippier failed to jump with Perisic and his header fell to Mandzukic as he was faster than Stones to react and fired home. With all the substitutions having been made England were down to ten men for the last few minutes as Trippier limped off injured and the final whistle blew as the England players slumped to the ground, many in tears. The 8,000 England fans inside the stadium stayed behind for an hour to sing and applaud their heroes. I found it all too much and headed home broken hearted, although I hadn't expected I had certainly dreamed. England fans had spent 264 million on World Cup Merchandise and England's 1980's style retro training shirt had sold out despite the price tag.

The Final would be between France and Croatia but I had suddenly lost all interest. England would have to face Belgium in the 3rd place play off but I knew that as before England would not put everything into this game following their disappointment and would no doubt lose the match. Around 5.3 million watched the whole game with another 3 million checking in and out to check the score. They must have felt the same as I did. England lost the game 2-0 but at least the FA got £16.6 million in prize money for coming fourth. Overall England had been a great success in the tournament which had been enjoyed across the country. Experts predict 5,000 extra births for next March!

Harry Kane tweeted 'Not the way we wanted to finish but so many positives to take from this experience. Travelling fans and everyone back home have been great - thank you. #ENG #ThreeLions #WorldCup'. Harry Kane was the winner of the Golden Boot with his 6 goals. I didn't take much interest in the World Cup Final once England were out but France went on to beat Croatia 4-2 to lift the trophy. It really could have been our time.

Ipswich Away – June,Terry, me, Taff (Adrian) and Nigel

Villa's relegation party at Huddersfield Away

Hull away – me, June, Ryan, James, Taff (Adrian) and Nigel

Pre season friendly away at Cheltenham with Cheikh Ndoye

Rotherham Away – June, Terry, Nigel, me and Taff

Reading Away last game of the season in fancy dress!

Me and Stephen on way to Charlton

Me and Che Adams before he left to join Southampton for £15 million

Garry Monk and me at the end of season awards

Blackburn Away – James, James, me, June, Taff, Ben, Nigel and mate

Chapter Twenty - Transfer Embargo

Blues began the 2018-19 season under transfer restrictions imposed by the EFL for breaching the Financial Fair Play Regulations and were under threat of a points deduction. Blues were also in trouble for signing Kristian Pedersen whilst under a soft transfer embargo (which no one understood) and for a while the EFL refused to register him. They really do hate Blues at the EFL.

The home and away kits this season were really nice. The home kit is a blue shirt with white trim on the shoulders and upper chest and white strips down the side seams and white shorts with blue strips down the sides and blue socks with white trim at the turnover. The away shirts were yellow with three blue strips on the shoulders, blue shorts with yellow stripes down the side seams and yellow socks with blue trim.

I had been having a lovely summer and it's been really hot. Today was no different as I headed off to Cheltenham for Blues pre season friendly against Cheltenham Town FC. Blues pre season so far had included a game in Austria which we lost 1-0 and a draw with a team in Munich, Germany and last night Blues played a first team against Doncaster Rovers at Solihull Moors which we won with a goal from Che Adams in the 87th minute.

Today I was traveling on the 'party bus' and we left St. Anne's at 10.30 and headed to a pub in Tewksbury called the Ember Inn which was only 20 minutes from the ground. We arrived in the sunshine and ordered drinks and a nice meal. There were soon Bluenoses everywhere, especially outside in the sunshine where our flags were proudly displayed on the fences. We had a lovely couple of hours there before heading off to Cheltenham.

As we arrived in Cheltenham there were Blues fans everywhere and I set about waving to them. Due to traffic we arrived at the Jonny Rocks Stadium with about 10 minutes to kick off, having been directed around the stadium once. We drew the line at the second attempt to send us around the stadium by the stewards and we went about disembarking outside the away turnstiles. There were a lot of Bluenoses inside and we had the end behind the goal and half way along the side.

This was a new ground for me, which doesn't happen often, so it was really nice. It was a happy atmosphere in the sunshine although there wasn't any singing, probably due to it being a friendly game. Garry Monk had pretty much put the kids out, to be honest, apart from Wes Harding, Marc Roberts and Cheikh Ndoye. The players had numbers on their shirts but no names so most of us struggled as to who was actually playing. The programme was of no help either as it gave a list of the Blues players but no numbers. I was disappointed that I would not see the first team players. On the other hand League Two Cheltenham Town fielded their first team.

It was an entertaining game though and Blues went ahead when Charlie Lakin scored on 26 minutes and it remained 1-0 at half time. Blues continued to dominate and Lubala headed home the second from a Lakin corner on 52 minutes. A third goal was disallowed before Blues won a penalty in the 89th minute. The 1,218 (amongst the 2,234 attendance) chanted for NDoye to take the penalty. There were loud chants of 'NDoye! NDoye!' and he looked surprised before gesturing to the bench asking if he should take it and Garry Monk put his thumb up. NDoye then headed towards the penalty spot as the Blues fans continued to chant his name but Lubala put the ball on the spot to take it instead and everyone booed. He did then step aside though and Cheikh NDoye smashed the ball in the net and the away end went wild.

At the end of the game the players came over to applaud us and Cheikh NDoye came over to the fans and I got my photo taken with him. 'Great Goal Cheikh' I said and he replied 'thank you' before high five'ing me and walking away. What a great day. I even managed to get an ice cream before boarding the party bus back to Birmingham.

Well, it's been sunny with no rain for weeks and today it decides to rain for most of the day which is a bit disappointing as Blues final friendly game is at St. Andrews today. It's still warm though and I never let the weather prevent me going to watch my beloved Blues. I headed to St. Andrews on my own today as June can't make it but I know lots of my other mates would be there and I headed to the Cricketers to see who was out. Surprisingly it was almost empty but Barry was up the bar so I joined him for a drink and also saw Liam who arrived not long after me.

I left Barry finishing his pint and headed to the ground where I bumped into Angela who was working on the turnstiles. Once inside I saw Harry, Terry, Nigel and Charlie and I soon joined them. It's brilliant to see them all again and exciting that a new season is about to begin. There has been lots in the paper about Blues having had a transfer embargo imposed on us (yet again!) which is probably why we have made no signings apart from Kevin Pederson and the rumour is that he may not be allowed to play for us. Once again at Blues it's a mess. I think we will struggle if we don't get players in as we have no cover for any injuries and most of the squad this season are youth players.

Today's team is pretty much the first team against Premier League Brighton's first team and we started brightly. Jota looked really good as did our young keeper Connal Trueman who will probably be our first choice this season as Garry Monk has frozen out David Stockdale and Thomas Kuszczak. Other bad news is that Davis Davis is out for a while with a fractured ankle although Issac Vassell should be back in a few weeks.

I was really enjoying watching Blues again and we looked really good. Maikel Kieftenbeld hit a 30 yard thunderbolt which flew into the net to make it 1-0 to Blues. I have to say it's one of the best goals that I have seen at St. Andrews for a long time and worth the admission fee alone. The fans thoroughly enjoyed it. There were a handful of fans from Brighton – bless em. Kieftenbeld's thunderbolt looked to have secured the win for Blues as we defended well and Trueman in goal looked solid but in the 90th minute the referee awarded Brighton a very soft free kick (it was never a foul!) on the edge of the penalty area and they equalised with the last kick of the game – undeservedly.

Although Blues deserved to win, 1-1 was a good result against Premier League opponents and we left the stadium happy and looking forward to the opening game against Norwich City next Saturday at St. Andrews.

There has been a lot in the press during pre season regarding Birmingham falling foul of the EFL's Fair Play rules and that the club are currently under a transfer embargo and that we can't sign any new players, including Kristian Pedersen who is currently playing in pre season games but has not been allowed to sign. It's a mess to be honest. Apparently there are 11 or 12 teams facing transfer embargos in the championship. The Vile have managed to get out of it despite big debts, by having new owners. Bloody typical! Anyway, just before the Norwich game it was announced that Blues could sign five players, and Pedersen was allowed to sign, although there are conditions which include that they must be free transfers!

Despite everything that is going on around Blues at the moment I was still really excited to be heading back to St. Andrews again for the start of a new season. It was a glorious sunny day as June, James and I headed to the Bar 8 for a pre match drink. There were Bluenoses everywhere and many had worn the new yellow away shirt – strange considering we were playing Norwich who play in yellow! This has got to be the only match of the season that I wouldn't wear yellow.

Once we had finished our drinks – which we enjoyed outside in the sunshine, we headed round to find big queues at the turnstiles. We made it into the ground in time for kick off though and the place was packed – nearly 22,500 including 2,300 Norwich fans. It looked amazing and the noise was brilliant as the Bluenoses cheered and sang. Although I don't expect much this season my heart is forever hopeful. I would settle for mid table to be honest, with the team we have, I just don't want another last day relegation fight as I don't think my heart can take it! A sentiment shared by many Bluenoses.

The game got underway and Blues were giving it their all, despite the heat, but went into the halftime break goalless. In the second half Blues played even better and went ahead with a great shot from Jacques Maghoma who fired in via the underside of the crossbar to make it 1-0. The stadium exploded and we celebrated loudly. 'Keep Right On' and 'Garry Monk's Blue and White Army' were sang.

At present Garry Monk has frozen out our 2 main goalkeepers (I don't know why) so we are playing youngster Connal Trueman and he was having a great game up to now but he could do nothing to prevent Norwich's equaliser when it came. I thought a couple of our defenders when brushed aside too easily and that we were a bit naïve. Disappointing to say the least. Blues continued to attack though and gained our reward when sub Viv Soloman Ottabor (recently returned from a loan spell at Blackpool) was put through to slot past the Norwich keeper and it was 2-1 and St. Andrews erupted!

It was in the 87th minute and sure to be the winner? Well, no! Blues had a throw in but managed to lose it, Morrison slipped and a Norwich player was clean through and he fired past Trueman in the 93rd minute to break our hearts and claim a point for Norwich. The match summed up Blues! Joys and sorrows indeed. We really should have won but instead had to settle for a point. There is still a long way to go though and I was still hopeful as I headed home.

Before the transfer window closed Garry Monk bought in 4 new players on loans and I admit to being somewhat surprised by a couple of them. Winger Connor Mahoney came from Bournemouth after spending last season on loan at Barnsley (who were relegated) and striker Omar Bogle came from Cardiff City. Bogle is a big Birmingham fan so hopefully he will do well for us. Goalkeeper Lee Camp came from Cardiff (having not played for them since he signed from Sunderland) and the feedback on the Sunderland fan sites is somewhat concerning as they all say he is the worse keeper they have ever seen! His interview does not help either as he talks about hopeful not making too many bad mistakes!

Perhaps the most surprising signing is Gary Gardener (Craig Gardener's brother) from rivals Villa. Everyone remembers when he scored against us and ran the length of the pitch to celebrate with the vilers. Mind you, the villa fans are more pissed off about it than us. It takes guts to cross the city on loan so we should all get behind him. On the signings Blues have made I think we are going to struggle again.

The coaches for Middlesbrough left St. Andrews 10 minutes late as usual at 0910 and we had 5 official coaches making the trip. The weather is changing too and is a little colder but at least it wasn't raining as we left Birmingham. We made the usual stop at the services the headed off to be met by the police for our escort into Middlesbrough and to the Riverside Stadium. There was no point heading for a pub as it was either into town or across the railway to their home pub which would not let anyone in with colours – which ruled all of us out. Brendan and the lads had tried but to no avail and we met them on their return.

Hence we headed into the away end and got drinks inside. There were already quite a few Bluenoses inside enjoying a pre match drink. Today 1,200 Bluenoses had the made the trip and many were in the lovely new yellow away shirt. I had worn the blue shirt as had June as we thought Blues would play in blue as Middlesbrough are red but today Blues had chosen to play in the yellow and blue away kit. I admitted that I would be more than happy with a draw today.

The game got underway and although Middlesbrough were nothing special they took the lead with their first chance of the game in the 13th minute as the Blues defence failed to stop Assombalonga from curling in a shot past Connal Trueman. Disappointing to say the least. Blues were trying to play good football but we couldn't score and despite Middlesbrough hitting the woodwork 3 times and Morrison clearing off the line, I still though Middlesbrough were beatable. I though our defence was weak and that Morrison was poor. In the second half Garry Monk did bring on Connor Mahoney, Omar Bogle and Viv Soloman-Otabor but we just couldn't get that equaliser. Mahoney and Bogle both looked promising though.

The game finished in a 1-0 defeat and after applauding the players we headed back to the coaches and the long trip home. It's still early days so we are all hopeful that Blues will improve and that the season will not end with another painful relegation battle.

A few days later I was again on my travels and this time it was just June and myself who were heading off to Reading on a Tuesday night for a game in the Carabao Cup (League Cup). I was proudly wearing the new yellow away shirt and enticed June to purchase one from the club shop before the coaches set off from St. Andrews. For once we arrived at the Madejski Stadium in plenty of time and as the weather was nice we headed around the stadium to the Reading end where they have good refreshment stalls and a seated area. It was already quite busy with many Bluenoses having the same idea and I had a lovely sausage and chips meal while June enjoyed a pork bap before heading into the away end.

I purchased a cider and set about watching the Blues video that was playing on the TV whilst the concourse filled up with Bluenoses, many in the away yellow shirt. There were 1000 Bluenoses who had travelled and were in good voice. And then I saw the team selection and my hope of a trip to Wembley for a League Cup Final died there and then. I knew Garry Monk was going to make changes as he is more concentrated on the league but I didn't think he would make 11 changes. Blues were basically playing the kids and reserves. In contrast Reading only made 5 changes and it showed.

It was a poor game against a poor Reading team. We made mistakes and several passes went astray. The match report may say different but I think I must have been at another game as I couldn't take any positives from this match and I thought it was clear that we wanted to exit the Cup at the earliest opportunity. I felt downhearted as it took me back to the dark days of last season when we were crap. We did have some great banter with the Reading fans who seem to have the same sense of humour as us but by the end they were just taking the piss. 'How shit must you be, we're winning at home!' rang out and we responded with 'his shit must you be, it's only 2-0!' So a few laughs were had.

It's only 3 games into the season and still no win but it's early days yet and we have to have faith in manager Garry Monk. There are still strange things going on at the club though as four administration staff have reportedly been sacked and with a transfer embargo and a possible points deduction I don't know what's going to happen in the future.

On the Friday night it was off to St. Andrews for the televised game against Swansea City who were relegated from the Premier League at the end of last season and they have had a good start to their season with two wins already. Once again Garry Monk will be coming up against one of his old teams (managed and played for). Despite the fact that it was a Friday night and being shown live there was a good crowd of 20,083 in great voice and the atmosphere was fabulous.

The game got under way and Blues totally dominated the most one sided game I have seen for a long time and how we didn't score I will never know. Blues had 17 shots to Swansea's 1. Blues did have to ball in the net but it was disallowed. The referee was awful and gave everything to Swansea. He was a disgrace. The second half Swansea came into it a bit more but were still dominated by Blues who had several more chances to score but just couldn't finish as well as their keeper making some good saves. It wasn't to be though and the game finished 0-0 and the wait for a win goes on. As Garry Monk said in his after match interview, we should be now sitting here with 6 points instead of 2. Jota got the Sky TV man of the match with an outstanding performance.

Five days later we were off to Bolton on a lovely sunny Wednesday in Birmingham but by the time we arrived in Bolton 3 hours 30 minutes later it was pouring with rain. It had stopped by the time we disembarked our coaches though but was still dull. This season 950 Bluenoses made the trip compared to 5000 last season which was probably due to the price increase. Last time it was £15 adults and £1 under 18's. This time it was £30 adults and £12 under 18's so a massive price hike. Perhaps they don't want us there after we completely out sang them last time. It was still a great atmosphere among the Bluenoses this time too though.

Once again Blues dominated the match but just couldn't put the ball in the net. Blues had 17 shots on goal compared to Bolton who had one chance which ex Blues player Will Buckley clearly put the ball in the net with his hand for the winning goal for Bolton. How this was missed by the officials I will never know! As manager Garry Monk said after the game, the referee (who was very poor and biased against Blues) cost us the game. So Blues lost the game 1-0, another game we should have won but I am still optimistic as there is a lot of positives to be taken from the way Blues are playing at the moment. It is very entertaining football and the results will come. It was a long journey back though as the M6 was closed for maintenance and we sped home via the A roads which left me feeling somewhat travel sick (something that I don't suffer with either so it must have been bad!). It settled once we were back on the motorway. Glad to get home though!

It was a nice sunny day as we headed off to Nottingham for Blues match against Nottingham Forest and today it was me, June, James and Terry who travelled on the coach as both Nigel and Charlie were away on holiday. It didn't take us long to get there and once we arrived Terry and James headed to the burger van and me and June headed off to Nottingham's famous chip shop which is near the ground. We bumped into Robert (Hoppy) Hopkins on the way and he warned us that there was a big queue out of the chippie. Not to be deterred we carried on and joined the queue and Hoppy appeared a few minutes later to add 'I told you there was a queue' as he laughed and headed off. It was worth it as the fish and chips was amazing. The fish was so big that I shared it with June and Terry when we arrived back at the stadium.

Then we headed into the away end and the 2,083 Bluenoses were in full voice. It was amazing and we never stopped singing for the entire match. We had brilliant banter with the Forest fans in the stand above us. The Forest fans weren't singing at first though so we kept ourselves happy with 'Keep Right On' and 'we hate Villa more than you' to each other. The sun was shining on the away end and I had worn my yellow away shirt and as luck would have it that was the kit that Blues were playing in today.

Blues started the game really strongly and we cheered them on. We were in heaven when Lucas Jutkiewicz rose to loop a header over the Forest keeper and into the net to make in 1-0 to Blues in the 21st minute. The away end went mental as the Blues players ran to us to celebrate. A Blues fan had been the first to reach Jutkiewicz and hug him before the other players caught up. Two other Bluenoses made it to the celebrating players and Blue smoke poured out from the flares that were set off when we scored. It was crazy, me, June, Terry and James had lungs full of blue smoke but it was worth it. The celebrations were amazing!

Blues had a couple more chances but went in at half time with a 1-0 lead and well worth it. The second half started much the same with Blues on top. Then on 72 minutes Che Adams turned on the edge of the penalty area and fired a shot into the bottom corner to make it 2-0 and cue more unbelievable scenes in the away end. Another blue flare was set off with someone picking it up and running around with it as the stewards chased him. It was fantastic.

Blues fans started having some fun with the Forest fans who were now silent, many had headed for the exits, and sang 'you're not famous anymore' and they responded (as always) with 'Champions of Europe'. This is when the fun really started as Blues sang 'you live in the past. Just like the Villa you live in the past'. Which I thought was hilarious. Of course it prompted another 'Champions of Europe' from the Forest fans and so Blues came back with 'you weren't even born! Champions of Europe, you weren't even born'. Brilliant! They really hated that and started throwing coins and a couple of bottles. June came away £2 better off!

To be honest, with 15 minutes to go it looked a certain win but Forest tried their luck with a long range shot from the edge of the penalty area and it beat Lee Camp in goal and it was 2-1. Typical Blues, I thought, and with only 2 minutes left Lee Camp parried a shot straight to their forward who beat him at the near post as he attempted to save it with his foot? I'm really not sure about this goalkeeper and I think we should have stuck to the young Connal Trueman. The Forest fans sang '2-0 and you fucked it up' and they were right. We sang 'Keep Right On' and didn't let it get to us. The game finished 2-2 and it was yet another game we should have won, I hope that this is not going to be the story of our season. At least we are playing really good football which is entertaining to watch and if we carry on the same I'm sure the wins will start coming.

I was quite hopeful that Blues would get that first win against QPR at St. Andrews but 21,155 saw a very poor game that finished in a 0-0 draw. QPR just flooded the midfield and we struggled to get through and ended up hitting long balls all the time. Basically a poor QPR side just dragged us down to their level and it really was the worse game I have seen for a while. I'm not too down though as it is only one match and Blues have played really well in all the other games (apart from the Cup game against Reading) and I still think once we get a win we will go from strength to strength.

I hade to rearrange my shifts in order to get to the local derby against West Brom due to the game being switched from the Saturday to the Friday night to suit Sky TV. It meant I had to work an early but at least I would make the match. I am so glad that I did make it as the atmosphere was brilliant and St. Andrews was rocking. There were 23,000 inside the stadium but many had been unable to get tickets due to new selling arrangements making it harder and some could not get tickets because of their post code. It really is poorly organised at the moment with this new fast pay card etc and it's not easy for people to make last minute decisions to attend the games.

Blues started the game really well and created several chances to keep the fans in good voice. At one point the entire stadium - Blues and West Brom sang 'shit on the Villa'. On 26 minutes the stadium exploded when Jota scored to put Blues 1-0 ahead and a couple of blue flares were set off in the Tilton causing blue smoke to fill the stadium. Brilliant scenes of celebration ensued. The Albion fans had been predicting that they were going to thrash Blues 4 or 5-0. The way Blues were playing there was no chance of that more the other way round. Three minutes later and Blues were awarded a penalty and up stepped Jota to take the kick. We all held our breath as he hit it towards the bottom right corner but their keeper got down to save it and we knew we would be left to rue it. It was still predominantly Blues but in the 39th minute the inevitable happened and West Brom scored the equaliser and we were stunned. 'Keep Right On' was belted out in stubbornness and we continued to get behind the team.

The second half got underway and Blues continued to dominate although West Brom did come into the game a bit more towards the end of the match but it finished in yet another draw that Blues really should have won. It's still a great result against one of the leagues top teams and the football from Blues is really good under Garry Monk so we can't complain despite feeling disappointed that we didn't win.

The following Wednesday we boarded the coaches and headed for Sheffield for the night game against Sheffield United who were doing very well at the moment and had recently smashed Villa 4-1 at Brammall Lane. It was a cold night and around 900 Bluenoses had made the trip and were in good voice as usual. The game got underway and Blues continued to play really great football. Despite being away from home we were still the better team although we just couldn't score tonight. Gary Gardener came closest when he hit the post from a free kick in the second half as Blues had 9 chances to the home teams 4. The outcome was yet another draw, this time 0-0 but still a very good result against a team flying high at home. We left the stadium in good spirits as we headed for the coaches to take us back to Birmingham. It was worth the late night.

On Saturday we were off on our travels again, this time to Leeds as Blues took on top of the table and unbeaten Leeds Utd. Despite Leeds charging an extortionate £37 Blues had filled the away section and were in good voice. There was some great banter going on between the Bluenoses and the Leeds fans. There were over 34,000 in the Stadium and Blues manager Garry Monk was returning to face one of his old teams. It was my mate Tracey's birthday back in Abu Dhabi and she is a massive Leeds fan so I text her a picture from outside Elland Road and wished her a happy birthday (not a win though).

The game kicked off with Blues playing in our fabulous Yellow away shirts and on 8 minutes Che Adams fired in a shot to put Blues 1-0 ahead and the away end erupted! It left the home fans stunned and we belted out Keep Right On. It got even better on 29 Minutes when Che Adams hit another shot from the edge of the penalty area which found its way into the far corner and it was now 2-0 Blues and unbelievable celebrations in the away end!

Blues fans started singing 'Leeds, Leeds are falling apart again!' and we were all enjoying ourselves although I was still a bit too apprehensive to think we could hang on and get our first win of the season and inflict Leeds first defeat. The singing and banter was brilliant although the Leeds fans were somewhat subdued now. They were giving Garry Monk lots of abuse as was to be expected as he had managed them. I didn't want half time to come as I wasn't convinced we would play as well in the second half.

The second half got underway and Leeds were really physical although Blues held firm until the 85th minute when Leeds got a goal back and proceeded to lay siege to the Blues goal. It seemed that the referee wanted to continue play until Leeds got level as he added 7 minutes of injury time but actually played 8 minutes! Blues held firm though and Goalkeeper Lee Camp pulled off a great save to preserve our lead and the away end erupted when the referee was forced to blow for full time. What a fantastic away win! We had great fun taunting the departing Leeds fans as we held our scarves aloft and sang 'Leeds, Leeds are falling apart again'. The singing continued as we made our way out of the stadium and back to the coaches. What a great away day and I was really happy on the journey back to Birmingham.

It was off to St. Andrews for the next game which concerned me a bit more than the Leeds game as Blues don't seem to do very well against sides at the bottom of the table and although it's still early days, Ipswich are currently sitting near the bottom and without a win. This did not bode well for me although I was still looking forward to the game. My mate June would be missing today as she was staying home to watch the Ryder Cup so I would miss her today.

As is usual this season a good crowd of 21,612 were in attendance but the atmosphere seemed really flat which is somewhat unusual. Maybe the players sensed it? Whatever it was it didn't get any better when Ipswich took the lead on 26 minutes when Nolan easily skipped passed Pederson to beat Lee Camp at his near post (seems to be happening a lot) and then Ipswich doubled their lead just before half time when Pennington was left totally unmarked to head home from a corner. Their small group of fans were in shock and sang 'how shit must you be? we're winning away'

I didn't know what to make of it and could only hope Garry Monk would give them a rocketing and that we would play better in the second half. That is exactly what happened as Garry Monk told them he would have substituted all of them but he didn't have 11 subs on the bench. It certainly worked as Blues were brilliant in the second half and the crowd responded and St. Andrews became a cauldron of noise again. It took only 3 minutes of the second half for Blues to half the deficit as the 'Duke' Lucas Jutkiewicz scored and the stadium exploded.

Blues were on fire and we created chance after chance with the home fans roaring them on. On 68 minutes as the ball bounced around inside the area Jutkiewicz smashed the ball into the net to claim Blues equaliser and his second of the game. He ran off in celebration as blue smoke filled the air from a flare set off in the Tilton and wild celebrations ensued.

In the 88th minute Ipswich had a player sent off as he cynically brought down Jacques Maghoma who was through on goal. Blues hammered the Ipswich goal but just couldn't get the winner we craved. Although it felt like 2 points dropped and we really should have won, I was heartened by the fact that last season under Steve Cotterill Blues would never have recovered from a 2-0 deficit or even 1-0 so there is much to be happy with.

A few days later on the Tuesday night we headed to Brentford and as the coaches surprisingly arrived early we headed into the nearby Griffin Pub. My nephew Stephen joined us from work despite being unwell with a cold/flu. It was lovely to catch up with him and he told me that they are arranging his wedding to Alice for next August on my moms birthday so that will be lovely. We then headed into the ground and onto the cold terraces. Blues took the lead and the away end erupted in celebration as blue smoke filled the air from a smoke bomb and it looked great.

Unfortunately Brentford equalised in the second half against the run of play and to add insult to injury a Brentford player cheated by falling to the ground holding his face and Kieftenbeld was sent off. Garry Monk went mad over the injustice of it and he too was sent off. The Blues fans were also up in arms and it was really bad that a dirty Brentford team and a crap referee could rob us of the 3 points. The red card was later rescinded for Kieftenbeld as it was shown that he never touched the player. The player should have got a ban for cheating the referee! Garry Monk had to serve out his ban though. The game ended in a 1-1 draw and we headed back to find our coaches with a great sense of injustice.

There was another good crowd at St. Andrews of nearly 20,000 when Rotherham came to town and I was amongst them to enjoy the atmosphere. I was weary once again as it was a newly promoted team that are not expected to do very much but haven't done too badly so far. The game kicked off and it took only 10 minutes to break the deadlock as Lucas Jutkiewicz headed home from a cross from Jota to make it 1-0 and we were on our feet celebrating. It was all Blues now and 3 minutes later we were 2-0 up when Jutkiewicz fired home from close range following several attempts in the area. More celebrations ensued! I didn't want half time to come as we were playing so well but it did and we went in 2-0 ahead for the break.

Blues started the second half just as well and on 68 minute Lucas Jutkiewicz completed a well deserved hat trick as he scored a cracker to make it 3-0 from a free kick which was passed to him to fire home and so began the celebrations. The game was pretty safe although Rotherham did pull a goal back on 77 minutes but Blues hung on the win 3-1 and collect all 3 points. Another great result! This now means that Blues have the longest undefeated run in England, most average headers won per game in all of the UK, Jota has the most assists in the league and the loudest fans in the league by decibel readings. Not bad eh! Garry Monks blue and white army.

The following weekend I was heading off on my holidays to sunny Tenerife for a well earned break but it did mean I would miss 3 Blues games so it was bittersweet. The first weekend I was away was just the international break and it was in Tenerife that I watched England win 3-2 against Spain after leading 3-0 at half time. Still a really good win though.

No matter how hard I tried I could not get a live stream for the Stoke game where 3,200 Bluenoses were giving a good account of themselves. This was a big game against a side only just relegated from the Premier League and managed by ex-Blues manager Gary Rowett. Everyone had been devastated when Gary Rowett was sacked despite rumours that he had constantly been asking for more money after talks with varies teams but has since shown his true colours after leaving Derby for a bigger job at Stoke as soon as it came available. Anyway, we were desperate to get a result against him as he always seems to get one over us.

I had to rely on live updates and texts from my mates and I was delighted when Che Adams scored on 81 minutes to put Blues 1-0 up. I had to smile when I heard that Gary Rowett was sent off before the end of the game and despite the referee adding several minutes of injury time Blues held on for the win and the Blues fans celebrated in style. So much so that the police had to walk them back to the station rather that on the usual buses. What a great result and our undefeated run continues.

I was still in Tenerife for the home game against Reading and I rushed back to our apartment from our evening meal in the hope of finding a live stream. Unfortunately I was to be disappointed and I had to make do with alerts and text messages from my friends at the game. Another good crowd at St. Andrews saw the first half end goalless but the second half saw a much improved Blues team take the lead on 49 minutes through Gary Gardener to put Blues 1-0 ahead. My mates said Gary Gardener was outstanding in this match. The 'Juke' Lucas Jutkiewicz added a second in the 70th minute which is how it remained until the 90th minute when Reading pulled a goal back the make the final score 2-1 to Blues. Our unbeaten run continues and that is now 3 wins on the trot as we continue to climb the table. I'm really looking forward to getting to a game once I get back home.

Once again I was relying on live score alerts and updates from my friends at St. Andrews for the game against Sheffield Wednesday on Saturday 28th October due still being in Tenerife on holiday. It was another good crowd of nearly 24,000 inside St. Andrews and I'm sure they were as disappointed as I was when Stephen Fletcher put Sheffield Wednesday ahead on 19 minutes. Blues didn't give up though and pressed to get back into the game. The equaliser came on 43 minutes when Connor Mahoney scored to send Blues into the break all square again at 1-1. Blues continued to look dangerous and the 'Juke' Lucas Jutkiewicz scored in the 80th minute to put Blues ahead. I was getting quite nervous listening to the updates and was therefore delighted when Che Adams scored the 3rd goal with six minutes remaining and the three points were in the bag. What a fantastic run Blues are on at present and we are getting ever nearer to the playoff places.

Due to a medical emergency in Tenerife my stay as extended and I was unable to make it to Derby game despite having match tickets and travel organised. At the time of kick off I was still miles away in Tenerife. My mate June went though and kept me updated and I followed the live updates on my iPad. I saw the first 15 minutes by live stream but that was then taken down, much to my disappointment. I did see Blues take the lead when Lucas Jutkiewicz scored to make it 1-0 which is how it stayed till half time.

The second half saw Derby up their game and they scored 3 goals to win the game 3-1. June said we were beaten by the best team we have played against this season so as disappointing as it is we have to take it on the chin. Hopefully we will bounce back next week when we play Hull City at St. Andrews and I will be there to cheer them on.

Chapter Twenty One - Che Will Tear You Apart Again!

It was a cold day when Blues entertained Hull City's at St. Andrews and although Hull were languishing in the bottom half they had begun to turns things around coming into today's game on the back of a good result against high flyers West Brom. The atmosphere was a bit subdued inside the stadium for some unknown reason despite there being a good attendance and Blues were soon 2-0 ahead with goals from in form Che Adams. So at half time it was a good 2-0 lead we took into the break but Hull came out looking a different side in the second half and turned the game on its head in 13 second half minutes as they scored 3 goals to storm into a 3-2 lead and we were stunned! This did then inspire Blues to attack Hull in waves and woke the St. Andrews crowd up too as they roared their team on.

It was an amazing second half as Blues threw everything at Hull and with 6 minutes remaining Che Adams scored to complete his hat trick and the stadium exploded in joy and relief! What a comeback! This time last year it was unheard of that Blues would recover from being 1-0 down let alone in circumstances like today, what an amazing difference Garry Monk has made! His name was being sang loudly and another great rendition of 'Keep Right On'. The game ended in a 3-3 draw and we all left the stadium fairly happy.

I was looking forward to the game against Villa as I thought it was about time we got a result against them and I felt this was our best chance for a while as all our players were now playing at their best under Garry Monk. It's always a nerve wracking time though and today's game was another early kick off over in the dark side which meant that me, Stephen, James and Steve were in the local football club social club by 8.30 am. There was a good crowd of Bluenoses already there and we had a good time and a 'team photo' before we ordered taxis to take us to Vile Park for the game.

We ended up arriving more near the Vile end but were soon spotted by stewards (because Steve was foolishly singing shit on the Villa) and moved into the away cordon which was swamped with police. Once inside the Blues end it was buzzing and loud as several songs were belted out. I met up with June and the game soon got underway. On 28 minutes Lucas Jutkiewicz scored in front of the Holte End to make it 1-0 Blues and the away end exploded and blue smoke filled the air. Me and Stephen went bonkers - it was brilliant!

Blues should have made it 2-0 not long after but of course we were left to rue it as Villa scored 2 goals against the run of play! Bloody typical. We were all gutted but continued to sing and belt out 'Keep Right On' putting the vilers to shame. Despite being behind at half time we still had faith that Blues could get back into the game. Our hopes were dashed just 6 minutes into the second half when the Vile got a 3rd goal. Blues were playing really well though in what was a cracking game and 6 minutes later Pederson smashed the ball home to make it 3-2 and game on again. I really thought we could rescue the game until Craig Gardener plus a couple of other players allowed a Vile player to run past them all and score and make it 4-2 which was not at all a true reflection of a game that Blues played so well in. That was how it stayed and we left feeling robbed again but at least we are playing really good football this season and competing with the top teams. Villa may be just above us at the moment but it won't be for long.

A few days after the Villa game and I was off to London for the midweek game against Millwall at the Den. The coach journey took quite a while and we arrived very early as the coaches had left Birmingham early to avoid the rush hour and the Millwall turnstiles were not even open yet. It was a cold evening so me and June headed to the Millwall cafe to get some chips to warm us up as we waited for the turnstiles to open. My nephew Stephen joined us not long afterwards as he had heard it was pay on the gate and decided to join us from work.

There were over 1500 Blues fans in attendance and it was the only stand that looked pretty full as the other 3 ends of the ground were very sparsely occupied and the stadium looked embarrassingly empty. Us Bluenoses were in great voice though and sang throughout the game. We took the piss out of the Millwall contingent relentlessly including 'nobody likes you - because your shit!'

Blues really needed a good result to get back on track and we hoped the team would pick themselves up and put in a good performance. Blues started really well and on 11 minutes Che Adams hit the post and the ball then hit a Millwall player and went in for an own goal! The away end erupted and a blue flare scorched the pitch as blue smoke filled the stadium. I was jumping around all over the place! Brilliant! It got even better when Millwall had a player sent off on 30 minutes for a bad foul on Mikel kieftenbeld and they were down to 10 men.

Being down to 10 men seemed to inspire Millwall and it became a tough game. Then on 76 minutes Michael Morrison scored and the away end celebrated again. The goal was right in front of the away fans and the noise was tremendous and I again jumped around wildly. A couple of minutes later Garry Monk brought Gary Gardener on for Kieftenbeld which meant that the two Gardener brothers were on the pitch at the same time for Birmingham for the first time. It prompted a rendition of the 'Toure' song that went 'Craigy, Craigy, Craigy, Craigy Craigy Gardener! Gary, Gary, Gary, Gary, Gary Gardener!' etc and it went on for a while. It was great fun.

The Millwall fans left way before the end to a chorus of 'is there a fire drill?' and the game ended with a fantastic 2-0 away win for Blues . Stephen headed off to catch the train and we headed back to the coaches very happy indeed. It would be a long trip through London and home but it was well worth the trip.

There was another good crowd of over 20,000 at St. Andrews for the visit of Preston who were currently on a good run of form. Ever the optimist I went for 3-0 on the Blues predictor though. Strangely enough the crowd were quite subdued for the first half in which Blues were below par but still managed to create a few chances and half time came with the match still goalless.

The second half started with a bang which really got the crowd on their feet as Maikel Kieftenbeld hit a long pass over the heads of both defenders and attackers straight to the keeper who managed to let it slip through his hands then his legs and into the goal! What an unbelievable goal! Kieftenbeld couldn't believe his luck as everyone ran to him to celebrate. The goalkeeper looked absolutely gutted as a lone Preston player went over to console him. I didn't know whether to laugh or celebrate so I did both. Manager Garry Monk had looked away when Kieftenbeld hit the pass and was cursing him when he heard the roar of the crowd and turned to see the ball in the net!

The goal kick started the Blues and the crowd into life and the fun started. On 61 minutes Colin crossed for Maghoma to fire a shot into the bottom left corner and double Blues lead. The stadium erupted again as we celebrated loudly. Even at 2-0 I still find it hard to relax but when Che Adams fired into the bottom right corner following a pass from man of the match Kieftenbeld I celebrated and finally relaxed, confident that the 3 points were now in bag. Such was Blues dominance we had 16 shots - 7 on target. Brilliant result and I headed home happy again. Blues are unbeaten at home for a very long time now.

I've got to say that I don't like playing Bristol City. I've never forgiven them for trying so hard to send us down a couple of years ago when we had to win to stay up. We had been 1-0 up with minutes to go and they were so desperate to try to relegate us that they even sent their keeper up to attack a corner and they had absolutely nothing riding on that match. I'm happy to say that they never succeeded and Blues won the game 1-0 so stuff them!

There were 21,000 inside St. Andrews to see Blues well and truly mugged! Despite several chances and Jutkiewicz hitting the woodwork in the last few minutes and 3 penalty appeals Blues lost to a poor goal to conceded from a corner which gave Bristol a 1-0 win. Blues still have an excellent home record though, with this defeat being only our second loss at home this season and since Garry Monk arrived last season. I went home disappointed but not disheartened.

It was a real rainy day as we headed north to Blackburn as a storm was in full flow and as I disembarked the coach by the Stadium in Blackburn to go and look for the badge seller the rain hit me full force. It was that torrential ice rain and I deeply regretted going to the badge seller as he had sold out of matchday badges and I was soaked so much with the ice rain directly into my face on the way back that I ended up with a bad cold which meant losing time from work - something I hate to do. I got straight back on the coach where the others were still nice and dry and we all waited a while before heading inside.

There were lots of Bluenoses and despite the cold we were in good voice. The game got underway and Blues were poor in the first half. We conceded after 16 minutes and then again just after kick off for the second half. Very disappointing. Monk then brought on Jota and Craig Gardener in a double substitution in the 56th minute which turned the game around.

Blues looked a different side and the fight back began when Blues were awarded a penalty in the 77th minute and Craig Gardener stepped up to fire the ball home and it was now 2-1 and game on. The fans were singing their hearts out and cheering the team on. Three minutes later and Che Adams shot into the bottom corner and the away end went mental. Blue smoke filled the air and we jumped around as we celebrated what had seemed like a very unlikely point. In fact we could have gone one to win the game and we all agreed that if we had 5 more minutes we would have won. What an inspired substitution by Garry Monk and we all sang his name. The game ended in a 2-2 draw and we went home happy despite the storm.

I was excited about the trip to Wigan as there would be nearly 5000 Bluenoses making the journey and I was anticipating a great atmosphere again. We arrived by coach early and headed towards the Red Robin pub only to find that it was already full of Bluenoses both inside and outside and the doormen were not allowing anyone else in. Therefore we headed back towards the stadium and decided to try the bar in Frankie and Benny's which proved to be a good decision as it was not packed and we easily obtained pre match drinks. After a couple of drinks we headed back to the stadium and joined the other Bluenoses in the packed away end. It was brilliant and everyone was in good voice.

The game got underway and Blues were playing in our yellow and blue away kit and looked to be playing well from the off. Che Adams scored on 26 minutes to put Blues in front and the away end exploded in celebration. The singing was non stop and just before half time Michael Morrison scored to make it 2-0 and more celebrations ensued.

The Blues fans made up over a 3rd of the 13,774 attendance and were making our presence known. We even got to sing 'Jingle Bells - oh what fun it is to see City win Away!' The second half began much like the first with Blues dominating and on 61 minutes Jacques Maghoma scored in front of the away end to make it 3-0 and we went mental! Amazing scenes ensued and 'Garry, Garry Monk!' was belted out. It was brilliant! We were all so happy with a great 3-0 away win. Blues are now 8th on the league.

There was loads of positive feedback on social media from the Wigan fans which included:

'Yeah, Birmingham fans were mad mate!'.

'Them Birmingham fans are something else'

'Aside from the bunch who were booted out early, fair play to the Birmingham fans, amazing support! Wish our fans were that vocal ☐'

'Fair play to the Birmingham City fans. Normally have a week of the rubbish on the wafc timeline from teams bringing far less than they did today. No rubbish, turned up in numbers, packed the away end and (sadly) probably had a cracking day.'

Garry Monk's verdict was "it was the last thing we said before we left the changing room, that there are 4,500 fans here who have come to support you guys. At this time of year, money can be scarce, we have to give them a performance as we have all season - with some heart and positive front foot football. I think we gave them that. They can have a really good Christmas Day now with three points and the atmosphere on Boxing Day I'm sure will be amazing. We're looking forward to it."

Needless to say once the hoards of Blues coaches left the car park we all had a very enjoyable trip back. We sang and chatted and were very excited about the forthcoming match against Stoke City on Boxing Day.

There was a big crowd of over 26,000 at St. Andrews on Boxing Day as Gary Rowett's Stoke came to town and Blues were looking to do the double over them. Even the Olympic Gallery was opened for the game. The atmosphere was electric and Blues were in great voice from the start. I was a bit anxious about the game as usual but really hoped we could win. Blues came roaring out of the pits with Jota nearly scoring after only 1 minute and we could have been a couple of goals in front before we did take the lead when Jacques Maghoma scored a spectacular goal as he curled in a shot from outside the penalty area on 43 minutes to send Blues into the break with a 1-0 lead. St. Andrews erupted and the noise was deafening as we all celebrated. The Stoke fans were silent.

The second half saw Stoke trying to make a comeback although Blues continued to play well. Mind you, it's always nerve wracking watching Blues even when we are in the lead. I remained stressed until Omar Bogle came on as substitute and unleashed a spectacular left footed shot from some distance which flew into the bottom corner of the net on 87 minutes and the place exploded. Blue smoke came from the Tilton and the celebrations began in earnest as we knew the win was ours. I was jumping around celebrating and I was so happy. When the referee finally blew his whistle the noise was deafening again as the majority of the 26,344 celebrated. Gary Rowett was getting a lot of stick from the Stoke fans and it wasn't long afterwards that he was sacked and his short time at Stoke came to an abrupt end. So I headed home happy. Blues are up to 7th and only 2 points off the play offs.

The last game of 2018 was at St. Andrews and a good crowd of 24,000 turned up as Blues decided to open half of the Olympic Gallery due to number of tickets already sold. Unfortunately they made the decision on matchday which meant they probably lost out on perhaps another 1000 fans. Still a good crowd though. I couldn't help but reflect on the difference from the same time last year when Blues were bottom of the league with 17 points and the lowest scorers in the EFL. This time Blues are 7th with 37 points and +10 goal difference, yes we are scoring for fun now. It's the first time in many years (since the 50's I think) that Blues have had 2 forwards with 20 goals by Christmas. So far Che Adams and Lucas Jutkiewicz have 21 between them. Good times I think. It was so miserable last season that this one has been a breath of fresh air so far and very enjoyable with the football under Gary Monk.

Unfortunately today's game turned into a hard fought battle as cheating Brentford came to town to bully, foul and dive in an attempt to gain a result. Yes same old Brentford! The referee was completely useless and lost the game early on. He should have stamped down on Brentford's constant fouls which would have prevented the brawls that followed. Brentford had 5 players booked and Maupay had to be substituted for his own good before he was sent off. He left the field to a crescendo of boos from the Blues fans. The match finished 0-0 and Blues were forced to settle for a point as well as a fair few bruises.

Garry Monks comments about the Brentford striker Neal Maupay was "he does it every game and he had one of our players sent off for exactly that reason in the last game. So we knew he was going to do it and unfortunately, I think everyone in football knows he does it, but he doesn't get punished for it. I think it was obvious the way they took him off the pitch he was going to get himself into trouble. That's in his make-up and a lot of Brentford's make-up and that's for them to decide whether that's what they want". Blues remain in 7th place and we have had a great festive period so far. I am really happy watching Blues play this season as there is always hope.

I had worked New Year's Eve and it had been an horrendously busy day and short staffed so I was knackered when I got up to travel to Sheffield on New

Year's Day but I was really looking forward to the trip. It is so different to this time last year with no stress at all as Blues sit comfortably in 7th place just outside the play offs. Everyone is just happy that we are not involved in the relegation scrap and anything extra is a bonus.

Surprisingly though, there were only 4 official coaches going and I heard that 1500 Bluenoses were heading to the game. I though we would have sold our allocation plus more for this game but I guess a lot of people would probably be nursing New Year hangovers and therefore decided not to venture out. Thanks to my sober/working New Year's Eve I was in good health (apart from being really tired) and was happy to meet up with all my friends on the coach where we took over the back seats and our flag was proudly on display across the back window.

We had a great catch up and a laugh on the way and before we knew it we were arriving at Hillsborough in Sheffield. Of course we immediately headed up the road to their famous chippy 'the Four Lanes' where there was already a massive queue of Blues fans that stretched out into the street. Terry said he didn't care if he missed the kick off as long as he got his fish and chips! I must say the mini fish and chips were wonderful and worth queuing for.

We then headed into the away end and although the concourse wasn't packed and buzzing with beer shampoos it looked there was way more than the said 1500 Blues fans in attendance. Blues played in our 'lucky' yellow shirts again but we didn't start very well and looked poor. Wes Harding decided to catch the ball in his arms about a foot from the sideline (why?) and from the resulting free kick Sheffield Wednesday took the lead. It looked like the ball went in in slow motion and I thought Lee Camp in goal should have saved it but looking at the replay later on TV I'm not so sure. It meant that Blues went in at half time 1-0 down.

Blues started the second half much better and it wasn't long before Che Adams got behind the Wednesday defence to fire home and the away end erupted. A blue smoke bomb was set off really close to us and we were all engulfed in thick blue smoke but it looked good and it was fun. Parity was restored although Wednesday had a few good chances but Lee Camp was outstanding and a new song was born - to the tune of 'our house' by madness which went 'Lee Camp - in the middle of our goal! Lee Camp - in the middle of our goal! Lee Camp'. It was great. The game finished 1-1 and Blues dropped down to 8th as Nottingham Forest beat Leeds to go above us. I'm not concerned though as I'm just happy to be clear of the bottom 3 and of course to be above the Vile.

It was a very happy trip home on the coach. I'm really lucky to have such a fun group of friends and we sang the Lee Camp song and 'Birmingham, Birmingham Ra Ra Ra' all the way home as well as chatting and laughing. What a great away day following the Blues!

I had been looking forward to the trip to the London Stadium since the draw for the FA Cup 3rd round paired Birmingham City with West Ham United and we had booked our train travel immediately. Unfortunately I was feeling really unwell with flu like symptoms but I didn't let this stop me and I headed to New Street station with June, James and Steve to get the 8.30 train to Euston. There was already loads of Bluenoses in New Street station and I chatted to Fidler who was also headed to the game with his daughter and mates.

The train journey went quite quickly and our train pulled into Euston at 0955am and we made our way by the London Underground to Liverpool Street and found our way into 'Dirty Dicks' which was really quiet compared to the nearby Wetherspoon's which was packed with Blues. I had already text Stephen (my nephew) to let him know where we were headed and he came into the pub not long afterwards along with several other Bluenoses including MIB Dave and Jeanette.

June and I had to leave to pub early to meet Nigel and Terry who had the extra ticket for Stephen in the Blues end, so we left the others enjoying their drinks while we got the tube to Stratford. Once we disembarked at Stratford it was a long walk to the stadium and I resisted the half half FACup scarves as I could not possibly buy a scarf with claret and blue on it! The London Stadium looked good but was spoiled by the claret and blue on it. It took us about 25-30 minutes for us the get to where Nigel, Terry and James were waiting for us and it was then like trying to get into Fort Knox! It began with two searches on the way to the turnstiles and then we had to undo our coats again once we got inside. It was ridiculous and it's not a friendly place at all. We were definitely not made to feel welcome.

Once inside I tried to get some hot food but failed miserably and had to settle for a packet of crisps and a mars duo (the chocolate had turned white!) for a total of £3.55 and had to be paid for by 'card only'. It doesn't feel like a proper football stadium, in fact it was totally soulless. We headed to our seats in the upper tier and the view was really good considering we are so far from the pitch. The others soon joined us and the atmosphere amongst the Blues fans was fantastic as 5200 of us belted out 'Keep Right On'. The overall attendance was 55,000 but the only noise came from the Blues fans. At times Blues sang 'is this a library?' as well as 'your support is fucking shit'. The song that really hit home with the West Ham fans was when we sang 'your not West Ham anymore!'

The sound of 5200 Bluenoses belting out Keep Right On was incredible as the game kicked off. It seemed to bounce of the roof and echo around the Stadium - fantastic! Unfortunately Blues conceded after only 2 minutes as Lee Camp only parried a shot which was then headed home by a West Ham player but even their cheer for their goal wasn't loud and was soon drowned out by 'Keep Right On!' Their stadium really is soulless and I am so glad we don't have to play at stadiums like this very often. I feel quite sorry for the West Ham fans who have lost their home ground and have to travel to a soulless pit like this. Blues had a great chance to equalise when Lucas Jutkiewicz had a header cleared off the line by Andy Carroll but we went in at half time 1-0 down but not outplayed.

At half time there was a mascot race as the West Ham mascot 'Hammerhead' challenged the Blues mascot Beau Brummie to a race. Of course Beau Brummie romped home and the Bluenoses sang 'he's one of our own' to Beau and then 'your fucking shit' to Hammerhead. I thoroughly enjoyed that bit of fun as there was no way I was heading back down all them stairs for a half time break! The second half got underway and Blues were playing really well and looked like we could get back into the game. Credit to Garry Monk for playing his strongest team although a a lot of that is probably because we only have 18 fit players at present. Blues just couldn't get the goal we need though and in stoppage time Andy Carroll scored the second for West Ham and our hopes were dashed.

At the end of the day Blues had not disappointed against a Premier League side and we had all enjoyed a great day out and a new ground to tick off our lists. It got quite tasty on our walk back to the station as the biggest police presence I have ever seen at a football match tried to keep the two sets on supporters separate. A West Ham fan threw horse shit over the bridge at the Birmingham fans and the Birmingham fans set a smoke bomb off (which made me jump out of my skin - along with several coppers) and a blue flare pumped blue smoke into the air. Some West Ham fans stood behind a line of police under a bridge as hundreds of Birmingham fans sang 'your not West Ham anymore!' at them and they didn't look best pleased.

As we walked back to the station the stewards held aloft big lollipops with GO on one side and STOP on the other and most of these had Birmingham City stickers on them which I found hilarious. It took us an hour to get away from the stadium then we headed to Baker Street and into the Wetherspoon's for a drink before catching the train from Marylebone back to New Street.

Apart from feeling so unwell and losing, it had been a great day out although I wouldn't be in a hurry to return to the London Stadium. West Ham fans took to twitter to comment that the Blues fans were the best they have had at the London Stadium this season. I think some of our songs hit the spot though as 'West Ham Transfers' said 'Not many chants by away fans wind me up but when Birmingham fans sang "you're not West Ham anymore" that cut deep. Proper deep'.

It was back to League action and Middlesbrough were in town and a big crowd had made it to St. Andrews and half the Olympic gallery was opened again. Middlesbrough were above us in 5th place and would prove to be a difficult opponent. In fact it was an awful first half as Middlesbrough played 4 defenders and 5 midfielders to stifle our game. The best news of the day was that Blues Isaac Vassell is back from injury after nearly a year out and is on the bench today after scoring 2 goals for the under 23's last week.

Middlesbrough managed to snatch the lead with one of the few opportunities they created and Blues went in 1-0 down at half time. We played much better in the second half despite the negative tactics of the Boro players as they constantly fell on the floor like they had been shot and stayed down for ages each time. The referee was a complete disgrace too as he gave everything to Boro and constantly penalised the Blues players. Che Adams was hacked down in the Penalty are for what looked a stonewall penalty but the referee instead booked Che Adams for diving! Shocking! He also didn't give a blatant handball in the Boro Penalty area as the crowd sang 'who's the wanker in the black'

With about 12 minutes to go Isaac Vassell prepared to come on and as he stood at the side of the pitch waiting to come on Che Adams turned his player on the edge of the box and fired in a cracking shot for the equaliser and St. Andrews exploded! What a brilliant goal. Once the celebrations were complete Isaac Vassell made his way onto the pitch from cheers from all around the stadium. It's brilliant to see him back. Blues were the best team in the second half and were creating lots of chances and looked like we could go on to win the game. However, 3 minutes later Blues were undone by a ball straight through the middle to Assombalonga who looked miles offside but ran through unchallenged to beat Lee Camp and totally against the run of play Blues were losing again. I could believe it.

Middlesbrough's football was awful and the crowd pointed this out as they sang 'Tony Pullis - your football is shit!' Blues played much better football and the Blues sang 'Garry, Garry Monk!' despite this defeat which we did not deserve. That's football though and we left the ground disappointed but happy that at least our football is good. At least we were cheered up by the Villa losing 3-0 at Wigan with all the Vile fans moaning on the radio on the way home! They are down to 12th while Blues remain in 8th position.

Because of Sky TV our next game against Norwich City had been moved to the Friday which meant a long away trip for a night game as well as a shift swap. It also meant that many of the Bluenoses who had been planning to go on the Saturday afternoon were now unable to travel and therefore our away support was severely affected and only 700 or so of us made the long trip in the cold. It doesn't bode well that we don't usually do very well when in front of the live cameras.

All this aside we boarded the official coaches that left St. Andrews at 2pm and finally arrived at Carrow Road just after 630pm. It was too late and too cold to head to a pub so we made our way inside to join the other Bluenoses already there. Norwich are flying high in 3rd place and I wasn't really expecting much from the game and I would be happy with a draw to be honest. Some good news came in the form of a new signing from Sweden. Blues are only allowed one addition in the January transfer window and he must be free and on a low salary due to the EFL embargo that Blues are currently forced to operate under. The new player is called Kerim Mrabti and is a 24 year old Swedish international and is a winger who can play as an attacking midfielder or striker.

The match got underway and it took only 13 minutes for Norwich to exploit our poor defending and score to make it 1-0. I was disappointed but 88 seconds later Jota put a brilliant pass through to Che Adams who smashed it into the net and the away end erupted. 'Keep Right On' was belted out as well as 'you're not singing anymore' to the nearby Norwich fans. Brilliant! The lead only lasted 8 minutes though as a Norwich player was allowed to shoot from outside the box and beat Lee Camp in the bottom right corner. Three minutes later and it was 3-1 as a Norwich player was unmarked to head home from a corner. All very poor goals to concede.

Blues were having an off day although we did still create chances but could also have conceded again. Maghoma was having an awful game and I was surprised that he was not pulled off as Monk made his 3 substitutions in the second half. Norwich played good football even though a lot of it was on the break and the referee gave most decisions to them. I was also amazed and disappointed at how subdued the away support had become. They didn't sing at all for the rest of the game which is really unusual for Blues so I'm guessing that the real singers were absent and mostly snowflakes had made the trip.

Four fans nearby sang constantly in the hope of inspiring the rest and me and June joined in but it was all to no avail and we trooped out of the ground disillusioned. I hope the real fans turn up for the next away trip to Swansea which will now also be played on a midweek night due to Swansea's continued involvement in the FA Cup. It was a very long trip home due to road closures (not that that bothers SKY TV one bit!) and arrived back at St. Andrews at 2am to find snow on some of the cars by where I live. Glad I left the heating on!

The next match was a rearrangement due to Swansea still being in the FA Cup, therefore our scheduled Saturday match was now going to take place the following Tuesday night and meant a long midweek trip to Swansea on a cold night. Loads of Bluenoses were now unable to go and had to return their tickets so there was just 900 of us that headed to Wales. This was still an excellent following though. The official coaches were 20 minutes late leaving St. Andrews due to a disturbance on the disabilities coach which involved K2 stewards as sandwiches were thrown! We all voted to leave them - especially as they always leave us behind!

It was a long trip down with a stop at the services which meant it took over 4 and a half hours. We sang 'we're all going on a European tour' and had a good catch up on the way. I entertained them with all the details of my trip to Kingsmeadow on the Sunday to watch Blues Ladies play the Champions Chelsea. I had driven to London with Terry and Harry and we stood with other Bluenoses including the Redditch lot on the terrace and we out sang the Chelsea lot as Blues ladies won 3-2 which was Chelsea's first defeat in 14 games (they had won their last 11 matches). It was a brilliant day!

Swansea City's Stadium would be a new ground for me as I had only been to the old ground years ago. It was hard to see it properly when we arrived as it was dark and the way that Swansea have their floodlights on the inside of the stadium it remained dark outside. It did look nice inside but it is just your average new flat pack stadium that they build these days and I didn't think it had any character really. Blues really need to get back to winning ways although I would be happy with a draw tonight.

The game kicked off and it was obvious from the start that the referee wasn't going to give us anything. In fact he was shocking, he moved their free kicks so much closer to goal that it was ridiculous and he went about trying to book as many Blues players as he could get away with. I am convinced (along with a few other Bluenoses) that the EFL have spoken to all their referees to give Birmingham nothing this season. The EFL have well and truly got it in for Blues, which is pretty obvious if you just look at what they keep doing to us.

Swansea went ahead on 22 minutes with a goal that went straight through Leed Camp in our goal but Blues refused to give up and Jacques Maghoma scored a similar goal to equalise on 35 minutes and it was all level again. Obviously the referee didn't like that and decided to send off our defender Kristian Pederson just before half time to ensure that we now had an uphill battle for the whole of the second half. We all though that Garry would sacrifice a striker and take Jutkiewicz off but were pleasantly surprised to see that he stuck with 2 strikers and went 4-3-2. Brilliant! Just when we thought we couldn't love him any more! Best manager for a long long time.

Blues started the first half strongly but as we were now playing 10 men against 12 (including the referee) it was no surprise when Swansea went 2-1 ahead in the 65th minute. We all sighed and couldn't see a way back but Vassell came on for Jutkiewicz and 2 minutes later we were level from a Jota free kick which was headed by Morrison and fumbled in for an own goal by Grimes for 2-2. We went mental in the away end as we celebrated. Then 4 minutes later the away end erupted again as Che Adams fired a cracker into the corner to give 10 men Blues the lead - 3-2! 'Che, Che will tear you apart again!' we sang to a stunned Swansea! We even sang the national anthem although it didn't have the same effect on the Swansea fans as it does on Cardiff fans!

A lot of the Swansea fans were heading to the exits and Blues sang 'we can see you sneaking out'. The 90 minutes were up and the board went up to indicate and extra 4 minutes - where did they come from? Oh yes I forgot, we are winning! Blues were giving their all but Lee Camp's kick somewhat surprisingly went out and Swansea came back at us and Wes Harding again allowed a cross into the box which was headed home with 20 seconds remaining to break our hearts. We had to settle for a point in an entertaining 3-3 draw in which 6 cards were shown to Blues players by an awful referee. Not a bad result but it really should have been a win. We now had a very long trip back with work in the morning and arrived at St. Andrews a little after 1am only to find all the cars frozen!

The following Saturday saw the visit of Martin O'Neil's Nottingham Forest and St. Andrews had 24,235 fans inside who were anticipating a hard game. There were around 3,000 Forest fans who were in good voice and occasionally taunted us with 'is this a library?' It took only 13 minutes to silence them as Jota scored a great goal to put Blues 1-0 ahead and the Blues fans sprang into life as a really loud rendition of 'is this a library!' was aimed back at the stunned Forest fans. Blues were playing well and at the half time break it was 1-0 to the home side.

I was happy but not able to relax as that is how it is with Blues despite us playing well. It went right to the wire as Forest had Yohan Benaloune sent off in the 91st minutes for blocking Che Adams shot on the goal line with his hand. As we all waved him off singing 'Cheerio!' Craig Gardener stepped aside for Che Adams to take the resulting penalty. Che calmly fired the ball into the bottom right hand corner before heading off to celebrate in front of the Tilton as he passionately pointed to the ground and shouted 'I'm staying right here!'. It was in response to the recent transfer window bids that had been received for him from both Southampton and Burnley which had both been turned down by the club and it was common knowledge that Che was happy at Blues and does not want to leave. What a refreshing change that is in this day and age. 'Is this a Library?' Was sang to the backs of the rapidly departing Forest fans and the whistle sounded to confirm a great 2-0 win for Blues which keeps us in 8th spot (still above the Vile).

There was great response online as fans took to Twitter: 'Che Adams scoring that pen pointing to the floor shouting I'm staying here has made my weekend' another said 'Che Adams celebration, tears in my eyes' and another saying 'how can you not love this club? Che Adams - best striker in the league'

Chapter Twenty Two - Points Deduction

Next it was off to London by train as Blues took on QPR at Loftus Road, a ground we all hate as the view is shocking with the majority of seats in the upper stand being restricted view - so much so that you cannot see the goal line beneath the stand. They will not give Blues the lower stand although they are happy to allow other teams fans such as Leeds and Sheffield but not Birmingham! It's about time they demolished the ground. There is only one way in and one way out via a very narrow concourse and it's so dangerous. Hence Terry, Nigel and Charlie were not going today. So it was me, June, James and Steve who headed to London to meet Stephen.

We arrived at Euston and got the tube to Shepherds Bush station (Shepherds Bush Market station was closed) and we walked to a pub called The Crown and Sceptre, which was already full of QPR fans but I recognised a few Bluenoses in there too. Me and June ordered Cheesie chips which we then had to eat whilst standing up although a nearby QPR fan let us put our plates on their table and I chatted to him about the match. He reckoned we would get something from the game but I wasn't so sure as QPR are one of our bogey teams. Stephen met us in the pub and it was great to see him again. Barry arrived with a friend so we said hello to him and he had a cheesie chip or two. Then it was off to the ground.

It was packed in the away end once we got inside and as I had one of the few unrestricted view seats I could actually see some of the goal line which was in marked contrast to last season. The Bluenoses were in great voice too and I happily joined in. The game got underway and Blues were on fire. The away end erupted when Che Adams fired home on 21 minutes and it was funny to see Bluenoses falling over each other in their celebrations. Five minutes later and Che got his second to make it 2-0 and wild celebrations ensued once again. Stephen and I could hardly believe it. It got even better when Harlee Dean headed in from a corner on 36 minutes and it was 3-0.Unbelievable scenes in the away end as we celebrated an unlikely score line.

Bluenoses were singing our hearts out for the entire time and it was great. Six minutes later the lively Jota curled in a lovely shot which hit the post but the on fire Che Adams was first to react and he fired home to rebound to unbelievable scenes as Blues went 4-0 up before half time! It was crazy! 'Che, Che will tear you apart again!' rang out from the away end. Stephen and I went mental and even the blokes in front of us turned round and hugged us as complete strangers were hugging each other and shaking hands. It was brilliant and I couldn't believe it. We sang 'easy' and 'can we play you every week?'. 'Garry, Garry Monk!' rang out loudly and 'Garry give us a wave' to which he responded by clapping us. The only blip on the horizon was that Blues manage to concede a soft goal from a corner in the last minute before half time to make the halftime score 4-1.

I thought this would now give QPR hope and inspire them in the second half, which it did. QPR scored within 3 minutes of the second half to make it 4-2 and they came at Blues persistently. Lee Camp made some good saves as Blues looked like they had imploded and were a different side from the one that was on fire in the first half. It was extremely stressful to watch especially when QPR got a 3rd goal on 80 minutes. It was agony in the away end as we are well aware how Blues are probably the only team who could throw away a 4 goal half time lead to draw or lose. Blues were hanging on and the fourth official put up the board with 4 minute of injury time and I set my stop watch. With only 20 seconds remaining the referee awarded QPR a penalty and my heart sank. The Bluenoses were in stunned silence as the player stepped up to take the penalty and I could barely watch.

Time seemed to stand still and then the player was making his run up before hitting it hard and low to Lee Camp's right but the ensuing celebrations came in the away end as Lee Camp made an unbelievable save and the rebound was cleared! I went mental as chaos broke out all around me amid incredible scenes. The final whistle sounded and the whole of the away end were singing 'Lee Camp! In the middle of our goal! Lee Camp!' to the tune of Madness 'Our House'. It went on for ages as Lee Camp made his way down the pitch to stand in front of us and pump his fist into the air as a massive cheer sounded!

I looked around and though that this had been one of those special games that would be talked about for years and one that I was privileged to have been part of. This is what loving Blues is all about! It had been a very special, although stressful day and we happily left the stadium with 3 precious points as we headed back to the station to go home. Even the fact that the train was packed and we had to stand the whole way home didn't spoil what had been a brilliant day out!

What a contrast the following game was as Blues took on Bolton at St. Andrews on a cold night. To be honest it was a very poor Bolton side that are currently struggling at the bottom end of the table and it showed. Blues failed to take their chances and the atmosphere for once felt flat as Bolton came to stop us playing football and then mugged us once again as we failed to defend a set piece and Bolton nicked a goal to win 1-0 and stun St. Andrews. A very disappointing night indeed.

It was back to St. Andrews again on the Saturday as Blackburn came to town and once again I thought this could potentially be another banana skin. It was a lovely day too as the sun shone and there were collections for 'Justice for the 21' to which everyone was contributing to. I had injured my back a few days previously and this was my first time out so I was trying to take it easy and my back was quite sore.

The atmosphere was a lot better today and the Bluenoses were up for it from the start. Blues began the game well and created a few very good chances before Che Adams fired home in the 16th minute followed by a loud rendition of 'Che, Che will tear you apart again!'. Blues were well on top and really should have put the game out of reach. As half time approached Blues seemed to lose momentum and eased off which invited Blackburn to come into the game more. It took only 7 minutes of the second half for Blackburn to grab the equaliser from a corner - a very poor goal to concede and my heart sank.

I though Blues were poor now and I was really disappointed when Monk took Jota off for Mahoney as I though Jota was having a great game and my heart sank even further. I was gutted 7 minutes from time when Blackburn snatched the lead with a cruel deflection although I felt it was coming as nothing was going our way. The Blackburn fans were celebrating and taunting the nearby Bluenoses but just 2 minutes later the ball was fed through to Che Adams who fired home from a tight angle and it was 2-2 and the Bluenoses were now taunting the stunned Blackburn fans. 'Che, Che will tear you apart again!' rang out and all the snowflakes who had left the ground after Blackburn's second goal had missed a cracker. Blues then had a free kick some way out which Gary Gardener hit towards the top corner and it was going in until the Blackburn keeper got a hand to it to tip it over and the points were shared.

It should have been a game that Blues won but at least we are still in 8th place and above the Villa and at least it's much better than this time last season. Che Adams has now scored 21 goals and beaten the record set by Steve Claridge (20 goals in a season) in 1994-95 and the first in the top 2 divisions since Trevor Francis in 1977-78! what a player he is!

It was a lovely sunny day when we headed for Bristol and it had been 16 degrees during the day - a record high for February and it added to the excitement. Today there was a full contingent of us. As well as me and June the lads were also joining us - Terry, Nigel, Charlie and James and by 4pm we were on our way and we arrived around 6.15 and walked down to the ground (apart from Terry who managed to get on the complimentary bus which dropped him at the home end!). There were 1,200 Bluenoses who had made the trip and the bar area outside the away end was buzzing. Me and June had a drink as the lads headed inside.

It was a great atmosphere and the Blues were in great voice. We all agreed that we would be happy with a point as Bristol are the in form team at the moment and before their recent defeat they had gone unbeaten for 13 games. They were also unbeaten at home for 2 months and were currently sitting in a playoff spot in 6th place in the league. Garry Monk made 2 changes as Jota and Maghoma were on the bench and Connor Mahoney and Kerim Mrabti were starting. The game kicked off and Blues were dominant in their bright yellow shirts (which have fast become my favourite away shirt of all time!) and threatened to take the lead with a couple of very good chances. Then the on fire Che Adams fired in a shot from 30 yards which came down off the bar and out again and looked very close to being over the line. Cue 'Che, Che will tear you apart again!'.

Blues deservedly went ahead just before half time when Connor Mahoney's shot was deflected past the Bristol keeper and we all went crazy in the away end. The singing was constant and brilliant and at half time we were extremely happy. The second half got underway and it took only 2 minutes for Blues to go 2-0 up as Morrison headed home from a free kick and he ran to the away end to celebrate as blue smoke filled the air and we all went crazy again! I couldn't believe it and the Bristol fans were stunned as we taunted them with 'no noise from the tractor boys!'. It really should have been 3 when Che Adams rounded their keeper but a defender made a fantastic clearance off the line.

Of course Blues then conceded a soft goal which gave Bristol hope and they then threw everything at us in the last few minutes including their goalkeeper as the referee added 5 minutes of injury time (where did that come from?) and did in fact played 5 minutes 38 seconds as I put my stopwatch on. It was tense as usual but that seems to be how it is with Blues, we always do it the hard way. Finally the whistle blew and the away end exploded in celebration and the players immediately headed over to us to celebrate and applaud us. They really are bonded with us these days, it brilliant! We headed back to the coaches very happy. This means Blues are in 8th place just 3 points off the play off places and 5 points and 5 places above the Vile. Happy days.

There was a lot of good feedback on social media from the Bristol City fans including "Ok we were poor tonight but I was impressed by them, the two up front were a handful all the time and they played some good stuff especially first half. They could be more of a threat than Derby and Forest. Fans were loud as well at times."

"The two up front, Adams and Jutkiewicz were a handful all night. I think they are one of the best teams I have seen down here this season."

"I thought Birmingham were outstanding 1st half. Strength, pace and movement. Their fitness was incredible which helped them to continually shut us down in the 2nd half."

"No complaints about the result. If we had got a late equaliser, we'd have robbed them. They were the better team and played the better football this evening, with their front two looking double strong. The ref might well have been poor this evening, but his decisions didn't impact the final score. Brum (unfortunately) were well worthy of the 3 points."

"Very impressed with Brum tonight, Monk out thought Jnr, set up his team to press and break, which they did effectively. Could have been 2-4. □ "

Just a few days later and I was off on my travels again, this time even further as we headed up north to Hull. There were 5 official coaches and I was traveling with our usual gang and as usual everyone was on form and we had a good laugh on the way. We arrived in plenty of time and me, June, James, Nigel, Adrian (Taff) and his grandson all headed across the car park to the Walton Social club which was already full of Bluenoses with a massive Blues flag on display outside. Terry and Charlie decided to give it a miss and head into the ground.

I saw a lot of Bluenoses that I knew in the social club and it was great to have a catch up over a nice cold cider. At 2.20 we headed back across the car park and made our way passed the sniffer dog and into the ground. There was a lot of Bluenoses who had made the trip but the rest of the stadium looked pretty sparse with lots of empty seats in the Hull stands. In fact the attendance was only 12,500 with about 2,000 being from Birmingham! The game got underway and Blues looked jaded to be honest. It was a poor performance from most of the players and we made a poor Hull side look good. Hull took the lead on 23 minutes and it looked offside to me - and to Lee Camp who protested to the linesman and referee. To make matters worse we then conceded a penalty in the second half to condemn us to a 2-0 defeat. Shame really as Blues could have moved into the play off places with a win.

So despite having 18 chances and 8 corners to Hull's 1 it was a rare defeat but we just have to get up again, dust ourselves off and carry on to the next game which is the big one as the Vile travel across 'our' city next Sunday. The trip home was a long one but we still managed a few songs and laughs and I got home and watched England Ladies play world champions USA in the She Believes Cup, although I fell asleep at half time!

I was half looking forward to today's game but half dreading it as the Vile seem to have all the luck against us these days. June picked up me and Stephen and we were at St. Andrew by 10am for the early kick off and there was already loads of Bluenoses about. The Royal George looked really busy, as did the Roost as we passed them on our way to the Cricketers. We also stopped to chat to Terry, James and Nigel who had just arrived on Tilton Road and after a bit of a catch up we carried on to the pub. There was lots of people I knew in the Cricketers and we had a good chat over our pre match pints and it also gave me a chance to catch up with Stephen. As we made our way back to St. Andrews we could hear the singing and I knew the place would be rocking.

When we got inside St. Andrews it was a cauldron of noise from the Blues fans and the stadium was packed to the rafters apart from half the Olympic Gallery which remained closed as it was above the Vile fans (how come they are allowed above us at Vile Park? and how come Wolves fans are above Blues at Molyneux and at Sheffield Utd - I could go on and on here but you get the picture). There was also a section of empty seats in the away end as it was clear they had not sold their allocation. When the players came out through a tunnel of flames (for the benefit of the live TV viewers no doubt) 'Keep Right On' was sang and the volume was incredible. We also had a really loud rendition of 'Shit on the Villa' which was sang all around the stadium (apart from the silent away end).

The game got underway and Blues dominated the first half but sadly the game will be remembered for so called Blues fan who ran onto the pitch in the 9th minute and punched Villa's Jack Grealish putting him on his backside before being detained and led from the pitch. Yes I know Grealish is a Vile little cheating scumbag but of course it's not acceptable that any attack on a player should happen and it does not reflect on the true supporters of Birmingham City. No doubt it will give our haters more ammunition to punish us and already some want to see us deducted points etc. No surprise there though as they all want to see us fall. No wonder we have a siege mentality these days. It really feels like there is a conspiracy against us from the EFL at the moment - especially when you look at all the refereeing decisions against us this season - totally shocking!

From the beginning the referee was giving the Vile everything and booking Blues players whenever he could. Poor Jutkiewicz was battered and kicked throughout and ended up with a bandage on his bloodied head but no free kicks were given against him. There was also a clear penalty appeal on Che Adams in the second half but of course it wasn't given. Villa then had one chance which, due to poor defending led to that scumbag Grealish scoring to rob us and win the game for them. He overdid the celebrations of course as 4 of them jumped into the away end with only Grealish getting booked (so how does that work then ref?). fair play to the steward who was lead away for kicking Grealish as he celebrated in the away end. No mention of the Vile fan who pushed a police woman to the floor at this point though? Of course not.

I was fuming as I left the stadium having been robbed again and having the clubs name tarnished yet again, the only thing that cheered me a bit was seeing Craig Gardener calling the Vile fans wankers. I bumped into Nigel on the way back to the car and we had a quick rant before heading back to our cars. It took ages to get away from the ground as we had had to park the other side due to our usual roads being closed to accommodate the Vile coaches in order to get them away from the ground quickly and safely (yes they all come on coaches!). So it was a bad day which left a bitter taste and the wait for victory over Vile goes on. Blues drop down to 11th place but at least we are having a good season and are doing so much better than recent years.

I was hoping for a much improved performance the following Wednesday when Millwall came to town especially as they were currently sitting near the bottom 3 having lost their last 5 games. Thinking about it though, this did not bode well for us as we are not good against lower league opposition. Unfortunately I was proved correct as over 20,000 turned up on a cold night to witness an awful performance from Blues as Millwall scored twice in the first half to leave with a 2-0 win over us. It was the first time during Garry Monks reign that I have heard boos at half time and the end of the match. Of course this is something I do not agree with as I think it is wrong to boo our own team and cannot possibly help the players in any way, shape or form. I left feeling really disappointed. Blues are now down to 12th in the league table.

I was really looking forward to the next game away at Preston as Blues were taking nearly 6,000 Bluenoses! Preston were flying high and were unbeaten in 13 games but I fancied Blues to get a result with a 6,000 traveling army, many of which were going via Blackpool! We were on the official coaches and had a fun trip up north and were soon arriving in Preston. Our coach had to park a long way from the ground as there were so many coaches (between 35-40 coaches) and it was pouring with rain. So it was hoods up and off to the stadium where Terry and Nigel got chips and curry sauce outside the ground as we tried to find a dry corner until the turnstiles opened.

As soon as the chips were consumed we headed to the away end to join the big queues to gain entry. Once inside we headed to the bar where James and I obtained pre match drinks. There was already loads of Bluenoses in the concourse and it wasn't long before they began singing. It was great. We soon headed up into the stands and joined in with the singing and looked forward to the game. The teams came out and the match was soon underway. Blues were dominant from the start and looked a different side from that which put in such a lacklustre performance against Millwall a few days ago.

The Bluenoses made up a third of the total attendance inside the stadium and got behind the team throughout as we created several chances. It was 0-0 at half time and Blues continued to dominate in the second half but were unable to convert any of our chances. As full time approached Blues threw everything at Preston in search of a deserved winner then on 94 minutes Preston broke from a Blues attack and forced a corner. With the last kick of the game Preston put the corner into the penalty area and a Preston player headed home to break our hearts and snatch a totally undeserved winner.

I was gutted and could not believe that we had been robbed once again! It was so unfair but I had to console myself with the fact that Blues played so well and if we continue to do so then we will get the wins that we deserve. I headed back on the long walk in the rain to the coaches feeling quite despondent once again especially with the EFL hearing looming. The EFL had been due to meet to decide our punishment the previous Monday but with their offices being in Preston they quickly realised that it would not be such a good idea to do so, with Blues bringing 6,000 (very annoyed) Bluenoses to the vicinity of their offices only a few days later and therefore postponed the hearing. Blues now had a siege mentality and the song of choice being 'fuck the EFL!'

About a week later the EFL met and decided to deduct Blues 9 points for breaching the Financial Fair Play and Blues went from 13th place and 7 points off the play offs down to 18th place and only 5 points clear of the relegation places. It's sad that the EFL hate Birmingham City so much. What about all the other clubs who have also breached the FFP including the Vile? One rule for us eh! I was quite despondent at the thought of yet another relegation battle - one that we have not deserved this season. Some think we have got off lightly as they were expecting a 12 point deduction but the EFL are not that stupid, there would have been more uproar if that had occurred. The only positive is that finally our transfer embargo has been lifted so, should we avoid relegation, we can now strengthen our team during the summer.

A week later and I was off on holiday for a much needed break and I headed off to Los Cristianos in Tenerife with my mom and sister for a bit of sunshine to recharge my batteries. Due to the rearrangement of the away game at West Brom to the Friday I would miss this game but would watch it live in a nearby bar. Despite it raining on a couple of occasions it was mostly lovely and I managed to relax. I also visited the markets and shops and spent my euros easily. It's so lovely to see the nice blue sea in the sunshine. We would sit on the front with a nice cold drink just taking in our surroundings and watching the boats come and go in the nearby port. I also watched the Montenagro v England game as England won 5-1 despite going a goal down early on. Great to see the Birmingham City flag on display as the teams came out. This means that England top our Euro 2020 group table with maximum points after two games and a goal difference of +9. Excellent.

I headed to Taylor's Bar in Los Cristianos in Tenerife for the Friday night game against West Brom on what was a bit of a chilly evening now that the sun was going down. Apparently we are having a bit of a sand storm coming over from Africa. The pub was getting busy and loud but the football would be shown on all the big screens so we got seats right in front of one of the big screens and ordered meals and drinks. The game kicked off at 8pm and although it was hard to hear the crowd due to the noise in the bar, I could see a packed away end and the Bluenoses looked to be in good voice.

It only took a dominant Blues side 7 minutes to take a deserved lead when Gary Gardner headed home from a corner and the Blues end went crazy and a blue flare landed on the pitch covering one end in blue smoke - it looked fantastic! That was how it stayed till half time as Blues went in 1-0 ahead. I knew it couldn't last though the way everything is going against us this season, including the poor refereeing (I still think there is a conspiracy against us). It took only 2 minutes of the second half for West Brom to equalise from a free kick that could have been defended better and it was 1-1. To our credit though, Blues continued to attack West Brom and we were rewarded when Lucas Jutkiewicz got his first goal since November with a header from a corner to put Blues 2-1 ahead.

Then disaster struck as Connor Mahoney won the ball a FOOT OUTSIDE the penalty area only for the referee to award a penalty! I couldn't believe it - it is the worst decision I have seen for a long time and it was unjustly 2-2. It was at this point that I knew it was not going to be our day again. I was proved correct as West Brom were allowed to get in a shot from outside the area which went straight through Lee Camps hands and we were losing 3-2. Blues threw everything at West Brom right up until the end and deserved at least a point but once again everything was against us. It's been a really difficult season with so much adversity. It says it all that Sky turned off their microphones at the away end and the referee gave a penalty for a tackle that took place a foot outside the penalty area! It seems everyone is against us! Never mind, we pick ourselves up and go again!

Leeds came to St. Andrews in second place in the Championship and looking good for an automatic promotion place whereas Blues were now 18th in the table thanks to the EFL deducting us points and both teams were in need of the points. Bluenoses had turned up in force today along with a fair few from Leeds and the atmosphere was brilliant amongst the 24,197 inside the ground. I was looking forward to the game but a bit apprehensive as Leeds are a really good side that are flying at the moment.

Garry Monk summed it up well in his programme notes when he said "it seems that decisions are going against us at the moment as well, which is something we have to deal with and not be affected by. Throughout any season you're going to have ups and downs and we've had our fair share of obstacles and restrictions, without doubt. But one thing that shines through time and time again is the attitude, determination and resilience of this group and you as a fan base." He also added "our target at the beginning of the campaign was to ensure that, at the least, we weren't fighting a battle at the wrong end of the table again. The Club has to endure that scenario too often in recent years. We had effectively achieved that goal when we reached the 50-point mark. We then had bigger possibilities to consider. However, since the news of the points deduction imposed by an EFL commission, those other possibilities have gone and we now find ourselves having to do it all over again."

The game kicked off and 'Keep Right On' echoed around the stadium. Blues were playing well and looked good. The only time we looked in danger was when a Leeds attempt hit the post and rebounded safely into the arms of keeper Lee Camp. Almost immediately Blues went on the attack with Jacques Maghoma hitting a ball across to Che Adams, which Lucas Jutkiewicz stepped over, and Che calmly collected the pass and fired a great shot into the bottom corner from around 20 yards out and St. Andrews exploded with noise! I jumped around wildly as we all celebrated. I couldn't believe we were winning 1-0 after 29 minutes and prayed that we could hold out.

Leeds were quite a physical team and were fouling our players relentlessly, picking up only 3 yellow cards in the process though. Gary Gardener had to be substituted at half time due to illness and David Davis came on in his place at the start of the second half and I began to worry. Then Kieftenbeld was fouled and had to be stretchered off with Wes Harding replacing him and I was now very worried. Blues were not playing as well now and to make matters worse Maghoma was having a poor game and kept losing the ball hence I was really surprised when Monk took off Mahoney, who was having a good game, and brought on Jota. Most of those around me felt that Maghoma should have been the one to make way for Jota.

As full time approached and Leeds threw everything at us, Blues had a couple of very good chances to kill the game with a second goal but the keeper made a couple of saves to keep us out. The fourth official then held up the board with 6 minutes of injury time and I set me stopwatch as everyone gazed at it over my shoulder. It was a nerve wracking last 6 minutes as Leeds attacked but Blues held firm and there were amazing scenes at the sound of the final whistle. Somewhat unusually most of the Blues fans had stayed to the end and really loud 'Fuck the EFL' resounded around St. Andrews in defiance of our points deduction. This was followed by a loud 'Keep Right On' and 'Garry, Garry Monk!' as the players and manager applauded the fans. It was brilliant! Blues are the only team to have done the double over Leeds this season.

Unfortunately most of the teams at the bottom won their games (typically) but Blues have now moved up to 17th place although we are still only 5 points off the relegation places due to Rotherham's surprise win over Nottingham Forest. Oh well, We're Birmingham City, we'll fight to the end!

Two days later came the very bad news that Maikel Kieftenbeld will be out for between 6 to 9 months after it was confirmed that he has damaged the anterior cruciate ligament in his right knee following the tackle by Leeds Kelvin Phillips. Blues will really miss him as he is such an influential player and it makes the run in all that more difficult.

A few days later and Blues had another big game with second place Sheffield United visiting St. Andrews bringing nearly 3,000 traveling fans with them. The official attendance was nearly 23,000 but there certainly didn't look that many in the ground as there were quite a few empty seats in the Tilton where a lot of season ticket holders had not bothered to make the effort. I was disappointed but the Bluenoses who were there were in good voice and got behind the team. Sheffield United are playing really well at the moment and I was not sure we would get anything from the game despite predicting a 2-1 win on the Blues predictor (I'm always optimistic).

Blues played really well and created a few good chances but Sheffield United scored with their first shot of the game on 38 minutes and their traveling fans celebrated. Amazingly only 4 minutes later Blues were back in the game as Michael Morrison scored from close range and St. Andrews erupted. "Your not singing anymore!" was directed at the now silent Sheffield contingent. Half time came at 1-1 and in the second half Blues continued to play well against a very good Sheffield side and we created a couple of very good chances. Jota fed a fantastic ball through to Che Adams who unleashed a superb shot which produced a fantastic save from the Sheffield keeper who tipped the ball over. Not long afterwards Jota fired in a shot which the Sheffield keeper saved low to his bottom left and kept the score at 1-1 which is how it finished. I was slightly disappointed that we hadn't won but overall this was a very good point indeed and keeps Blues in 17th place 6 points off Rotherham who are 3rd from bottom.

It was an early morning for the Ipswich trip as I was getting picked up by June at 8am to get the coach from St. Andrews which was due to leave at 9am. Great to see the gang again and we had 6 official coaches heading to Ipswich for the game. We stopped on the way at the services at Cambridge and although it should have only been for 30 minutes we ended up waiting a further 30 minutes for one of the Blues stewards and therefore we were late leaving. We all found this quite frustrating especially as we were looking forward to heading for the great chip shop in Ipswich that Terry and Nigel went to last time they were there. Hence I gave up the idea of a pub and agreed to join the lads, as did June.

When we arrived it was nice and sunny and we walked into the centre to a lovely chip shop called 'the Ipswich Chip Shop' and it was lovely. There was a nice seated area inside and once we had all obtained our chips, fish etc, which James very kindly paid for (thanks James) we sat down and tucked in. I had run across to the shop to get beers and when we came out and opened our cans (Nigel's was a bottle so the chip shop man opened his bottle with a spoon!) it was hailing! Hence we spent about 5 minutes under cover drinking before braving the weather and heading to the ground.

When we arrived at the ground we went over to see the Bobby Robson statue and had photos taken by it. As we left Nigel tapped the statue and said "sorry Bobby but we've got to send you down today' and we all smiled and headed to the away end. If Ipswich failed to win today their relegation to League One would be confirmed and they currently sat bottom of the Championship. It must have been made even worse as their rivals Norwich are top of the table. Inside there were 1,700 Bluenoses and we were looking forward to the game.

The teams came out and Blues were playing in yellow with blue shorts as was expected and we started really well. Ipswich looked a poor side and it didn't take long for Blues to take the lead and the away end celebrated. 'Your going down' rang out and 'we'll meet again'. Blues also sang 'there's only one Mick McCarthy' - a reminder to the Ipswich fans that they should have been more careful of what they wanted as they had been comfortably under McCarthy till they all complained that his football was boring and called for him to be sacked. We also sang 'minus points and we're better than you!'. Bluenoses were singing a lot and the team were playing well but not putting our chances away. This did worry me a bit but as Ipswich were so poor I couldn't see them getting back into it as Blues went in 1-0 up at half time.

I was wrong though as Blues conceded in the first half and it was 1-1. I'm beginning to dread the first 5 minutes of the second half as this seem to be when we concede most of our goals. Ipswich had their tails up now and Blues we now very poor. We gave the ball away so much and defended poorly. It seemed we were now just sitting back and trying to hang on. Blues did create more chances but again we failed to take them. Blues fans had gone a bit quieter now but did sing 'we're Birmingham City, we're sending you down' and 'we've got the Monk, Super Garry Monk, I just don't think you understand, Harry spent the lot, Cotterill lost the plot, we've got super Garry Monk!'

The final whistle sounded and the game ended 1-1 which meant that Ipswich were relegated and some of their players dropped to the ground in despair. Blues sang 'ka sa ra sa ra, whatever will be will be , your going to Shrewsbury!' to the departing Ipswich fans. At least the hail had stopped and we headed back to the coaches. As Rotherham came from 2 goals down at Stoke to draw this meant that Blues were still 6 points clear of the relegation places but we dropped to 18th as QPR won their game.

We had a brilliant trip back as we laughed and sang all the way. Very funny when a Bluenose mooned at some Ipswich fans who were making gestures as us. June put some 80's top of the pops on and we sang and laughed. Great fun. I was back in the house just after 9pm so I got to watch the football league show. Another great trip following the Blues.

It was a beautiful sunny Good Friday when I next headed to St. Andrews for the match against Derby. There were Blues fans everywhere in their Blue home shirts and lots in our lovely yellow away shirts. I must admit this season's yellow Adidas away shirt has been my favourite away shirt ever. It was great to meet up with our group outside the ground and it was roasting as we chatted in the sunshine before heading into the stadium. It had been rumoured that there would be loads of empty seats in the KOP and Tilton stands due to many having to work the bank holiday but that proved to be rubbish as over 23,000 were inside the stadium which also included a large following from Derby of around 3,000.

Despite their numbers I thought the Derby following was poor as they were quiet for most of the game. The match got under way and it took only 4 minutes for a lively Blues team to take the lead as Lucas Jutkiewicz scored from a corner to make it 1-0 and it was his 13th goal of the season - a record for him. Derby then did their usual trick of hitting us on the counter attack as a long ball over the top caught out our defence and the Derby player lobbed Lee Camp to score and level the game at 1-1. Personally I thought it was offside and there was only 7 minutes on the clock. The Derby fans woke up and sang 'its all gone quiet over there'.

Blues continued to attack Derby and just 11 minutes later we took the lead again from another corner that Michael Morrison fired home to make it 2-1. This prompted a really loud version of 'it's all gone quiet over there!' in response to the Derby fans. Brilliant! We did a really loud 'Keep Right On' too. The crowd was buzzing. Ten minutes later Derby were level as Blues failed to defend a cross which was easily headed home by a Derby player and it was 2-2 with only 28 minutes played. Derby fans celebrated but that was the last we heard of them to be honest as it just inspired the Blues fans to sing 'Keep Right On' again. It was 2-2 at half time and despite dominating the second half and Lucas Jutkiewicz hitting the post the game finished 2-2. Not a bad result really as Derby are in contention for a play off place but still a game we could have won.

It had been an entertaining game apart from the constant moaning from the Derby players who were forever surrounding the referee with their complaints. It did result in one Derby player receiving a yellow card and Ashley Cole being serenaded with 'Ashley Cole - is a fucking arsehole' from the Bluenoses who have a long memory. It dates back to the time when we were newly promoted after a 16 year absence and in our first match away at

Arsenal he dived to get one of our players sent off - which was later rescinded!

In other games third from bottom Rotherham threw away a lead to lose 4-3 at Swansea and the other teams around the bottom drew apart from Wigan who amazingly won 2-1 at Leeds (3rd place) with only ten men. So Blùes are in 18th spot but 7 points clear of the relegation places which means a draw at Rotherham on Easter Monday will see Blues mathematically safe.

I woke up really early on the morning of the trip to Rotherham and it was a lovely sunny day. I was feeling really excited about the trip, I'm not sure if it was because of the lovely sunshine or the opportunity to ensure our Championship survival following Blues points deduction. As it was so lovely and sunny I decided on the yellow away shirt and was soon on our way to St. Andrews to join the others to take our place on the coaches. Blues were taking 7 official coaches and we set up our flag in the back window and were buzzing all the way to Rotherham. Me, Nigel and Taff had on the yellow shirts and said we reckoned Blues would play in yellow whereas June and Terry wore blue and were convinced we would play in blue as we always play in blue when we play Rotherham away.

The coaches arrived at the New York Stadium at 1.30pm (we didn't leave till 11.30am) and immediately headed for the nearby food van where we had hot dogs and pork baps - lovely. Once we had consumed these in the sunshine we headed into the ground where we obtained drinks and discovered Blues were indeed playing in yellow to the delight of me, Nigel and Taff. Twenty minutes before kick off we headed to our seats and June and I had fantastic seats in row A which meant we were standing just to the left of the goal and leaning against the barrier. We had to dodge a few balls in the warm up and the away end looked fantastic with a sea of blue and yellow singing in the sunshine. There was a massive Blues flag which was being passed over the heads of all the Bluenoses.

The teams came out to a wall of noise from the away end and the game got underway. Blues looked nervous and Rotherham looked like they were going to fight for their lives as they needed to win to stand a chance of avoiding relegation. Blues only needed a point. It took only 22 minutes for things to go pear shaped as a Rotherham player handled the ball before firing it into the net and surprise surprise the officials allowed it to stand and Blues were 1-0 down. Blues then played poorly, giving the ball away often and it could have been worse than just 1-0 score line at half time. To make matters worse the Blues fans became really quiet so I'm guessing that we had a lot of snowflakes here today amongst the 2,573 traveling fans. In previous times

Bluenoses would have been singing irrespective of the score and would have got behind the team if they were losing.

Obviously Garry Monk had a word and tweaked it at half time, playing a diamond which brought Jota and Maghoma into the game more. It only took 11 minutes of the second half for Blues to be level as Jacques Maghoma beat a handful of red shirts to fire home and spark delirium in the way end as he ran to the Bluenoses behind the goal. I jumped up and the chain on my handbag broke sending it flying. I carried on celebrating anyway and held aloft my 'we're Birmingham City, we'll fight to the end' scarf as a blue flare landed on the pitch and we were soon engulfed in blue smoke. Seven minutes later Che Adams beat his player and put in a great ball for Jota to calmly fire home and spark amazing celebrations in the away end. The usual songs were being belted out such as 'Keep Right On', 'Che, Che will tear you apart again' and 'Garry, Garry Monk!'.

Rotherham were now desperate to get back into the game and throwing everything at us and we were wondering why it always had to be this stressful. The fourth official held up the board showing 5 minutes of injury time and we all sighed. Then Maghoma broke through and laid the ball to Mbrati who fired home his first goal for the club to spark unbelievable scenes in the away end as Bluenoses spilled over the barrier as they attempted to celebrate with the players. Stewards and security had panic attacks and attempted to grab as many as they could and push others back over the barrier that they were now trying to climb. Meanwhile my handbag had flown over the barrier and I was attempting to get the attention of one of the security guys to pass it back - which I eventually did. It was brilliant! Unfortunately several Bluenoses were escorted out and arrested as apparently its against the law to celebrate and have fun nowadays.

When the final whistle went to signal Blues 3-1 win and ensure safety and another season in the Championship, the celebrations began as the players came over to join us. They really were unbelievable scenes as both fans and players looked ecstatic. We sang '9 points and we still stay up!' and a really loud version of 'fuck the EFL'. There was also 'you can stick your 9 points up your arse!' It was brilliant. A few of the Blues players threw their shirts into the crowd and Garry Monk made his way over to celebrate with us as well and we sang 'Garry, Garry Monk!' I held my scarf up and ended up on lots of Facebook groups including the Birmingham Mail and official Blues site as the photographers took pictures. Very funny! This took Blues up to 17th place and 10 points off the relegation places so mathematically safe. There was load of positive feedback from the Rotherham fans too who said:

Jock's Gloves: It was inevitable that they would go on to win. Everyone in the stadium felt it. It did seem like they were celebrating a great victory at the end.

Casper-64-Frank: I don't know what Garry Monk's team talk went like at half time but they came out a different side second half. They dominated that second half especially midfield and marked us out of the game up front. Best team won, Brum were a much better side.

Abbie: find me a better set of fans in the Championship - absolute class every single time.

The Rotherham Advisor (newspaper) reported 'At the final whistle. When he was at his lowest ebb, when a thrilling campaign had finally lurched too far out of the Millers' grasp , Rotherham's manager stayed true to himself. He was hurting yet he stayed hugged to the touchline and waited for the Birmingham players. They were in no rush as they were celebrating long and hard in front of the loudest and best New York away following of the season after making absolutely certain of their own survival.

But he waited.

In time, he shook hands with every single one of them before turning away, taking his despair down the tunnel with him. A leader. Decent man, a good human being, right to the very end.'

I like the trip to Rotherham and I hope they manage to stay up but I feel they have too much to do and will probably take the 3rd relegation spot.

The last home game of the season was upon us and I was looking forward to the game against Wigan even though there was nothing to play for. I am just happy that there is no last game stress of avoiding relegation and it has been a really interesting season. I wasn't expecting a good game though, as both teams were safe and Garry Monk would probably take the opportunity to rest his players with knocks and bruises along with Harlee Dean who had undergone surgery for a hernia problem that he had been struggling with and Michael Morrison who had picked up an injury against Rotherham. This meant a completely new central defence.

It was a good end of season attendance of 23,645 and although in good voice to begin with it was a lot more subdued than our usual relegation battles. Blues did get off to a great start though, with Lucas Jutkiewicz scoring after only 2 minutes and the stadium erupted. That was probably as good as it got for Blues as we failed to convert any of the other chances we created, and we had several, and Wigan managed to snatch an equaliser after 48 minutes. We have conceded so many goals in the first 5 minutes of the 2nd half! The game finished in a 1-1 draw and many of us stayed behind for the players lap of appreciation and as there was no relegation battle nobody invaded the pitch at the final whistle which allowed the lap of appreciation to commence fairly soon.

It was lovely to see all the players and the families as the walked around the pitch applauding the fans and great to see Garry Monk enjoying the moment. He has been absolutely fantastic since he came to Blues. He has turned the team around and bonded with the Bluenoses. It is so nice to watch great attacking football again. It has been a slog watching Blues play with only 1 up front for many years and to now have 2 strikers is amazing and so great to watch. Long may it continue! I headed home very happy. Rotherham had lost at West Brom despite taking the lead and they had taken the last relegation place.

As much as I was looking forward to the trip to Reading it was also tinged with sadness that such a fantastic season was coming to an end. I love the last away game because so many Bluenoses adhere to tradition and come in fancy dress. Because it was so stressful last season June and I had not done the fancy dress - too scared to jinx it but this season we were quite happy to don fancy dress once again. We had decided upon the 2 girls from Abba with June wearing the white Abba outfit (she has brown hair) and I wore the blue outfit with silver stars on the flares and a long white wig (even though I have blonde hair I wanted to get the look right). We both had fantastic 70's style white patent boots with heels that looked brilliant. To top it off we had face jewels and I had blue 'festival' glitter on my face!

We traveled by coaches that left early morning (15 minutes late as always seems to be the case) as it was a 12.30 kick off and we arrived at the Majestic Stadium at 11.00. My nephew Stephen was already there and laughed when he saw us dressed up. We met Adrian 'Taff' who was the only bloke in our group who had made the effort and he looked really cool dressed as a 'blue monk'. We headed to the food vans and got sausage, chips etc, which was really nice although Nigel dropped his sausage on the floor. Then it was into the ground to obtain pre match drinks.

There was a party atmosphere inside the away end as songs were sang and there was some good outfits on show. I liked the 4 men dressed as the Spice Girls, they were really good. I also liked the Beatles in their sergeant pepper outfits, the convicts, the banana's and the baby. Once we were up in the stands we joined in the singing and the game got underway. The Bluenoses then spotted a lad in the nearby Reading end wearing a Vile shirt (yes they really are that obsessed with us) and a loud version of 'Shit on the Villa' rang out. This idiot responded by standing up and gesticulating to the away end and he instantly regretted his actions as loads of singing from the entire away end was directed at him.

He looked embarrassed now but his mate decided to swap shirts with him and put the Vile shirt on and stood up and tried to taunt the Blues end before he was pounced on by the stewards who lead him from the ground. Many of the nearby Reading fans had applauded him - what a bunch of idiots! They have gone right down in my estimation now, apart from the few who gave him the 'wanker' sign as he was led out.

The game was a typical end of season affair with nothing to play for and it showed. There were a few changes to the team as Garry Monk rested some of his bruised players but they all played really well. The match finished 0-0 and Blues finished the season unbeaten in 7 games. Although the Bluenoses sang a lot at the end of the game as the players came over to applaud our support I had felt that they were unusually quiet throughout most of the game. I'm beginning to worry that a lot of the snowflakes and corporate are getting tickets instead of the real fans who sing their hearts out no matter what. I hope we don't lose this support as this is what Birmingham City are all about.

We headed back to Birmingham talking about how much we have all enjoyed this season which even a 9 point deduction couldn't spoil and only strengthened our resolve. Blues finished in 17th place (should have been 14th really!) and easily 12 points clear of the drop despite the EFL trying to send us down. We have been treated to some great football this season and really should have had more points from many of the games we played. There is so much to look forward to next season.

Norwich were promoted as champions and received the trophy at Villa Park after beating Villa 2-1. Its the first trophy the villa fans have seen at villa park for 23 years - and it's not theirs - ha ha. Sheffield United were promoted in 2nd place and the play offs were sadly won by the Vile. Rotherham, Bolton and Ipswich were relegated to League One with Luton - Champions, Barnsley- 2nd coming up to the championship.

The following weekend saw the last games in the Premier League which actually went to the wire this year with Manchester City winning the title with a 4-1 win at Brighton that meant that Liverpool's 2-0 win against Wolves saw them finish in second place just a point behind the champions. Cardiff, Fulham and Huddersfield were relegated to the Championship.

The FA Cup was won by Manchester City who thrashed Watford 6-0, not something people want to see really. Unless it's Villa getting humiliated of course. Manchester City completed their domestic treble by beating Chelsea on penalties in the League Cup Final. Boring to see them win everything though.

Blues average home attendance over the season was 22,483 with the highest being 26,631 against the Villa and the lowest was 19,795 against Rotherham. Garry Monk had turned Blues into a really good side and I was really looking forward to next season with him in charge especially as he would have money in the transfer market and not have his hands tied by a transfer embargo.

However, in June is was reported that the relationship between Monk and Ren had broken down and we all began to get nervous knowing what our owners are capable of. Sure enough Garry Monk was sacked on 18th June and Bluenoses everywhere were outraged! How could our owners be so stupid? Monk was the best thing to happen to Blues in many years. I had met him at the players awards and he was a really nice man.

According to Ren, Garry Monk was sacked because of 'his attempt to use a single agent in transfer deals and his refusal to adapt the team's style of play' whilst sources close to Monk disagreed with this. The Club statement called for a change in the football philosophy. The sacking was badly received by most Blues fans and the club said they were not actively looking for a permanent manager and Pep Clotet was appointed caretaker head coach. The remainder of the backroom staff stayed in post.

It's never dull being a Bluenose but I wonder what the future holds for us now and what next season will bring. I know one thing though - it won't be boring!